Strategic Marketing Management

Alexander Chernev

Kellogg School of Management

Northwestern University

Fifth Edition

D1509681

Strategic Marketing Management

Fifth Edition | September 2009

ISBN-13: 978-0-9825126-3-0

ISBN-10: 0-9825126-3-5

Table of Contents

About the Author

Alexander Chernev is an associate professor of marketing at the Kellogg School of Management, Northwestern University. He holds a PhD in Psychology from Sofia University and a PhD in Business Administration from Duke University.

Dr. Chernev's research applies theories and concepts related to consumer behavior and managerial decision making to develop successful marketing strategies. He serves on the editorial boards of top research journals, including *Journal of Marketing, Journal of Marketing Research, Journal of Consumer Research, Journal of Consumer Psychology*, and *International Journal of Research in Marketing*. Dr. Chernev's research has been published in leading marketing journals and has been quoted in business and popular press, including *Business Week, Forbes, Newsweek, The Wall Street Journal*, and *The New York Times*. He has written numerous teaching cases focused on corporate planning, marketing strategy, and brand and customer management.

At Kellogg, Dr. Chernev teaches marketing management, strategic marketing, marketing research, and behavioral decision theory in the MBA, PhD, and executive education programs. In addition to teaching, he advises companies around the world on issues of strategic marketing planning and analysis, business innovation, brand and customer equity, new product development, and customer management.

Foreword

Marketing is both an art and a science. Many of its practitioners view marketing as an art, in which both intuition and creativity play a major role—a popular view, particularly in the advertising and sales spheres. Yet, if marketing plans were to be based primarily on intuition and creativity, they would be less effective and less credible to senior management and the company's stakeholders and collaborators. What gives marketing its growing respect and impact is the development and use of a broad range of scientific and analytic tools.

Over the past decades, the field of marketing has accumulated numerous tools. They help define goals and target markets, and facilitate positioning, differentiation, and branding. These tools, however, are usually scattered within marketing textbooks and fail to come together in a clear framework. Here lies the unique contribution of *Strategic Marketing Management*. This concise book presents the major tools and decision processes involved in planning and controlling marketing.

The theory presented in this book is based on three cornerstone ideas:

The first idea is that an offering's ultimate success is determined by the soundness of the five key components of its business model: goal, strategy, tactics, implementation, and control, or the G-STIC framework. This framework is used to streamline a company's marketing analyses and deliver an integrative approach to marketing planning.

The second idea is that when developing its offerings, a company should strive to create value for three key market entities: target customers, the company, and its collaborators. An offering's value proposition, therefore, should be optimized to deliver superior value to target customers in a way that enables the company and its collaborators to reach their strategic goals. These three types of value—customer value, collaborator value, and company value—comprise the 3-V framework, which is the foundation of strategic marketing analysis.

The third idea is that a company's marketing activities can be represented through the process of designing, communicating, and delivering value to its key constituencies, or the D-C-D framework. This framework offers a novel interpretation of the traditional 4-P approach to capture the dynamic nature of the value management process.

The second part of the book applies these ideas to common business problems, such as increasing profits and sales revenues, developing new products, extending product lines, and managing product portfolios. By linking the theory to practical applications, this book offers a structured approach to analyzing and solving business problems and delineates a set of methodologies to ensure a company's success in the market.

Student testimonies are evidence that this book is very helpful for analyzing marketing cases in the classroom. This book is also very helpful to managers involved in the development and implementation of marketing plans. I further recommend it to senior executives to improve their understanding of what constitutes great marketing analysis and planning.

A company's main focus should be on maximizing value to the customer, the company, and its collaborators. This can be achieved by applying the strategic marketing framework outlined in this book.

Philip Kotler
S. C. Johnson Distinguished Professor of International Marketing
Kellogg School of Management
Northwestern University

Acknowledgments

This book has benefited from the wisdom of my current and former colleagues at the Kellogg School of Management at Northwestern University: Nidhi Agrawal, Eric Anderson, James C. Anderson, Robert Blattberg, Anand Bodapati, Miguel Brendl, Bobby Calder, Timothy Calkins, Gregory Carpenter, Anne Coughlan, Patrick Duparcq, David Gal, Kent Grayson, Sachin Gupta, Karsten Hansen, Julie Hennessy, Dawn Iacobucci, Dipak C. Jain, Robert Kozinets, Lakshman Krishnamurthi, Angela Lee, Sidney Levy, Prashant Malaviya, Eyal Maoz, Vikas Mittal, Vincent Nijs, Christie Nordhielm, Yi Qian, Mohan Sawhney, John Sherry, Jr., Louis Stern, Brian Sternthal, Alice Tybout, Philip Zerrillo, Florian Zettelmeyer, and Andris Zoltners. I would like to acknowledge the help of Pierre Chandon (INSEAD), Akif Irfan (Goldman Sachs), and Ryan Hamilton (Emory University) for their valuable comments.

I owe a considerable debt of gratitude to Philip Kotler, one of the leading thinkers in the field of marketing, who through his insightful writings sparked my interest in marketing. I am also indebted to Jim Bettman, Julie Edell Britton, Joel Huber, John Lynch, John Payne, and Rick Staelin at the Fuqua School of Business at Duke University for their advice and support at the outset of my academic career.

Marketing as a Business Discipline

Marketing is too important to be left to the marketing department.
David Packard, co-founder of Hewlett-Packard

A great deal of confusion exists about the essence of marketing. This confusion stems from a more general misunderstanding of marketing as a core discipline. Managers often think of marketing in terms of tactical activities, such as sales, advertising, and promotions. In fact, within many organizations, marketing is thought of as an activity designed to support sales by helping managers sell more of the company's products and services.

Marketing is far more than tactics. In addition to specialized tactical activities, such as sales and advertising, marketing also involves strategic management, which is the foundation for the success of its tactical elements. This view of marketing as a central business function that permeates all areas of an enterprise is the basis of the strategic marketing theory outlined in this book. Marketing as a business discipline can be conceptualized as follows:

Marketing is the art and science of creating and managing successful exchanges.

An important aspect of marketing is that it is both an art and a science. Marketing is an art because it is driven by managers' creativity and imagination. At the same time, marketing is a science because it represents a body of knowledge that offers a systematic analysis of marketing phenomena. The scientific aspect of marketing that focuses on the logic underlying the process of creating and managing successful exchanges is the essence of strategic marketing.

The term *exchange* is key to understanding the essence of marketing. The core activity of a market is the exchange of goods and services among market participants. Consequently, the role of marketing is to create new exchanges by introducing new offerings and to manage the existing exchanges by building sustainable relationships between the company and its customers and collaborators.

The ultimate goal of marketing is to ensure the long-term success of an exchange. To be successful, an exchange should create value to all relevant participants. Because the main function of the marketing exchange is to create value, the concept of value is central to marketing. Thus, an offering's success is determined by its ability to create value for the relevant market participants: target customers, the company, and its collaborators.

Marketing management aims to ensure that a company's offerings create superior value for target customers in a way that enables the company and its collaborators to achieve their strategic goals.

Optimizing value for target customers, collaborators, and the company is the key principle that serves as the foundation for all marketing activities. Because

1

value optimization is the fundamental marketing principle, value management permeates all aspects of designing an offering's strategy and tactics. Business success can be achieved only when an offering's value is optimized for its target customers, the company, and its collaborators. Failure to create value for any one of the relevant market participants inevitably leads to an inefficient marketing exchange and market failure.

Part One

The Framework for Marketing Management

Introduction

The central role of marketing in a company's business activities and the increasing complexity of these activities call for the development of a systematic approach to analyzing and managing the different aspects of the marketing process. Such a systematic approach to providing a logical structure for organizing complex information can be achieved by using frameworks.

Frameworks are the cornerstones of marketing analysis because they offer a simplified description of complex processes and provide a general solution to a variety of industry-specific problems. Frameworks streamline the decision process by providing managers with a common view of how to frame the problem, a universal approach to identifying alternative solutions, and a shared vocabulary with which to discuss the issues. Because of their level of generality, frameworks rarely offer solutions to specific marketing problems. Instead, they provide a general algorithm that, when applied to a specific scenario, allows managers to identify the optimal solution. Using a framework calls for abstracting the problem at hand to a more general scenario for which the framework offers a predefined solution, and then applying this solution to solve the specific problem. Thus, by relying on the abstract knowledge captured in frameworks, a manager may effectively sidestep the trial-and-error-based learning process.

The frameworks advanced in this book reflect the processes by which a company develops and manages its offerings. They outline a generalized approach to analyzing and managing different aspects of the marketing process and delineate a set of methodologies to identify and solve specific marketing problems.

The processes by which a company develops and manages its offerings are captured by the G-STIC framework. The G-STIC framework—an acronym for goal, strategy, tactics, implementation, and control—implies that the actions a manager takes on a day-to-day basis should follow five steps: set a *goal*, develop the *strategy*, design the *tactics*, define the *implementation* plan, and identify the *control* metrics to measure the success of the proposed action (Figure 1).

Figure 1. The G-STIC Action-Planning Framework

The G-STIC framework serves as the organizing principle for the first part of the book, as follows:

- The big-picture approach to *marketing management* is outlined in Chapter 1, which introduces the G-STIC framework as an overarching approach to marketing planning.

- The key decisions involved in setting a company's *goal*—defining its focus and identifying performance benchmarks—are discussed in Chapter 2.

- The key components of developing an offering's *strategy*—identifying target markets and developing a value proposition—are outlined in Chapter 3.

- The *tactical* aspect of marketing management is discussed in Chapter 4, which outlines the seven key elements of an offering's marketing mix: product, service, brand, price, incentives, communication, and distribution.

- The *implementation* component of marketing management is addressed in Chapter 5 which discusses the timeline and logistics of executing an offering's strategy and tactics.

- The *control* aspect of action planning is discussed in Chapter 6, which outlines its performance evaluation and environmental analysis components.

The overview of the key aspects of marketing management defined in the G-STIC framework is followed by a detailed discussion of the essential components of its strategy (Parts II and III) and tactics (Part IV). A discussion of approaches to managing growth is outlined in Part V. Finally, Part VI presents the basics of writing a strategic marketing plan and reviews the relevant financial concepts and marketing metrics.

————————————— Chapter One —————————————

The Big Picture

Vision without action is a daydream. Action without vision is a nightmare.

Japanese proverb

Marketing management involves making a series of decisions aimed at ensuring the success of a given offering, a product line, or the entire company. The key aspects of the marketing management process are the focus of this chapter.

Marketing Management as a Process

On the most general level, marketing management can be represented as a three-step process: analyzing the situation, developing an action plan, and implementing this plan (Figure 1). Situation analysis calls for evaluating the company and the environment in which it operates for the purpose of identifying markets in which the company can successfully compete. Situation analysis is followed by the development of an action plan(s) for each of the identified target markets. Action planning is then followed by an implementation, which executes the action plan.

Figure 1. Marketing Management as a Process

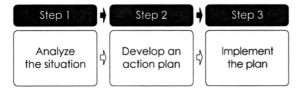

The three aspects of marketing management—situation analysis, action planning, and implementation—are discussed in more detail in the following sections.

Situation Analysis

Situation analysis aims to provide an overview of the company and the environment in which it operates, and to identify potential markets in which it will compete. Situation analysis can be viewed as a three-stage process that involves (1) evaluating the company and the environment in which it operates, (2) identifying potential target markets, and (3) selecting target markets in which to compete.

Situation analysis typically begins with analyzing five key factors: (1) potential *customers* whose needs the company can fulfill with its offerings, (2) the *company,* its goals, core competencies and strategic assets required to develop offerings to serve these customers, (3) potential *collaborators* who are likely to be working with the company on these offerings, (4) current and potential *competitors* with similar offerings targeting the same buyers, and (5) the economic, technological, sociocultural, regulatory, and physical *context* in which the company operates. These five factors are often referred to as the "Five C's."

Situation analysis typically leads to the selection of a target market(s)—a subset of customers to whom the company will tailor its offerings. Selection of a target market is determined by two main factors: (1) market attractiveness, which reflects the degree to which a particular market enables the company to achieve its strategic goals, and (2) market compatibility, which reflects the company's ability to serve this market by creating superior value to its target customers and collaborators. A detailed discussion of the process of identifying target markets is offered in the second part of this book (Chapters 7–11).

Following the selection of a target market is the development of an action plan that details the process of creating and managing the company's offering(s) aimed at this market. The process of developing an action plan is discussed in more detail in the following section.

Action Planning

The action plan comprises five key elements: goal, strategy, tactics, implementation, and control. A systematic analysis of these five elements is referred to as the G-STIC framework. The G-STIC framework implies that a manager's actions (e.g., product and service design, branding, pricing, sales promotions, communication, and distribution) should follow directly from the company's overall strategy, which, in turn, should enable the company to achieve its goal. In this context, the development of an action plan involves the following five steps: set a *goal*, develop the *strategy*, design the *tactics*, define the *implementation* plan, and identify the *control* metrics to measure the progress toward the set goal (Figure 2).

Figure 2. The G-STIC Framework for Action Planning

The G-STIC approach to action planning is outlined in more detail in the following sections.

Setting a Goal

Every action that a company undertakes should be consistent with a well-defined goal. Setting a goal involves two decisions: identifying the focus of the company's actions and defining the specific performance benchmarks to be achieved.

- The *focus* identifies the ultimate criterion for a company's success (e.g., net income, profit margins, sales revenues, or market share).

- *Benchmarks* define the quantitative and temporal aspects of the goal.

For example, a goal may involve increasing earnings per share (focus) by five percent (quantitative benchmark) by the end of the fiscal year (temporal benchmark). The process of setting strategic goals is discussed in more detail in Chapter 2.

Developing a Strategy

Strategy outlines the master plan of actions aimed at achieving the company goal. Strategy development involves two key components: identifying the target market and designing the offering's value proposition.

- The *target market* describes the key aspects of the market in which the company aims to create a successful value exchange. The target market is defined by the following five factors: (1) *target customers* for whom the company will tailor its offering, (2) the *company* introducing and managing the offering, its core competencies and strategic assets, (3) *collaborators* working with the company on this offering, (4) *competitors* with offerings that provide similar benefits to the target customers, and (5) the economic, technological, socio-cultural, regulatory, and physical *context* in which the company operates.

- The *value proposition* describes an offering's ability to create value for all relevant market participants—target customers, the company, and its collaborators. Because of its crucial role in ensuring the market success of an offering, optimizing these three aspects of the value proposition is the key aspect of an offering's strategy. The essence of the offering's value proposition is captured in its *positioning*, which aims to create a distinct image of the offering in a customer's mind.

The processes of defining the target market and designing the offering's value proposition are discussed in more detail in Chapter 3.

Designing the Tactics

Tactics identify how the desired strategy is translated into a set of specific actions. Marketing tactics are defined by seven key elements, often referred to as the marketing mix: product, service, brand, price, incentives, communication, and distribution. These marketing mix variables are summarized below.

- The *product* aspect of the offering captures its key functional characteristics. Products typically change ownership during purchase; once created, they can be physically separated from the manufacturer and distributed to end users via multiple channels.

- The *service* aspect of the offering also captures its key functional characteristics and is in many respects similar to the product aspect. However, unlike products, services do not necessarily imply a change in ownership of the offering; instead, they offer the right to use the service within a given time frame. Because they are created and consumed at the same time, services also tend to be inseparable from the service provider.

- The *brand* is a marketing tool used to identify the offering, differentiate it from the competition, and create value that goes beyond its product and service characteristics.

- The *price* reflects the monetary aspect of the offering; it refers to the amount of money the company charges for the benefits provided by its offering.

- *Incentives* offer solutions, typically short-term, aimed at enhancing the value of the offering by providing additional benefits and/or reducing costs.

- *Communication* aims to inform target customers about the availability of the offering and highlight its particular characteristics.

- *Distribution* involves the channel through which the offering is delivered to customers.

The tactical aspect of an offering can be represented by the processes of *designing, communicating,* and *delivering* value. The processes of designing, communicating, and delivering value incorporate the seven marketing mix variables discussed above, such that the product, service, brand, price, and incentives comprise the value-design aspect of the offering; communication captures the value-communication aspect; and distribution reflects the value-delivery aspect of the value management process. The tactical aspect of managing a company's offering is discussed in more detail in Chapter 4.

Defining the Implementation Plan

The implementation component of market planning outlines the timeline and the logistics of executing an offering's strategy and tactics. Developing an implementation plan involves three key components:

- Developing the business *infrastructure* necessary for implementing the action plan.

- Designing the *processes* used by the company to implement its strategy and tactics.

- Setting the implementation *schedule* identifying the sequence and time frame in which individual tasks will be performed.

The key aspects of implementation planning are discussed in more detail in Chapter 5.

Identifying Controls

The control aspect of managing an offering aims to ensure adequate progress toward the set goal. It encompasses two key activities: evaluating the company's performance and analyzing the environment in which the company operates.

- *Performance evaluation* involves analyzing the outcomes of the company's actions relative to its goals.

- *Environmental analysis* aims to identify changes in the environment in which the company operates and, when necessary, make adjustments to the company's actions.

The key elements of the control aspect of action planning are discussed in more detail in Chapter 6.

The Big Picture

The five components of the action plan can be represented in the form of a pyramid, as shown in Figure 3. Thus, the action plan begins with an outline of the goals that identify the company's focus and the performance benchmarks to be achieved. The goal analysis is followed by a description of the company's strategy, which involves defining the target market(s)—customers, collaborators, competitors, the company, and the context in which they operate—as well as outlining the offering's value proposition to target customers, the company, and its collaborators. The strategy analysis is followed by a description of marketing tactics, which involve the processes of designing, communicating, and delivering value. The tactical analysis is followed by an implementation plan that identifies the infrastructure, processes, and the timeline involved in translating the planned strategy and tactics into reality. The control aspect of action planning outlines a policy for evaluating the company's performance and analyzing the environment to ensure adequate progress toward the set goal. The use of G-STIC analysis in developing a marketing plan is further discussed in Chapter 25.

Figure 3: The G-STIC Action-Planning Pyramid

The action-planning process described by the G-STIC framework can be related to the situation-analysis aspect of marketing management illustrated in Figure 1.

Both situation analysis and action planning involve identifying markets that a company can successfully serve. The key difference between situation analysis and action planning is that situation analysis evaluates the environment for the purpose of identifying market opportunities (threats) and deciding whether to pursue these opportunities (respond to threats). Action planning builds on the situation analysis to formulate a course of action for creating a successful value exchange in the *already identified* market(s). In cases where situation analysis leads to the identification of multiple target markets, each individual market requires the development of its own action plan (see Chapter 24 for more detail).

Implementing the Action Plan

The implementation stage of marketing management involves a series of actions that aim to execute a company's action plan. The implementation stage of managing an offering (Figure 1) is directly related to the implementation aspect of the action plan (Figure 2). Both concepts depict a set of processes involved in the execution of a company's plan. Unlike the implementation aspect of the action plan (Figure 2), which involves the development of a *plan* aimed at executing a company's strategy and tactics, the implementation stage of managing an offering (Figure 1) involves the actual *actions* the company undertakes to turn its plan into reality.

In theory, the implementation of the proposed course of action should directly follow the implementation processes outlined in the company's action plan. In reality, however, this often is not the case. The discrepancy between the plan and the reality can be a result of changes in the environment in which the company operates, as well as management errors made during the implementation (e.g., not following the actions prescribed by the marketing plan, not following the schedule, and/or misinterpreting the changes in the marketing environment).

The implementation aspect of marketing management is an iterative process in which the company executes its strategy and tactics while simultaneously monitoring the outcome and modifying the process accordingly (Figure 4). This monitoring and adjustment enables the company to take into account the changes in the market in which it operates (i.e., changes related to customers, collaborators, competitors, and the context), as well as the changes in its own goals and resources.

Figure 4. Implementing the Action Plan

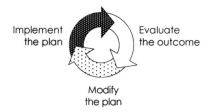

Implement
the plan

Evaluate
the outcome

Modify
the plan

The successful implementation is a function of the soundness of the underlying strategic plan. Therefore, the rest of this book focuses on the processes by which a company develops a strategy and tactics aimed at fulfilling its long-term goals.

Summary

The central role of marketing in a company's business activities and the increasing complexity of these activities call for the development of a systematic approach to analyzing and managing the various aspects of the marketing process. Such a systematic approach to providing a logical structure for organizing complex information can be achieved by using the frameworks introduced in this chapter.

On the most general level, marketing management can be represented as a process involving three key steps: analyzing the situation in which the company operates, developing an action plan, and implementing this plan. The focus of this chapter is the development of an action plan, a process captured by the G-STIC (goal, strategy, tactics, implementation, and control) framework.

The key aspects of the G-STIC framework are discussed throughout the entire book. The process of setting strategic goals is detailed in Chapter 2, the development of a marketing strategy is outlined in Chapter 3 and discussed in more detail in Parts II and III (Chapters 7–14), marketing tactics are summarized in Chapter 4 and discussed in more detail in Part IV (Chapters 15–20), implementation planning is discussed in Chapter 5, and performance evaluation and control are discussed in Chapter 6.

Additional Readings

Aaker, David A. (2007), *Strategic Market Management* (8th ed.). New York, NY: John Wiley & Sons.

Kotler, Philip and Kevin Lane Keller (2008), *Marketing Management* (13th ed.). Upper Saddle River, NJ: Prentice Hall.

Kotler, Philip (1999), *Kotler on Marketing: How to Create, Win, and Dominate Markets*. New York, NY: Free Press.

Lehmann, Donald R. and Russell S. Winer (2007), *Analysis for Marketing Planning* (7th ed.). Boston, MA: McGraw-Hill/Irvin.

Walker, Orville C., Jr., John W. Mullins, and Harper W. Boyd, Jr. (2008), *Marketing Strategy: A Decision-Focused Approach* (6th ed.). London: McGraw-Hill.

---------- Chapter Two ----------

Setting a Goal

If you don't care where you're going, it doesn't make a difference which path you take.
Lewis Carroll, English mathematician and writer

The development of an action plan begins with setting a goal, which provides a strategic direction for a company's marketing activities. The key aspects of the process of defining a marketing goal are the focus of this chapter.

Overview

Every action that a company undertakes should be consistent with its strategic goal(s). Because of the central place it plays in a company's strategic planning process, setting a goal plays a pivotal role in determining a company's overall success. Without a well-defined goal, an organization can neither design an effective marketing strategy nor evaluate the success of its current activities.

Setting a goal involves two decisions: (1) identifying the *focus* of the company's actions (e.g., net income, sales revenues, market share) and (2) defining the specific quantitative and temporal *benchmarks* to be reached (Figure 1).

Figure 1. Setting a Marketing Goal: The Big Picture

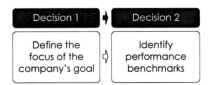

The two key aspects of setting a goal—identifying the focus and defining performance benchmarks—are discussed in more detail in the following sections.

Goal Focus

The focus of a company's goal defines the ultimate criterion for success. Goals vary in their level of generality: some goals reflect outcomes that are more fundamental than others. Therefore, a company's goals can be represented as a hierarchy headed by a company's ultimate goal, which is implemented through a set of more specific, actionable goals.

The ultimate goal reflects the desired outcome associated with a given offering, product line, or the entire company. Common examples of ultimate goals involve maximizing a company's net income, earnings per share, and return on investment. The ultimate goal does not necessarily need to be directly linked to monetary outcomes. For example, a company's goal may involve increasing customer/social welfare or facilitating other, more profitable and strategically important offerings.

In addition to setting an ultimate goal, a company often identifies a series of subgoals (also referred to as objectives or strategic initiatives) that, when acted upon, will enable it to reach its ultimate goal. Unlike the company's ultimate goal, which is typically defined in terms of a company-focused outcome (e.g., net income), subgoals can focus on other market factors as well. In particular, five common types of actionable subgoals can be identified: customer-focused goals, collaborator-focused goals, company-focused (internal) goals, competitor-focused goals, and context-focused goals.

- *Customer goals* aim to elicit a specific action from target customers (e.g., increasing purchase frequency, switching from a competitive product, or making a first-time purchase of this type of product), that will enable the company to achieve its ultimate goal. To illustrate, a company might decide to increase net income (ultimate goal) by increasing sales volume from its current customers (customer-focused subgoal). Because the customers are the ultimate source of a company's revenues and profits, a company's ultimate goal typically involves a customer-focused subgoal.

- *Collaborator goals* aim to optimize a company's relationships with its current collaborators (e.g., achieving a greater level of collaboration) as well to form new alliances.

- *Company goals* involve internal actions, such as reducing the costs of goods sold, improving the effectiveness of the company's marketing actions, and optimizing research and development costs.

- *Competitive goals* involve actions that aim to improve a company's market position, such as creating barriers to entry, securing proprietary access to scarce resources, and establishing market leadership.

- *Context goals* aim to improve the economic, technological, socio-cultural, regulatory, and physical environment in which the company operates. For example, a company might also set the goal of improving the social welfare, preserving the environment, and/or changing the regulatory context in which it operates.

The nature of the identified subgoals determines the action plan that follows. To illustrate, the goal of increasing the rate of adoption of an offering by new customers calls for a corresponding action such as increasing the offering's benefits and/or decreasing its costs, developing a targeted communication campaign, and/or enhancing the offering's distribution coverage. The goal of preventing a competitor's market entry might involve actions such as a preemptive launch of a new offering, lowering the prices on the company's existing offerings, and/or securing the company's dominant position in distribution channels. The relationship between a company's ultimate goal, its different subgoals, and the corresponding action plans is illustrated in Figure 2.

Figure 2. Identifying Actionable Goals

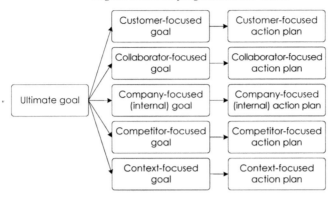

Performance Benchmarks

In addition to determining the focus, setting a goal also involves identifying the performance benchmarks the company needs to achieve. There are two types of goal-specific benchmarks: quantitative and temporal.

- *Quantitative benchmarks* define the specific milestones to be achieved by the company with respect to its focal goals. For example, benchmarks such as "increase market share by 2%," "increase retention rates by 12%," and "improve the effectiveness of marketing expenditures by 15%" quantify the selected goal. Quantitative benchmarks can be expressed in either relative terms (e.g., increase market share by 20%) or absolute terms (e.g., achieve annual sales of one million units).

- *Temporal benchmarks* identify the time frame for achieving a particular quantitative benchmark. Setting a timeline for achieving a goal is a key strategic decision because the strategy adopted to implement these goals is often contingent on the time horizon. To illustrate, the goal of maximizing next quarter profitability will likely require a different strategy and tactics than the goal of maximizing long-term profitability. The time horizon for achieving an offering's goals could also be a source of conflict among the company's stakeholders. For example, short-term investors and many analysts tend to focus on the short-term performance reflected in a company's quarterly results, whereas longer-term investors tend to focus on the long-term prospects of the company reflected in a company's strategic plan.

To illustrate, a company's ultimate goal may involve generating net income (focus) of $10B (quantitative benchmark) by the end of the fourth quarter (temporal benchmark). A customer-specific goal may involve increasing market share by 10% by the end of the fourth quarter. A collaborator-related goal might involve securing 45% of the distribution outlets by the end of the fourth quarter. An internal goal might involve lowering the cost of goods sold by 25% by the end of the fourth quarter.

A company's performance benchmarks reflect its outlook for the future. An optimistic view of the company's growth prospects typically results in growth-oriented goals (e.g., increasing profit margins, sales revenues, or market share). In contrast, a pessimistic view of the company's growth prospects (e.g., stemming from weakening demand, increasing competition, or a decline in the overall economic conditions) can result in status-quo goals (e.g., preserving current profit margins, sales revenues, or market share) or even decline-stabilization goals (e.g., slowing the decline in profit margins, sales revenues, or market share). In general, when setting future goals, a company can use three types of reference points: (1) its current *goal*, (2) its current *performance*, and/or (3) the untapped *market opportunity* (i.e., opportunity gap). The relationship among these three reference points is illustrated in Figure 3.

Figure 3. Reference Points for Setting Performance Benchmarks

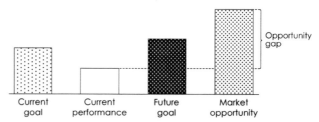

Setting growth-oriented performance benchmarks calls for a balance between maximizing the company's performance and having a realistic view of the market opportunity. More aggressive goals indicate a company's desire to take full advantage of market opportunities, whereas more conservative goals indicate the desire to minimize the risks associated with pursuing unproven growth prospects.

Summary

Setting a goal typically involves two decisions: (1) identifying the focus of the company's actions and (2) identifying the specific benchmarks to be reached. The focus of a company's goal defines the ultimate criterion for success and can be represented as a hierarchy headed by this ultimate goal, which is implemented through a series of more specific, actionable goals. The ultimate goal reflects the desired outcome associated with a given offering, product line, or the entire company. Unlike the ultimate goal, which is typically defined in terms of company-focused outcome (e.g., net income), actionable subgoals often focus on other entities, such as target customers, collaborators, competitors, and the context in which the company operates. Both the company's ultimate goal and its actionable subgoals involve two types of benchmarks: (1) quantitative benchmarks, which define the specific milestones to be achieved by the company with respect to its focal goals, and (2) temporal benchmarks, which identify the time frame for achieving a particular quantitative benchmark.

Additional Readings

Aaker, David A. (2007), *Strategic Market Management* (8th ed.). New York, NY: John Wiley & Sons.

Kotler, Philip and Kevin Lane Keller (2008), *Marketing Management* (13th ed.). Upper Saddle River, NJ: Prentice Hall.

Lehmann, Donald R. and Russell S. Winer (2007), *Analysis for Marketing Planning* (7th ed.). Boston, MA: McGraw-Hill/Irvin.

———————— Chapter Three ————————

Developing a Strategy

*All men can see the tactics whereby I conquer, but what
none can see is the strategy out of which victory is evolved.*
Sun Tzu, Chinese military strategist

The term *strategy* comes from the Greek *stratēgia*—meaning "generalship"—used in reference to maneuvering troops into position before a battle. In marketing, strategy refers to a company's master plan designed to achieve a particular goal. Developing a marketing strategy involves two key components: identifying the target market and developing the offering's value proposition. These two aspects of marketing strategy are the focus of this chapter.

Overview

Delineating an offering's strategy involves two key decisions: (1) identifying the target market (i.e., target customers, collaborators, competitors, company, and context) and (2) developing the offering's value proposition (Figure 1). Arriving at these two decisions is often an iterative process in which the identification of the target market drives the development of the value proposition. At the same time, a company's ability to develop a superior value proposition for certain customers is a key factor in deciding which markets to pursue.

Figure 1. Marketing Strategy: The Big Picture

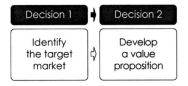

The two components of strategy development—identifying the target market and developing a value proposition—are discussed in more detail in the following sections.

Identifying the Target Market

Identifying the right target market is the key to developing a successful marketing strategy. The process of identifying a target market is guided by the company's ability to develop an offering that can satisfy a particular need of its target customers better than the competition and in a way that creates value for the company and its collaborators.

Identifying a target market involves five types of analyses: (1) customer analysis, (2) company analysis, (3) collaborator analysis, (4) competitor analysis, and (5) context analysis. These five factors are often referred to as the "Five C's" and are illustrated in Figure 2.

Figure 2. Target Market Analysis: The 5-C Framework

The key aspects of target market analysis are discussed in more detail below.

- *Customer analysis* involves identifying potential buyers for whom the company will tailor its offering. Identifying target customers—a process commonly referred to as targeting—typically involves two decisions: (1) selecting which customers to serve and (2) identifying actionable strategies to reach these customers.

  Selecting target customers (also referred to as strategic targeting) is guided by the company's ability to fulfill customer needs better than the competition in a way that creates value for the company and its collaborators. Because fulfilling customer needs is central to the success of an offering, target customers are typically identified through their underlying needs. Selecting target customers through their needs, however, is difficult because these needs are, in most cases, not readily observable. Therefore, identifying observable (actionable) characteristics that enable the company to reach customers with these needs (also referred to as tactical targeting) is essential for developing an effective and cost-efficient targeting strategy. Typical actionable characteristics involve demographic (e.g., age, gender, and income), geographic (e.g., country, region, and postal codes), psychographic (e.g., personality, moral values, and lifestyle), and behavioral characteristics (e.g., user status, purchase frequency, and price sensitivity).

  The process of identifying target customers often involves grouping customers into segments, such that customers within each segment are likely to respond in a similar fashion to the company's offerings. This process of dividing customers into groups, commonly referred to as *segmentation*, aims to improve the effectiveness and efficiency of a company's marketing activities by ignoring the nonessential differences among customers within each segment and treating these customers as if they were a single entity. The processes of segmentation and targeting are discussed in more detail in Chapter 7.

- *Company analysis* builds on the selected target market to define the particular business unit (e.g., a department, division, branch, or the entire company) that will manage the offering and to evaluate resources (e.g., core competencies and strategic assets) that will enable this unit to create superior value to target customers, the company, and its collaborators. A more detailed discussion of a company's ability to create superior value to target customers is offered in Chapter 8.

- *Collaborator analysis* builds on the selected target market to identify entities that work with the company to design, communicate, and deliver value to target customers. Collaboration can occur in several areas: product design, service development, branding, pricing, incentives management, communication, and distribution. For example, companies can collaborate to develop a product (research and development collaboration), create a customer incentive (promotional collaboration), and/or deliver the offering to the customer (channel collaboration). A more detailed discussion of different aspects of collaboration is offered in Chapter 9.

- *Competitive analysis* involves identifying current and potential competitors, as well as their goals and resources. Competitors are entities with offerings that aim to fulfill the same needs of the same target customers as the company's offering. Because competitors are defined relative to the needs of the target segment, the competition often goes beyond the traditional industry-defined categories. For instance, Coca-Cola competes not only with other cola producers such as Pepsi, but also with producers of all products that could potentially fulfill the same need, such as juice, bottled water, and milk. A more detailed discussion of different aspects of competition is offered in Chapter 10.

- *Context analysis* involves evaluating the relevant aspects of the environment in which the company operates. The key context factors include the economic, technological, socio-cultural, regulatory, and physical environment in which the marketing exchange takes place. A more detailed discussion of the marketing context is offered in Chapter 11.

Identifying target customers is crucial for defining the other aspects of the market. Because customers in different target segments vary in their needs and are likely to respond in different ways to the company's offering, each target segment defines its own market and requires its own analysis. To illustrate, different target customers might be served by different competitors, require a different set of collaborators (e.g., different distribution channels), be managed by different business units of the company, and/or operate in a different economic, technological, socio-cultural, regulatory, and physical context.

Developing a Value Proposition

The development of a value proposition is the key aspect of creating and managing a value exchange. An offering's success is ultimately determined by its ability to create value for the relevant market participants: target customers, the company, and its collaborators. Optimizing these three types of value—a process captured in the 3-V framework—is not only the basis for developing a successful value proposition, but is also the key factor for the success of a company's entire marketing strategy (Figure 3). A more detailed discussion of managing company, customer, and collaborator value is offered in Chapters 12–14.

Figure 3. Developing a Value Proposition: The 3-V Framework

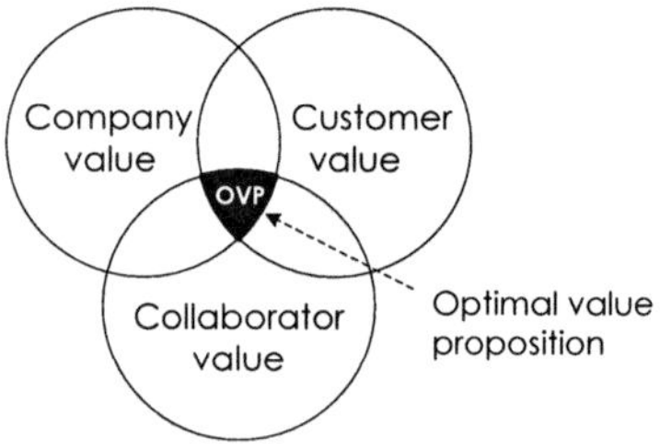

An important component of an offering's value proposition is its *positioning*. Positioning reflects the most important aspect(s) of an offering's value proposition to create a distinct image of the offering in a customer's mind. Unlike the value proposition, which captures *all* of the benefits and costs of an offering, positioning captures only the most important aspect(s) of the offering's value proposition. To illustrate, safety is one of the many aspects of Volvo's value proposition that the company chose to position its cars in the minds of its customers. Thus, positioning aims to present the offering in a way that accentuates its primary benefit(s), providing customers with a compelling reason to choose this offering. The key aspects of developing a value proposition and a positioning strategy are discussed in more detail in Chapter 12.

The Big Picture

The two aspects of strategy development—identifying an offering's target market and developing its value proposition—are an iterative process in which the value proposition is determined by customer needs, and the selection of a target customers is, in turn, determined by the company's ability to create superior value for these customers. Thus, the development of a marketing strategy involves simultaneously identifying the target market—a process captured in the 5-C framework—and evaluating the company's ability to create value for target customers, collaborators, and company stakeholders—a process captured in the 3-V framework. These two aspects of strategy development are illustrated in Figure 4.

Figure 4. Managing the Value Exchange

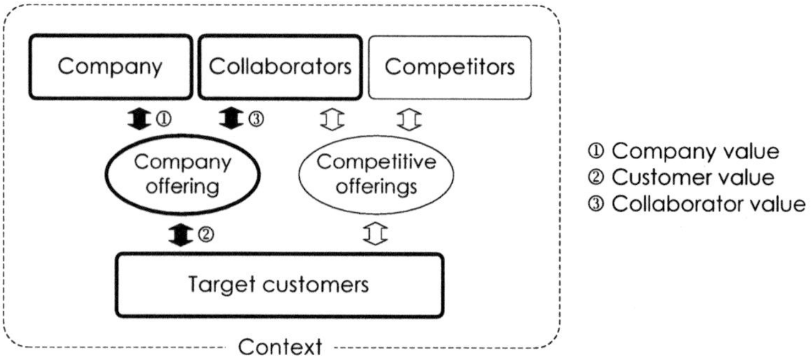

The process of identifying a target market and developing a value proposition can be illustrated using the example of the iPod, the digital music player from Apple.

- The iPod's primary target *customers* are individuals (predominantly teenagers and young adults) with a need for mobile access to music/video recordings who are able to afford the iPod's price tag. For these customers, the iPod creates *value* by offering a revolutionary digital music player that lets them store music and video content in their pockets and listen to or view it wherever they go.

- Apple's *collaborators* include companies like PortalPlayer, which provided the firmware and software platform for the iPod, and Pixo, which developed the design and the user interface. The iPod creates *value* for these collaborators by providing a highly visible offering that serves as a showcase for their capabilities. Apple's collaborators also include content providers, such as Sony, EMI, Universal, and Warner record labels. For these collaborators, iPod and iTunes create *value* by offering an alternative distribution channel to reach a desirable target audience. Apple's collaborators also include a diverse set of retailers: mass merchandisers (e.g., Wal-Mart), consumer electronics retailers (e.g., Best Buy), and specialized Apple resellers. The iPod creates *value* for its distributors by attracting customers to their stores and helping them increase their sales revenues and net income.

- From a *company* perspective, the iPod builds on Apple's core competency of customer-focused product development and strategic assets, which include technological, design, and marketing expertise; its existing customer base; and the power of its brand. For Apple, the iPod creates *value* by offering a steady stream of revenues, and by providing a platform for product development that enabled Apple to extend its digital player product line (e.g., iPod Shuffle and iPod Nano) and launch new products such as the iPhone.

- iPod *competitors* include Zune (Microsoft), Zen (Creative Labs), Sansa (Sandisk), and Insignia (Best Buy), which offer similar benefits and target the same customers. The success of the iPod is determined by its ability to deliver superior value (relative to these competitors) to its target customers and collaborators.

- The iPod's success is also a function of the *context* in which it is being sold and used. Among the relevant context factors for the iPod are the overall economic conditions (which affect consumers' disposable income), technological developments (e.g., the development of alternative data compression technologies and their compatibility with Apple's proprietary AAC and Apple Lossless formats), and regulatory factors (e.g., regulations guiding the copyright and licensing of digital content).

To succeed, an offering must create superior value to target customers, the company, and its collaborators. Because an offering's ability to deliver superior customer value is a function of the underlying customer needs, a company must develop distinct strategies for serving each target segment it decides to pursue. Thus, when targeting multiple customer segments, a company must evaluate—for each segment—its core competencies and strategic assets, its collaborators and competitors, as well as the relevant context factors. A more detailed discussion of targeting multiple customer segments is offered in Chapter 24.

Summary

Strategy outlines the master plan of actions aimed at achieving the company goal. Strategy development involves two key components: (1) identifying a target market and (2) designing the offering's value proposition for target customers, the company, and its collaborators.

Identifying target markets begins with identifying potential buyers for whom the company will tailor its offering. The process of identifying target customers involves two decisions: selecting which customers to serve and which to ignore (strategic targeting), and identifying actionable strategies to reach these customers (tactical targeting). The process of identifying target customers is discussed in more detail in Chapter 7. Identifying target customers is followed by defining the other aspects of the market: the company, its collaborators and competitors, and the context in which the company operates (5-C framework).

The value proposition is the key aspect of an offering's strategy. The key principle in developing a value proposition is that it should be optimized to deliver superior value to target customers in a way that enables the company and its collaborators to reach their strategic goals—a concept captured by the 3-V framework. The process of developing and managing a successful value proposition is discussed in more detail in Chapters 12–14.

Relevant Frameworks: The 3-C Framework

The 3-C framework, advanced by the Japanese strategist Kenichi Ohmae, suggests that a manager should focus on three key factors for success: the company, the customer, and the competition. By understanding these three factors and integrating them into a strategic framework (or, to use Ohmae's terminology, a strategic triangle), the company can achieve a sustainable competitive advantage. The 3-C framework suggests that managers need to evaluate the business environment in which they operate: the strengths and weaknesses of their own company, the needs of their customers, and the strengths and weaknesses of their competitors. The 3-C framework is simple, intuitive, and easy to understand and use—factors that have contributed to its popularity.

An important limitation of the 3-C framework is that it does not explicitly account for two important market factors: collaborators and context. Despite the important role collaborators (e.g., suppliers and distributors) play in developing and delivering a company's offerings, they are not part of the 3-C model. Furthermore, the 3-C framework does not explicitly account for the variety of economic, technological, socio-cultural, regulatory, and physical factors that compose the context in which the company operates. Because of these limitations, marketing analysis can be better served by the more comprehensive and up-to-date 5-C framework (customers, company, collaborators, competitors, and context).

Additional Readings

Aaker, David A. (2007), *Strategic Market Management* (8th ed.). New York, NY: John Wiley & Sons.

Kotler, Philip (1999), *Kotler on Marketing: How to Create, Win, and Dominate Markets*. New York, NY: Free Press.

Lehmann, Donald R. and Russell S. Winer (2007), *Analysis for Marketing Planning* (7th ed.). Boston, MA: McGraw-Hill/Irvin.

Ohmae, Kenichi (1982), *The Mind of the Strategist: The Art of Japanese Business*. New York, NY: McGraw-Hill.

Chapter Four

Designing the Tactics

Strategy without tactics is the slowest route to victory.
Tactics without strategy is the noise before defeat.
Sun Tzu, Chinese military strategist

Tactics reflect the means employed to translate the desired strategy into a specific set of actions. In the military, tactics refers to the deployment of troops during the battle. In marketing, tactics denotes a set of specific activities—commonly referred to as the marketing mix—employed to execute a given strategy. The key aspects of developing marketing tactics are the focus of this chapter.

Overview

An offering's tactics involve a set of specific activities employed to execute a given strategy. The tactical aspect of an offering can be represented as a process of designing, communicating, and delivering value to target customers, collaborators, and the company. These three aspects of marketing tactics—designing, communicating, and delivering value—are referred to as the D-C-D framework (Figure 1).

Figure 1. Marketing Tactics: The D-C-D Framework

These three aspects of marketing tactics are defined by a set of specific decisions referring to specific tactical elements discussed in more detail in the following section.

The Key Tactical Elements

A company's tactics involve seven different elements: product, service, brand, price, incentives, communication, and distribution. These tactical elements, commonly referred to as the marketing mix, are summarized below.

- The *product* aspect of the offering captures some of its key functional characteristics. Products typically change ownership during purchase; once created, they can be physically separated from the manufacturer and distributed to end users via multiple channels.

- The *service* aspect of the offering is in many respects similar to the product aspect, with two main exceptions: change of ownership and separability. Unlike products, which typically change ownership at purchase, services do not necessarily imply a change in ownership; instead, the customer acquires the right to use the service within a given time frame. Furthermore, unlike products, which can be physically separated from the manufacturer, services are usually delivered and consumed at the same time; as a result, they cannot be inventoried or distributed through independent channels.

- The *brand* is a marketing tool used to identify the offering, differentiate it from the competition, and create value that goes beyond its product and service characteristics Brand identity and differentiation are achieved on dimensions such as name, logo, symbol, character, slogan, jingle, and packaging. Brand value is typically achieved by creating meaningful brand associations.

- The *price* reflects the monetary aspect of the offering; it refers to the amount of money the company charges for the benefits provided by its offering. In dynamic markets, the monetary value of the offering is determined not by price alone; it is also a function of various monetary incentives, such as volume discounts, price reductions, coupons, and rebates. Even though companies typically consider monetary incentives as part of their promotional activity, from a customer's perspective, many of these incentives are viewed as an integral component of an offering's price.

- *Incentives* enhance the value of the offering by providing additional, typically short-term, benefits and/or by reducing costs. Incentives may be divided into two categories: monetary, such as volume discounts, price reductions, coupons, and rebates; and nonmonetary, such as premiums, contests, and rewards. In contrast to monetary incentives, which typically aim to reduce an offering's costs, nonmonetary incentives typically aim to enhance the offering's benefits.

- *Communication* aims to inform target customers about the availability of the offering and highlight its particular characteristics. The message may involve any of the first five marketing mix variables: product, service, brand, price, and incentives. For example, a company may choose to promote the benefits of a product or service, communicate the meaning of its brand, publicize its price, and inform customers about its current incentives.

- *Distribution* captures the channel through which the offering is delivered to customers. Distribution is not limited to delivering the company's products and services to customers; it can involve the other marketing mix variables as well. To illustrate, brand delivery involves enabling customers to experience the brand (e.g., Disney World theme parks and Niketown retail stores function as channels delivering Disney and Nike brands to customers). Similarly, price delivery involves the channels for collecting customer payments, as well as for processing reverse payments (e.g., refunds). In the same vein, incentive delivery involves the mechanisms for distributing and implementing incentives (e.g., processing coupons and rebates).

The seven marketing mix variables—product, service, brand, price, incentives, communication, and distribution—can be related to the processes of designing, communicating, and delivering value, as shown in Figure 2. Here, product, service, brand, price, and incentives compose the value-design aspect of the offering; communication captures the value-communication aspect; and distribution reflects the value-delivery aspect of the value-creation process.

Figure 2. The D-C-D Marketing Mix Framework

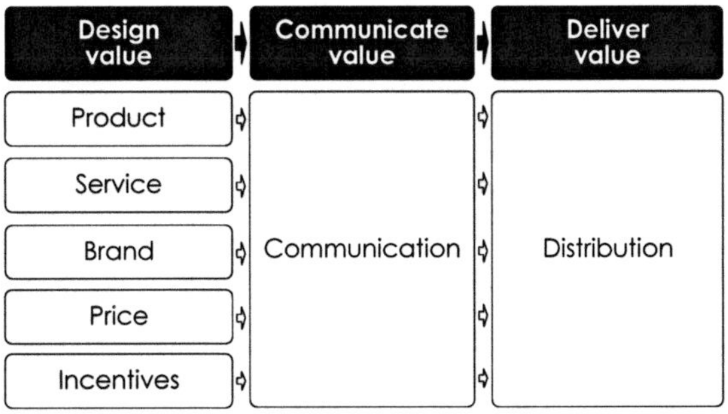

To illustrate, consider the processes of designing, communicating, and delivering value in the case of the Apple's iPod:

- *Designing value.* The value-design aspect of the marketing mix involves five key components: product, service, brand, price, and incentives. For example, the product aspect of the iPod reflects the functionality offered by the digital player, such as hard drive capacity, display, battery life, design, and user-friendly interface. The service aspect of the offering involves the service and technical support that come with the product, as well as augmented services such as iTunes. The brand aspect is defined by the Apple and iPod brands, which differentiate this offering from other functionally similar offerings by Microsoft, Dell, and Sony. The price reflects the retail price at which the iPod is being sold to customers. Incentives include monetary rewards such as price reductions, coupons, and educational discounts, as well as nonmonetary rewards such as free music/video downloads.

- *Communicating value.* Communication aims to inform target customers about the benefits of iPod and iTunes, enhance the iPod and Apple brands, and inform customers about the price of the iPod and the relevant incentives. This information is conveyed to target customers through various media formats such as advertising, public relations, personal selling, and product placement in newscasts, movies, and talk shows.

- *Delivering value.* The distribution component encompasses the channels used to deliver the offering to end-users. Thus, the iPod product is delivered through various direct and indirect channels such as Apple's online store, its brick-and-mortar retail stores, and other retailers such as Best Buy. The music download service is delivered through Apple's iTunes website, and diagnostic and repair service is delivered though its brick-and-mortar stores, as well as through various resellers. The Apple brand is delivered through its website and its brick-and-mortar retail stores, which enable customers to experience the essence of the Apple brand. The price is delivered through the retailers, who collect payments from customers and, when necessary, adjust payments made (e.g., price-matching adjustments and refunds). Finally, incentives such as free music downloads are delivered through the iTunes website.

Marketing Functions and Market Entities

An offering's marketing mix describes the marketing functions involved in the process of designing, communicating, and delivering value to target customers, collaborators, and the company. Marketing functions can be implemented by the company managing the offering, as well as by its collaborators and/or customers. To illustrate, the value-design function, such as product development, can be outsourced to specialized research and development companies, the value-communication function is often implemented by advertising agencies, and the value-delivery function is typically implemented by the retail channel members.

Each of the key market entities involved in the value-delivery process—the company, its collaborators, and its customers—can perform one or more of the value-delivery functions: designing, communicating, and/or delivering value (Figure 3). For example, advertising agencies can play a significant role in both designing the value of the offering (e.g., by facilitating the building and managing of the offering's brand) and communicating its value (e.g., by creating awareness of the offering's benefits). Similarly, distribution channels can play an important role in designing the value of the offering (e.g., by customizing the product, augmenting the service, setting the price, and managing incentives), communicating the offering's value, as well as delivering the actual offering to target customers.

Figure 3. Marketing Functions and Market Entities[1]

Market entities	Marketing functions		
	Design value	Communicate value	Deliver value
Company	✓	✓	✓
Collaborators	✓	✓	✓
Customers	✓	✓	✓

Value creation through collaboration represents a fundamental shift away from the traditional business paradigm in which value is created in the company and then delivered to the customer to a new paradigm in which the value is jointly created by the company, its collaborators, and its customers. This value co-creation approach extends beyond the company's efforts in being customer-centric. Customer centricity calls for optimizing the company's business activities from a customer's standpoint. In contrast, value co-creation calls for involving customers and collaborators in the very process of designing, communicating, and delivering value. Thus, value co-creation is in the heart of the business models of companies like Harley-Davidson, Wikipedia, and YouTube.

Summary

Tactics identify how an offering's strategy is translated into a set of specific actions. Marketing tactics are defined by seven key elements, often referred to as the marketing mix: product, service, brand, price, incentives, communication, and distribution.

Conceptually, the tactical aspect of an offering can be represented by the processes of designing, communicating, and delivering value (referred to as the D-C-D framework). The processes of designing, communicating, and delivering value may be related to the seven marketing mix variables, such that product, service, brand, price, and incentives compose the value-design aspect of the offering; communication captures the value-communication aspect; and distribution reflects the value-delivery aspect of the offering.

Each of the key market entities involved in the value-delivery process—the company, its collaborators, and its customers—can perform one or more of the value-delivery functions: designing, communicating, and delivering value.

Relevant Frameworks: The 4-P Framework

The 4-P framework offers a relatively simple tool for planning and analyzing the execution of a given marketing strategy. According to this model, there are four key decisions that managers must make with respect to a given offering: (1) what features to include in the product, (2) how to price the product, (3) how to promote the product, and (4) in which distribution channels to "place" the product. These four decisions, often referred to as the marketing mix, are captured by the four P's: product, price, promotion, and place.

The 4-P framework is often misconstrued by managers who try to fit in other factors starting with "p" rather than focus on the underlying logic. For example, a common misinterpretation of the four P's involves including concepts such as positioning, people, personnel, processes, and productivity as one of the marketing mix variables. Positioning is not a marketing mix variable; rather, it is part of a company's overall strategy, which is then implemented through a particular combination of the marketing mix variables. In the same vein, people are typically viewed as an integral part of the company rather than as part of an offering's marketing mix. Another common misinterpretation of the 4-P framework concerns the use of "placement" instead of "place." The term "placement" refers to a promotional strategy that involves embedding a product in various forms of entertainment.

The 4-P framework has a number of important limitations. The most obvious is the absence of separate service and brand components. Because it was developed to explain the process involved in marketing consumer packaged goods, the 4-P framework does not explicitly account for the service element of the offering—a key drawback in today's service-oriented business environment. Furthermore, the brand is not explicitly considered as a separate marketing mix variable and is, instead, viewed as part of a company's product and/or promotion decisions.

Another potential limitation of the 4-P framework concerns the term "promotion." Promotion is a very broad term that includes two distinct types of marketing variables: incentives (e.g., price promotions, coupons, and trade promotions) and communication (e.g., advertising, public relations, and personal selling). While it is a common accounting practice to combine these factors, they each have a distinct impact on business processes. Thus, incentives tend to enhance the offering's value, whereas the primary role of communication is to inform customers about the offering. Therefore, for the purpose of marketing analysis, incentives and communication should be considered separately.

Finally, the use of the term "place" as an element of the marketing mix may be questioned. As the process of delivering the company's offering to customers becomes increasingly complex, it is more accurate to refer to this process as "distribution" or "channel" rather than simply as "place," a term rarely used in contemporary marketing analysis.

Because of the limitations of the 4-P framework, marketing analysis is better served by the more comprehensive and up-to-date D-C-D framework. In fact, the 4-P approach may be interpreted in the context of the D-C-D value-management framework, such that product and price represent the processes of creating value, promotion represents both the value-design and value-communication aspects of the offering, and place represents the value-delivery aspect of the offering (Figure 4).

Figure 4. The 4-P and the D-C-D Frameworks

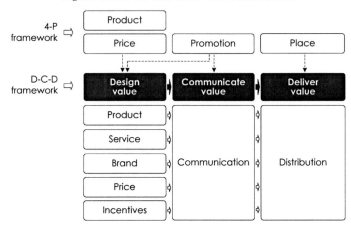

Additional Readings

Aaker, David A. (2007), *Strategic Market Management* (8th ed.). New York, NY: John Wiley & Sons.

Kotler, Philip and Kevin Lane Keller (2008), *Marketing Management* (13th ed.). Upper Saddle River, NJ: Prentice Hall.

Kotler, Philip (1999), *Kotler on Marketing: How to Create, Win, and Dominate Markets*. New York, NY: Free Press.

Lehmann, Donald R. and Russell S. Winer (2007), *Analysis for Marketing Planning* (7th ed.). Boston, MA: McGraw-Hill/Irvin.

Walker, Orville C., Jr., John W. Mullins, and Harper W. Boyd, Jr. (2008), *Marketing Strategy: A Decision-Focused Approach* (6th ed.). London: McGraw-Hill.

Notes

[1] The checkmarks in each box indicate that each collaborator can potentially contribute to the value-creaction process by designing, communicating, and/or delivering specific aspects of the offering's value to target customers.

Chapter Five

Defining the Implementation

Nothing comes merely by thinking about it.
John Wanamaker, U.S. merchant, founder of Wanamaker's department store

The development of the strategic and tactical aspects of an offering is followed by defining an implementation plan that outlines how an offering's strategy and tactics will be put into action. The key aspects of developing an implementation plan are the focus of this chapter.

Overview

The implementation plan delineates the specific activities involved in executing an offering's strategy and tactics. The development of an implementation plan involves three key decisions: (1) developing the business *infrastructure*, (2) designing the underlying business *processes*, and (3) determining the implementation *schedule* (Figure 1).

Figure 1. Implementation Management: The Big Picture

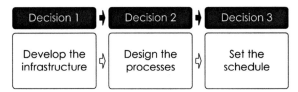

These three aspects of developing an implementation plan—developing the infrastructure, designing the processes, and setting the schedule—are described in more detail in the following sections.

Developing the Infrastructure

The business infrastructure involved in the implementation of a company's offering has two aspects: company infrastructure and collaborator infrastructure.

- The *company infrastructure* determines the formal relationships among different entities within an organization. Based on the degree of centralization and specialization, three common organizational structures can be identified: functional, divisional, and matrix. The functional structure organizes employees based on their function (e.g., research and development, manufacturing, marketing, finance). The divisional structure organizes employees based on the type of product or market involved, such that each division is responsible for a certain product/market and manages its own functional resources. The matrix organization combines the functional and divisional approach in a way that preserves the functional structure while creating specialized teams responsible for a particular product or market. These three types of organizational designs are discussed in more detail at the end of this chapter.

- The *collaborator infrastructure* determines the formal relationships among the company and its collaborators. Thus, to achieve greater effectiveness and cost-efficiency in managing a particular offering, a company might decide to out-source to a third party the implementation of different aspects of its marketing mix, including product manufacturing, customer support (e.g., call centers), branding, managing incentives, communication (e.g., advertising and public relations), and distribution. A more detailed discussion of different aspects of the collaborator infrastructure is offered in Chapter 9.

Designing the Processes

Implementation processes depict the specific actions that need to be taken to execute an offering's strategy and tactics. These processes involve managing the flow of information, goods, services, and money. In this context, several types of implementation processes can be identified: strategic planning, resource management, product management, service management, brand management, price management, incentives management, communication management, and distribution management.

- *Strategic planning processes* include activities leading to the identification of an offering's target market (customers, collaborators, competitors, company, and context), and defining the offering's value proposition. These processes typically involve gathering information about the target market (i.e., marketing research) and using this information to evaluate alternative courses of action, as well as ultimately deciding on the specifics of the offering's action plan.

- *Resource management processes* involve activities focused on managing human resources (e.g., recruiting, performance evaluation, compensation, and professional development), functional resources (e.g., manufacturing capacity), and financial resources required for the implementation of a given offering. Resource management involves the acquisition of resources that are new to the company and the allocation of existing resources across a company's business units.

- *Product management processes* involve activities used by the company to design (e.g., identify the key product attributes) and manufacture (e.g., procurement, inbound logistics, and production) a given offering.

- *Service management processes* involve activities that aim to design (e.g., identify the key service attributes) and implement (e.g., oversee installation, support, and repair activities) the service aspect of an offering.

- *Brand management processes* involve activities that aim to design (e.g., determine the identity and the meaning of the brand) and manage an offering's brand.

- *Price management processes* involve the specific price-setting (e.g., setting retail prices and wholesale price schedules) and price-management (e.g., modifying existing prices) activities.

- *Incentives management processes* involve activities that aim to design (e.g., identify the type and nature of customer and collaborator incentives) and manage (e.g., distribute and process coupons and implement temporary price discounts) an offering's incentives.

- *Communication management processes* involve activities that aim to design (e.g., identify the message, media, and the creative solution) and manage (e.g., produce the advertisement and place it in the appropriate media channel) an offering's communications.

- *Distribution management processes* involve activities that aim to design (e.g., determine the optimal channel structure) and manage (e.g., warehousing, order fulfillment, and transportation) an offering's distribution system.

Setting the Schedule

The process of setting an implementation schedule involves deciding on the timing and the optimal sequence in which individual tasks should be performed to ensure effective and cost-efficient completion of the project. The two project management techniques most commonly used to plan, schedule, and control complex projects are the Critical Path Method (CPM) and the Program Evaluation Review Technique (PERT). A more detailed discussion of CPM and PERT is offered at the end of this chapter.

Once the optimal sequence and duration of the key implementation tasks have been determined, the next step involves the development of an implementation chart. This chart maps the individual tasks and their timeline in a format that enables a manager to easily identify the optimal sequence and duration of these tasks in the context of the entire project. The implementation chart can involve a box-and-arrow representation of the individual tasks, illustrating the CPM/PERT decision process. A very popular method of representing the implementation plan, referred to as the Gantt chart, involves using bars to visually represent the timeline and duration of each individual task. A more detailed discussion of Gantt charts is offered at the end of this chapter.

Summary

The implementation plan delineates the activities involved in executing an offering's strategy and tactics. The development of an implementation plan involves three key decisions: developing the business *infrastructure*, designing the underlying business *processes*, and setting the implementation *schedule*.

The implementation infrastructure involves two aspects: company infrastructure (i.e., functional, divisional, or matrix) and collaborator infrastructure. Implementation processes involve the actions required to execute an offering's strategy and tactics. Several types of processes can be identified: strategic planning, resource management, product management, service management, brand management, price management, incentives management, communication management, and distribution management.

Setting an implementation schedule involves deciding on the project timeline and the optimal sequence in which individual tasks should be performed to ensure effective and cost-efficient completion of the project. The two project-management techniques most commonly used to plan, schedule, and control complex projects are the Critical Path Method (CPM) and the Program Evaluation Review Technique (PERT). The implementation schedule is typically presented in the form of a chart (e.g., Gantt chart) used to guide the implementation process.

Relevant Concepts: Organizational Infrastructure

Functional Structure: A structure in which employees are organized based on their function (e.g., research and development, manufacturing, marketing, accounting/finance, and human resources; Figure 2).

Figure 2. Functional Organizational Structure

Divisional Structure: The divisional structure organizes employees based on the type of product or market, such that each division is responsible for a certain product/market and manages its own functional resources (Figure 3). In particular, *product structure* groups employees based on the company's products or services, with each division representing a separate product (or product line). For example, Buick, Cadillac, and Chevrolet are different divisions of General Motors, each one managing its own set of offerings. *Market structure*, on the other hand, groups employees based on the target markets the company serves. Target markets are typically defined based on a relevant criterion that requires a distinct set of assets and core competencies. Common criteria used in developing market-focused organizational structure involve readily observed factors such as customer type (business vs. consumer), customer behavior (e.g., high-volume vs. low-volume buyers), and geographic location. Note that not all functional areas might be allocated across divisions; a company with a divisional structure might also have a number of centralized units (e.g., research and development, human resources, and accounting and finance).

Figure 3. Divisional Organizational Structure

Matrix Structure: The matrix structure combines the functional and divisional approach in a way that preserves the functional structure, simultaneously creating specialized teams responsible for a particular product or market (Figure 4). As a result, some employees end up having two managers: a functional manager and a product/market manager. Because of its flexibility, the matrix structure is very common in large organizations; it is also fairly complex, which makes it more difficult to implement.

Figure 4. Matrix Organizational Structure

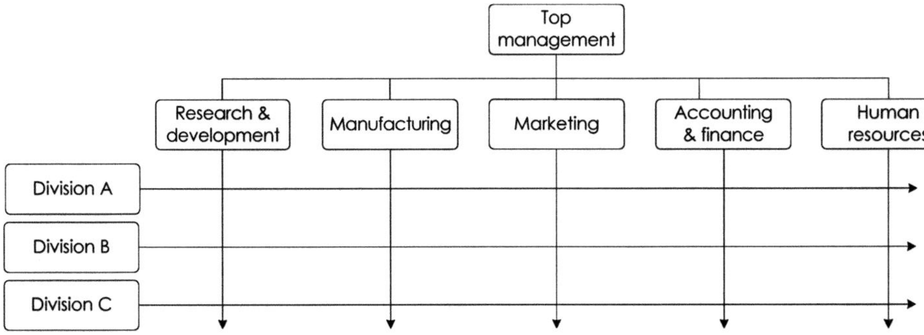

Relevant Concepts: Project Scheduling

Critical Path Method (CPM): A mathematically derived algorithm for scheduling project activities. CPM calculates the longest path of planned activities to the end of the project, as well as the earliest and latest that each activity can begin and end while keeping the project on schedule. CPM is based on the notion that the implementation of a project is controlled by a relatively small set of activities that make up the longest time path through the activity network (i.e., the sequence of activities that adds up to the longest overall duration). The goal of CPM, therefore, is to identify these "critical" activities and use them as the backbone (often referred to as the critical path) of the project schedule. The advantage of identifying these key activities is that it allows the other less crucial activities to be planned around the activities composing the critical path.

CPM typically involves six key steps: (1) identify the specific activities and milestones associated with the project, (2) determine the optimal sequence of individual activities (i.e., which activities must precede and which must follow others), (3) develop a "network" diagram representing the individual activities and their relationship (e.g., sequence), (4) estimate the time and cost allocated to each activity, (5) determine the longest time path through the network (also referred to as the critical path), and (6) monitor the project implementation and, when necessary, modify the network.

The process of identifying the critical path is illustrated in Figure 5. Here specific outcomes are depicted by circles and individual activities are depicted by arrows; the numbers associated with each arrow indicate the duration (e.g., in weeks) of the corresponding activity. Analysis of the relationship between the different outcomes indicates that Outcomes C and D need to be completed prior to achieving the desired Outcome E, Outcomes A and B need to be achieved prior to achieving Outcome C, and Outcome A needs to be achieved prior to achieving Outcome D. Analysis of the time necessary to complete each individual activity further indicates that the longest path through the network is A-C-E (12 weeks). Hence, A-C-E is the critical path that should be used as the backbone in scheduling the remaining activities.

Figure 5. The Critical Path Method: An Illustration

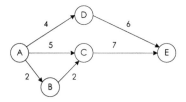

Project Evaluation and Review Technique (PERT): A method for analyzing the tasks involved in the implementation of a given project. Conceptually, PERT is very similar to CPM in that both models employ the notion of critical path and involve the same six implementation steps. The key distinction between the two is the manner in which the duration of a given activity is estimated. Unlike CPM, which relies on a single duration estimate, PERT involves calculating a weighted average of three different estimates of the expected completion time (optimistic, most likely, and pessimistic). Recent extensions of PERT and CPM enable managers to control resources other than time and costs, making these models general enough to be applicable to most business implementation tasks.

Gantt Chart: A bar chart illustrating the timeline for managing a particular project. Named after Henry Gantt—an American mechanical engineer and management consultant—this chart typically indicates the start and the finish dates of the key project tasks. The typical Gantt chart is a matrix that lists on the vertical axis all the tasks to be performed and on the horizontal axis lists a description of each task (e.g., estimated task duration, skill level needed to perform the task, and the individual/team assigned to the task); horizontal bars represent the starting time and duration of each task (Figure 6). Depending on the nature of the project, the time frame can be expressed in hours, days, weeks, months, or any other time units.

Figure 6. Gantt Chart: An Illustration

Activity	Timeline (weeks)									
	1	2	3	4	5	6	7	8	9	10
Activity A										
Activity B										
Activity C										
Activity D										

Additional Readings

Jeston, John and Johan Nelis (2008), Business Process Management: Practical Guidelines to Successful Implementations (2nd ed.). New York, NY: Elsevier.

Lewis, James P. (2006), Fundamentals of Project Management (3rd ed.). New York, NY: AMACOM.

Madison, Dan (2005), Process Mapping, Process Improvement, and Process Management: A Practical Guide to Enhancing Work and Information Flow. Chico, CA: Paton Press.

Chapter Six

Identifying Controls

Put all your eggs in the one basket and—WATCH THAT BASKET.
Mark Twain

To ensure successful implementation of its strategy and tactics, a company must develop a set of controls to monitor the progress toward its goal. The key aspects of developing marketing controls are the focus of this chapter.

Overview

Marketing controls aim to evaluate a company's progress toward its strategic goals and monitor for changes in the environment in which the company operates. The control aspect of managing an offering involves two activities: (1) *performance evaluation*, which involves evaluating the company's current performance, and (2) *environmental analysis*, which involves evaluating the environment in which the company operates for potential opportunities and threats (Figure 1).

Figure 1. Marketing Controls: The Big Picture

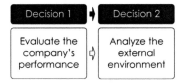

The two aspects of marketing controls—evaluating the company performance and analyzing the external environment—are discussed in more detail below.

Performance Evaluation

Performance evaluation involves evaluating the outcomes of the company's actions vis-à-vis its goals. Performance evaluation can lead to one of two outcomes: adequate goal progress or performance gaps.

- *Adequate goal progress* indicates that the company is on track to achieving its goal(s).

- *Performance gaps* signify a discrepancy between the desired and actual performance on a key metric. To illustrate, a decline in an offering's market share reflects a performance gap between the company's desire to strengthen its market position and the actual decrease in market share. An overview of some of the commonly used marketing metrics is offered in Chapter 27.

In cases when performance evaluation reveals a gap, the first step is to identify its primary actionable cause—a cause that the company can act on and devise action to remove. Because the environment in which the company operates is reflected in the five C's, the causes leading to a performance gap can be derived from the 5-C framework. Thus, five types of performance-gap causes can be identified: (1) causes stemming from the behavior of target *customers* (e.g., a change in customers' needs), (2) causes resulting from the behavior of the company's *collaborators* (e.g., an increase in the channel margins), (3) causes related to the *company's* own actions (e.g., an increase in internal costs), (4) causes attributed to *competitors'* actions (e.g., the launch of a competing offering), and (5) causes related to the economic, technological, sociocultural, regulatory, and physical *context* in which the company and its collaborators operate (e.g., a downturn in the overall economic conditions).

Once the primary actionable cause has been identified, the next step involves modifying the current action plan to remove the cause and put the company back on track toward achieving its goal. The key principle in modifying the action plan is that the changes should directly follow from the already identified primary actionable cause of the performance gap. To illustrate, if a decline in sales volume stems from deteriorating product quality resulting from inferior raw materials, then the logical solution is to develop a plan to improve product quality by identifying alternative sources of raw materials (e.g., replacing suppliers). The key aspects of the process of evaluating a company's performance are illustrated in Figure 2.

Figure 2. Marketing Controls: Performance Evaluation

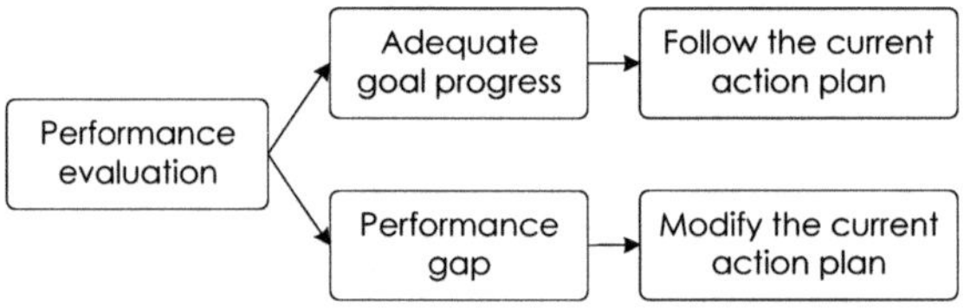

Environmental Analysis

Environmental analysis aims to identify changes in the environment in which the company operates and, when necessary, adjust its business activities to better reflect the new environment. Depending on their impact on the company, most environmental factors can be viewed as either opportunities, threats, or as neutral.[1]

- *Opportunities* are factors that are likely to have a favorable impact on the company's offering. Factors typically considered opportunities involve the introduction of new, favorable government regulations, a decrease in competition, or an increase in consumer demand.

- *Threats* are factors that are likely to have an unfavorable impact on the company's offering. Factors typically considered threats involve the introduction of new, unfavorable government regulations, an increase in competition, or a decline in consumer demand.

- *Neutral factors* are largely irrelevant to the company's business. Because they are unlikely to have a material impact on the company's performance, they are usually not taken into account in the subsequent analyses.

Once the key opportunities and threats have been identified, the next step involves modifying the current action plan to take advantage of the opportunities and counteract the impact of threats. The basic principle in modifying the action plan is that the changes should directly address the identified opportunities/threats. To illustrate, a company may respond to changes in the overall economic conditions by modifying its pricing and/or incentives strategy. The key aspects of environmental analysis are illustrated in Figure 3.

Figure 3. Marketing Controls: Environmental Analysis

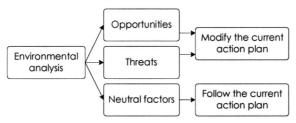

The Role of Controls in Marketing Management

Performance evaluation and control processes can be summarized as shown in Figure 4. The company's current and new marketing plans are organized using the G-STIC (goal, strategy, tactics, implementation, and control) framework, whereas the control aspect involves evaluating the offering's current performance (success or performance gap) and monitoring the environment for changes (i.e., identifying new opportunities and/or threats).

Figure 4. Marketing Controls as a Process

Current plan	Control		New plan
Goal	Performance evaluation	Environmental analysis	Goal
Strategy			Strategy
Tactics			Tactics
Implementation			Implementation
Control			Control

The key principle in revising the marketing plan is that changes should be directly linked to the identified primary actionable cause of the problem (in the case of performance gaps) and/or to the identified opportunities and threats. Thus, if the primary cause of the company's inability to achieve its goals is that these goals are unrealistic, then the solution is to set new and more realistic goals. If the primary cause is inefficient strategy, then the solution involves redesigning the existing strategy in a way that maximizes value for all relevant market participants (e.g., identifying new target markets; modifying the overall value proposition of the offering to customers, company, and/or its collaborators; and launching a new product). Similarly, if the problem has been attributed to suboptimal tactics, then the solution needs to focus on optimizing the marketing mix variables. If the cause of the problem is poor implementation, then the solution needs to focus on improving the processes underlying implementation and training or replacing the people managing these processes. Finally, if the cause of the problem is using inadequate controls, then the solution should focus on developing adequate measurements to evaluate the company's progress toward its goals.

Summary

The control aspect of managing an offering aims to ensure adequate progress toward the set goal. It encompasses two key activities: evaluating the company's performance and evaluating the environment in which it operates.

Performance analysis involves evaluating the outcomes of the company's actions vis-à-vis its goals and can lead to one of two outcomes: (1) success, which indicates adequate progress toward the established goal or (2) a performance gap that represents a discrepancy between a company's desired and actual performance on a key metric (e.g., net income).

Environmental analysis enables the company to identify changes in the environment in which it operates and, when necessary, adjust its business activities to better reflect the new environment. Environmental factors can be classified into one of three categories: (1) opportunities, which involve a favorable set of circumstances, (2) threats, which involve an unfavorable set of circumstances, and (3) neutral factors, which have no impact on the company's business activities.

The two control aspects of managing an offering—performance evaluation and environmental analysis—are used to evaluate an offering's performance vis-à-vis its marketing plan and, when necessary, modify this plan to better reflect the current situation.

Additional Readings

Aaker, David A. (2007), *Strategic Market Management* (8th ed.). New York, NY: John Wiley & Sons.

Kotler, Philip and Kevin Lane Keller (2008), *Marketing Management* (13th ed.). Upper Saddle River, NJ: Prentice Hall.

Koller, Tim, Marc Goedhart, David Wessels, and Thomas E. Copeland (2005), *Valuation: Measuring and Managing the Value of Companies* (4th ed.). Hoboken, NJ: John Wiley & Sons.

Lehmann, Donald R. and Russell S. Winer (2007), *Analysis for Marketing Planning* (7th ed.). Boston, MA: McGraw-Hill/Irvin.

Note

[1] The environmental analysis performed as part of marketing controls is very similar to the situation analysis preceding the development of an action plan (Step 1 in Figure 1, Chapter 1). The key difference is that whereas the situation analysis involves a comprehensive evaluation of the environment for the purpose of developing a *new* action plan, environmental analysis as a part of marketing controls focuses primarily on the changes in the environment in the context of the company's *existing* action plan.

Part Two

Situation Analysis and Identifying Target Markets

Introduction

Situation analysis and identifying target markets are the foundation for developing a successful marketing strategy. Situation analysis involves five aspects: (1) customer analysis, (2) company analysis, (3) collaborator analysis, (4) competitor analysis, and (5) context analysis. These five factors—commonly referred to as the "Five C's"—are illustrated in Figure 1.

Figure 1. The 5-C Market Analysis Framework

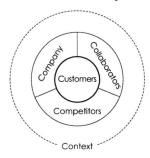

The 5-C framework serves as the organizing principle for this part of the book, as follows:

- *Customer analysis* involves identifying potential buyers for whom the company will tailor its offering. Identifying target customers involves three decisions: (1) grouping customers into segments, such that customers within each segment are likely to respond in a similar fashion to the company's offerings; (2) selecting which segments to serve and which to ignore; and (3) identifying actionable strategies to reach the selected segments. These decisions are discussed in more detail in Chapter 7.

- *Company analysis* builds on the selected target market to define the particular business unit that will manage the offering and to evaluate resources—core competencies and strategic assets—that will enable this unit to create superior value for target customers and collaborators. The key aspects of company analysis are discussed in Chapter 8.

- *Collaborator analysis* builds on the selected target market to identify entities that work with the company to design, communicate, and deliver value to target customers. The essential components of collaborator analysis are the focus of Chapter 9.

- *Competitor analysis* involves identifying the key current and potential competitors, as well as evaluating the competitive intensity of the selected target market. The key aspects of competitor analysis are discussed in Chapter 10.

- *Context analysis* involves evaluating the relevant aspects of the environment in which the company operates. The five aspects of context analysis—economic, technological, socio-cultural, regulatory, and physical—are the focus of Chapter 11.

Situation analysis and identifying target customers are crucial for defining the other aspects of the market. Because customers in different target segments vary in their needs and are likely to respond in a different fashion to the company's offering, each target segment defines its own market and requires separate analysis. Thus, different target customers tend to be served by different competitors, require a different set of collaborators (e.g., different distribution channels), are managed by different business units of the company, and/or operate in a different economic, technological, socio-cultural, regulatory, and physical context.

Chapter Seven

Customer Analysis

I don't know the key to success, but the key to failure is trying to please everybody.
Bill Cosby

Understanding customer needs and identifying market opportunities is the starting point in formulating a company's marketing strategy. A key aspect of customer analysis involves identifying groups of customers with similar preferences (segments) and deciding which segment(s) to target. These two strategic decisions—segmentation and targeting—are the focus of this chapter.

Segmentation

Segmentation is the process of dividing customers into groups with similar characteristics. The process of segmentation is based on the idea that the effectiveness and efficiency of a company's marketing activities can be improved by ignoring the nonessential differences among customers within each segment and treating these customers as if they were a single entity. Thus, through segmentation, the company can reduce the heterogeneity (i.e., diversity) in the marketplace and deal with a relatively small number of customer segments.

Grouping customers into segments serves two main functions. First, it optimizes the *effectiveness* of the offering by identifying the key differences among customers in order to develop a customized offering for each segment. Second, it optimizes the *cost-efficiency* of the offering by identifying the irrelevant differences among customers in order to deliver the same offering to customers within each segment. Thus, the key benefit of segmentation is in allowing the company to optimize marketing expenditures by grouping customers who are likely to respond in a similar fashion to the company's offerings. The key disadvantage of segmentation is that grouping customers into segments does not take into account potentially important differences that may exist among customers within each segment.

Segmentation, Mass Marketing, and One-to-One Marketing

The concept of segmentation can be better understood when considered in the context of two alternative marketing approaches: mass marketing and one-to-one marketing. Mass marketing refers to a scenario in which the same offering is given to all customers. A classic example is the strategy adopted by Ford's Model T, in which a single type of car was offered to all customers. In contrast, in one-to-one marketing, the company's offering is customized for each individual customer. *Haute couture*—made to order high-end clothing—exemplifies the one-to-one marketing strategy. In this context, segmentation can be viewed as a compromise between the mass-marketing approach and the one-to-one approach (Figure 1). By recognizing the diversity of customer needs, segmentation allows the company to design offerings that meet the needs of its customers better than the mass-marketing approach. The downside of segmentation vis-à-vis mass marketing is that developing different offerings for each segment could potentially lead to higher product development, communication, and distribution costs.

Figure 1. Segmentation, Mass Marketing, and One-to-One Marketing.

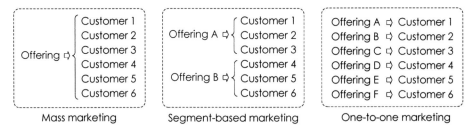

In cases when it is not cost-efficient to develop an individual offering for each customer (as advocated by the one-to-one approach), segmentation enables companies to streamline their product lines by developing offerings for groups of customers with similar needs. However, because grouping customers inevitably ignores some of the differences within each group, segmentation may decrease the effectiveness of the company's offering by not fully customizing the offering to fit the needs of individual customers.

An important issue in segmenting markets is determining the extent to which a market should be segmented and how large each segment should be. Segment size could potentially vary between a single segment encompassing the entire market (mass marketing) and multiple segments of one customer each (one-to-one marketing). As a general rule, segmentation is beneficial when the incremental value from effectively meeting the needs of resulting segments and from optimizing the communication and distribution strategies outweighs the costs of developing separate offerings for each segment. To illustrate, when the cost of customization is relatively high (e.g., durable goods manufacturing), companies tend to develop offerings that serve relatively large segments, whereas in industries where the cost of customization is low (e.g., online information delivery), segmentation can yield relatively small segments.

The process of segmentation is illustrated in Figure 2, in which customers vary on two factors represented by color and shape. In this context, there are three possible segmentation strategies: by color, by shape, and by color and shape. The choice of a particular segmentation criterion is a function of the degree to which this criterion captures strategically important aspects of customer reaction to the company's offering. The depth of segmentation, on the other hand, is determined by the degree of differences among potential buyers, such that more heterogeneous markets are typically associated with a greater number of customer segments. To illustrate, the three scenarios shown in Figure 2 vary in the depth of the underlying segmentation: Compared with Segmentations I and II, the depth of Segmentation III is greater, as evidenced by the larger number of segments and the lower within-segment heterogeneity.

Figure 2. Market Segmentation Strategies

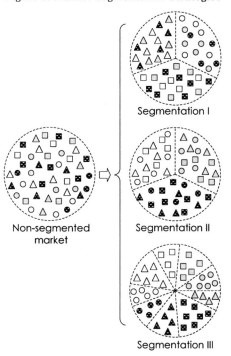

Criteria for Segmentation

When segmenting the market, the company's goal is to produce segments that differ in ways that are meaningful for marketing purposes. Thus, segmentation should yield groups of customers that vary in their response to the company's offering: Customers in the same segment should react in a similar fashion to the offering, while customers in different segments should vary in their response.

As a general rule, a good segmentation should yield segments that are mutually exclusive and collectively exhaustive: They should be sufficiently different from one another so that they do not overlap, and, at the same time, identified segments should include all customers in a given market. This can be achieved by using well-defined criteria to segment the market.

Value-Based vs. Profile-Based Segmentation

Two main criteria are used to divide customers into distinct segments: value factors and profile factors.

- *Value-based segmentation* groups customers based on their needs and the benefits they seek from the company's offerings. Value-based segmentation criteria can include three different types of factors: (1) functional factors, such as quality, performance, aesthetics, reliability, durability, and safety; (2) monetary factors, such as willingness to pay, financing preferences, and promotion preferences; and (3) psychological factors, such as image and social status.

- *Profile-based segmentation* captures some of the observable customer characteristics. In consumer marketing, four types of such characteristics are commonly used: demographic, geographic, psychographic, and behavioral. Each of these characteristics comprises one dimension of the customer profile:

  - *Demographic profile* includes factors such as age, gender, income, education, social status, and stage in the life cycle.

  - *Geographic profile* includes location identifiers such as country, region, city, postal code, and area code.

  - *Psychographic profile* includes relatively stable individual traits, such as personality, moral values, and lifestyle.

  - *Behavioral profile* captures customers' actions related to the company's offering, such as user status, distribution channel used, volume purchased, frequency of repurchase, price sensitivity, promotion sensitivity, and loyalty.

In business marketing, profile-based segmentation, referred to as *firmographics*, is based on factors such as location, size of company, industry, purchasing process, growth, and profitability.

User-Based vs. Occasion-Based Segmentation

Depending on the nature of the segmentation criterion, most segmentations fall into one of two categories: user-based and occasion-based. User-based segmentation groups customers based on their relatively stable individual characteristics, which are likely to determine their needs and/or behavior across different purchase and consumption occasions. To illustrate, a customer may have a strong preference for fast food (e.g., burgers and fries) across different consumption occasions.

In contrast, occasion-based segmentation groups customers based on purchase and consumption occasions. By focusing on usage occasions rather than on the individual characteristics of the customer, occasion-based segmentation implicitly assumes that the same customer is likely to display different needs depending on the occasion. For example, when buying wine, a customer's preference may vary as a function of the occasion (for cooking, for daily consumption, for a special occasion, or for a gift).

User-based segmentation is more appropriate in settings in which customers' needs are relatively stable across purchase occasions and, hence, can be used as a reliable predictor of their behavior on any particular purchase occasion. In contrast, occasion-based segmentation is more useful in cases in which customer needs vary across purchase occasions, and the same customer is likely to fall into different usage-based segments. To illustrate, the preference for regular versus light (diet) soft drinks is fairly stable across individuals and calls for user-based segmentation. In contrast, because the preference for a particular soft drink flavor is likely to vary over time for each individual depending on the usage occasion, in this case, occasion-based segmentation is more appropriate.

Targeting

The concept of targeting is used in two different contexts: (1) as a process of selecting which customers to serve and which to ignore and (2) as a process of identifying the actionable characteristics describing the customers that the company wishes to serve. These two aspects of targeting are discussed in more detail below.

Strategic Targeting

The strategic aspect of a company's targeting decision involves identifying which customers (segments) to serve and which to ignore (Figure 3). Strategic targeting reflects a company's decision to develop an offering that matches the needs of a particular set of customers, as well as customized communication and/or distribution activities to reach these customers. The basic principle underlying the selection of target customers is an offering's ability to deliver superior value to these customers in a way that enables the company and its collaborators to achieve their strategic goals. Because it is guided by the company's ability to fulfill customer needs better than the competition, strategic targeting is typically derived from value-based segmentation rather than from profile-based segmentation.

Figure 3. Strategic Targeting

- Target segment A
- Target segment B
- Target segment C

One of the key issues in strategic targeting analysis is identifying which criteria to use in selecting target customers. In general, three types of targeting criteria can be distinguished: (1) the inherent attractiveness of customers in a given segment; (2) the segment's compatibility with the company's strategic goals, competencies, and assets; and (3) the company's ability to serve the segment better than the competition. These three criteria are discussed in more detail below.

- *Segment attractiveness* reflects the ability of a particular segment to deliver value to the company and its collaborators. Segment attractiveness is a function of two key factors: (1) the long-term revenue potential of the customers in this segment and (2) the cost of reaching these customers. The revenue potential of the segment is typically determined by factors such as segment size, growth, buying power, and inherent loyalty. The cost of reaching customers in the segment, on the other hand, is a function of the company's ability to effectively and cost-efficiently communicate and deliver the offering to these customers.

- *Segment compatibility* reflects the ability of the company to deliver value to the target customers in a way that enables the company and its collaborators to achieve their strategic goals. Segment compatibility is a function of two key factors: (1) the degree to which serving this segment is consistent with the company's strategic goals and (2) the degree to which the company has the resources (e.g., competencies and assets) necessary to serve this segment.

- *Competitive advantage* reflects the company's ability to fulfill the needs of target customers better than the competition. A company's competitive advantage is, to a large degree, a function of the extent to which the competencies and assets necessary to deliver value to the target segment are unique and difficult to imitate by competitors.

Successful targeting requires that a segment meet all of these criteria; failure to meet even one criterion will impede the company's ability to succeed in delivering superior value to target customers in a way that benefits the company and its collaborators. To illustrate, the fact that a particular segment is inherently attractive is not a sufficient reason to target this segment; it is also imperative that serving this segment is consistent with the company's goals and that the company has the resources to deliver value to this segment in a way that cannot be matched by competitors.

Tactical Targeting

Unlike strategic targeting, which involves deciding which customers to target and which to ignore, tactical targeting involves developing an effective and cost-efficient plan to communicate and deliver the offering's value to the already selected target customers. Recall that strategic targeting is typically derived from a value-based segmentation that is not readily observable to the company—a fact that complicates the company's ability to communicate and deliver its offering to target customers in an effective and cost-efficient manner. In the absence of direct contact with its target customers, a company would need to communicate the value proposition of its offering and make it available to everyone, so that its target customers are aware of the offering and are able to obtain it. This approach, however, often is not cost-effective, especially when the targeted customer segment is relatively small. In cases of multiple offerings by the same company, there is also a risk of customer confusion and/or sales cannibalization if all of the offerings are made available to all potential customers. To address this issue, companies often use readily observable profile characteristics to identify the value-based target segments. For example, airlines tend to identify customers' price sensitivity based on their observable purchase behavior, such as advance purchase, flexibility of travel plans, and length of travel. This process of identifying value-based segments by linking them to certain observable and actionable characteristics is the essence of tactical targeting.

The efficiency of tactical targeting is a function of the fit between the value-based target segment (customers who share a particular need) and the readily identifiable target segment (customers who share certain identifiable profile characteristics). Visually, the efficiency of a company's targeting strategy can be represented by the overlap between the value-based target segment (identified in the process of strategic targeting) and the identifiable profile-based segment (Figure 4). The greater is the overlap, the more efficient the company's targeting approach.

Figure 4. Tactical Targeting

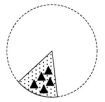

▲ Value-based segment (unobservable)
⊡ Profile-based segment (observable)

In the ideal scenario, the identifiable segment perfectly matches the value-based segment (e.g., Figure 4). In reality, however, achieving such an ideal fit is a challenging task. In this context, three types of errors can be made in tactical targeting: (1) the value-based target segment may be identified too broadly; (2) the target segment may be identified too narrowly; or (3) the target segment may be misidentified (Figure 5). The first type of error, often referred to as a "shotgun approach," leads to inefficient targeting because the company will likely spend significant resources reaching customers who are not interested in its offering. In contrast, the second type of error, often referred to as "oversegmentation," leads to inefficient targeting because the company will likely overlook customers interested in the offering. The decision as to which of the two types of errors the company should accept is a function of the relative benefits and costs and should be consistent with the company's overall goals and strategy. Finally, the third type of error involves misidentifying target customers—a scenario in which the company's communication and distribution efforts are directed to a segment that does not include its target customers.

Figure 5. Common Targeting Errors

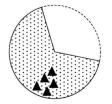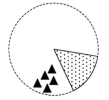

Broad target identification   Narrow target identification   Target misidentification

▲ Value-based segment (unobservable)
⊡ Profile-based segment (observable)

Targeting Multiple Segments

A company might target either a single segment or multiple segments. When targeting multiple segments, a company's goals often vary across segments. Furthermore, because different target segments vary in their needs, they often have a different set of competitors and collaborators, rely on different core competencies and strategic assets of the company, and are influenced by different aspects of the overall context in which the company operates. In the same vein, different segments typically require different marketing mix variables, different implementation plans, and different controls. This implies that each individual segment requires its own offering with its own action plan, as illustrated in Figure 6.

Figure 6. Targeting Multiple Segments

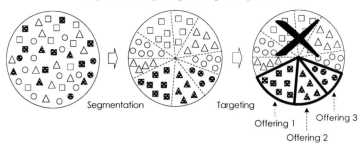

The process of identifying multiple target markets and managing multiple offerings comprising a company's product line is discussed in more detail in Chapter 24.

Summary

Understanding customer needs and identifying market opportunities is the starting point in formulating a company's marketing strategy. A key aspect of customer analysis involves identifying groups of customers with similar preferences (segments) and deciding which segment(s) to target.

Identifying target customers involves determining potential buyers for whom the company will tailor its offering. Identifying target customers typically involves three key decisions: (1) dividing customers into groups with similar characteristics (also referred to as segmentation), (2) selecting which customers to serve and which to ignore (also referred to as strategic targeting), and (3) creating an effective plan to reach these customers (also referred to as tactical targeting).

Segmentation is the process of dividing customers into groups with similar characteristics. The process of segmentation is based on the idea that the effectiveness and efficiency of a company's marketing activities can be improved by ignoring the nonessential differences among customers within each segment and treating these customers as if they were a single entity. As a general rule, a good segmentation should yield segments that are both mutually exclusive and collectively exhaustive. In other words, identified segments should be sufficiently different from one another so that they do not overlap; at the same time, these segments should include all customers in a given market.

Two main factors are used to divide customers into distinct segments: value factors and profile factors. Value-based segmentation groups customers based on their needs and the benefits they seek from the company's offerings. Profile-based segmentation captures some of the observable customer characteristics. In consumer marketing, four types of characteristics are commonly used: demographic (e.g., age, gender, income, and education), geographic (e.g., country, region, and city), psychographic (e.g., personality, moral values, and lifestyle), and behavioral (e.g., user status, volume purchased, and price sensitivity). In business marketing, profile-based segmentation is usually based on firm-specific factors (e.g., location, company size, and industry).

The strategic aspect of a company's targeting decision involves identifying which customers (segments) to serve and which to ignore. Because it aims to optimize the value to customers, the company, and its collaborators, strategic targeting is typically derived from value-based segmentation rather than from profile-based segmentation. The targeting decision is guided by three key criteria: (1) the inherent attractiveness of the customers in a given segment, (2) the segment's compatibility with the company's strategic goals, competencies, and assets, and (3) a company's ability to serve the segment better than the competition.

The tactical aspect of a company's targeting decision involves developing an effective and cost-efficient plan to communicate and deliver the offering's value to the already selected target customers. In particular, tactical targeting links the (typically unobservable) value-based segments to specific observable and actionable characteristics. Common tactical targeting errors result in three types of biases: segments defined too broadly (i.e., shotgun targeting), segments defined too narrowly (i.e., oversegmentation), and segments that are misidentified.

Relevant Concepts

Demographics: A set of characteristics used to describe a given population. Demographics commonly used in marketing include factors such as population size and growth, age dispersion, geographic dispersion, ethnic background, income, mobility, education, employment, and household composition.

Firmographics: The key characteristics of an organization, typically used for segmentation purposes. Firmographics include factors such as location, company size, industry, purchasing process, growth, revenues, and profitability.

Heterogeneous Market: Market composed of customers who vary in their response to a company's offering.

Homogeneous Market: Market composed of customers likely to react in a similar manner to the company's offering (e.g., they seek the same benefits, have similar financial resources, can be reached through the same communication means, and have access to the offering through the same distribution channels).

Niche Strategy: Marketing strategy aimed at a distinct and relatively small customer segment.

Additional Readings

McDonald, Malcolm and Ian Dunbar (2004), *Market Segmentation: How to Do It, How to Profit from It*. Amsterdam: Elsevier.

Weinstein, Art (2004), *Handbook of Market Segmentation: Strategic Targeting for Business and Technology Firms* (3rd ed.). New York, NY: Haworth Press.

Gordon, Ian H. (2002), *Competitor Targeting: Winning the Battle for Market and Customer Share*. New York, NY: John Wiley & Sons.

Chapter Eight

Company Analysis

If you don't have a competitive advantage, don't compete.
Jack Welch, former CEO of General Electric

Companies often encompass multiple business units targeting distinct customer segments. Accordingly, company analysis involves two key aspects: (1) analyzing individual business units and (2) analyzing the relationships among individual units comprising a company's business portfolio. These two aspects of company analysis are the focus of this chapter.

Strategic Business Unit Analysis

A strategic business unit (SBU) is an operating company unit with a discrete set of offerings sold to an identifiable group of customers, in competition with a well-defined set of competitors. A key aspect of analyzing an SBU involves evaluating its strategic assets and core competencies.

Strategic Assets

Strategic assets are the company's resources that (1) are essential for the success of the company's business and (2) differentiate the company from its competitors. From a marketing standpoint, a company's strategic assets could include some or all of the following factors: business infrastructure, collaborator networks, human capital, intellectual property, brands, customer base, synergistic offerings, access to scarce resources, and access to capital.

- *Business infrastructure* involves four types of assets: (1) manufacturing infrastructure, comprising the company's production facilities and equipment; (2) service infrastructure, which includes assets such as call-center facilities and customer relationship management solutions; (3) supply-chain infrastructure, integrating the manufacturing and service assets into an effective and efficient value-delivery process; and (4) management infrastructure, which involves the company's business management culture.

- *Collaborator networks* comprise two types of factors: (1) vertical networks, in which collaborators are located along the supply chain (e.g., suppliers and distributors), and (2) horizontal networks, in which collaborators are not an integral part of the company's supply chain (e.g., research and development, manufacturing, and promotion collaborators). The key to creating sustainable collaborator networks is designing offerings that deliver superior value to the company's collaborators while building relationships that result in switching costs for collaborators (e.g., integrating collaborators' systems into the company's operations).

- *Human capital* involves factors such as the technological, operational, business, and customer expertise of the company's employees. The key to creating sustainable human capital is delivering superior value to the company's key employees and building relationships that enhance the loyalty of these employees.

- *Intellectual property* covers the legal entitlement attached to an intangible asset. Two types of intellectual property can be the source of a competitive advantage: (1) industrial property, which includes inventions, industrial designs, and identity marks such as trademarks, service marks, commercial names and designations, including indications of source and appellations of origin, and (2) copyright, which includes literary and artistic works, such as novels, plays, films, musical works, drawings, paintings, photographs, sculptures, and architectural designs.

- *Brands* create competitive advantage in two ways: (1) by identifying the company and/or its offering and (2) by differentiating it from the competition. The most common brand elements include the brand name, logo, symbol, character, jingle, and slogan. Using these elements, brands provide unique value to customers, the company, and its collaborators.

- *Existing customer base* serves as a competitive advantage by facilitating the acceptance of a company's current and new offerings and by impeding the acceptance of competitive products.

- *Synergistic offerings* are a strategic asset to the degree that they facilitate customer acceptance of related company offerings. To illustrate, the Windows operating system can be viewed as a strategic asset for Microsoft because it facilitates customer adoption of related software offerings.

- *Access to scarce resources,* such as geographic locations and natural resources, is a strategic asset because it provides the company with a distinct competitive advantage.

- *Access to capital* may be considered a strategic asset in cases where it provides the company with a unique competitive advantage. For example, access to capital can influence the resources at a firm's disposal to carry out its strategy: to sustain a price war, to develop new products, and to implement a communication campaign.

Core Competencies

Core competencies reflect a company's ability to perform various business tasks in an efficient and effective manner. A competency is considered core if it strategically differentiates the company from its competitors. A competency that is central to a company's business operations but is not unique is generally not considered a core competency, because it does not meaningfully differentiate the company from its competitors. Thus, a core competency involves expertise in an area essential to the company's success, allowing the company to satisfy customer needs better than the competition in a way that enables the company and its collaborators to achieve their strategic goals.

There are four key functional areas in which a company can establish a core competency: business management, operations management, technology development, and customer management. These four areas are discussed in more detail below.

- *Business management.* Competency in business management refers to proficiency in effectively managing business processes, such as identifying business goals, designing strategies and tactics to achieve these goals, and implementing the company's business plan. Business management competency also involves the company's ability to build the collaborator network required for the efficient functioning of the business (e.g., relationships with suppliers and distributors). This competency typically leads to strategic benefits such as business model leadership. To illustrate, Dell's core competency in business management resulted in a direct distribution business model that was one of the key reasons for its success. Other examples of companies with demonstrated competency in business management include McDonald's, Blockbuster, Starbucks, Wal-Mart, and Amazon.com.

- *Operations management.* A competency in operations management refers to an expertise in supply-chain management. Companies with this competency are proficient in optimizing the effectiveness and cost-efficiency of the business processes. This typically leads to the strategic benefit of cost leadership in the marketplace. For example, Wal-Mart's competency in operations management is reflected in its dominant position as the low-cost player in the market. Other examples of companies with demonstrated competency in operations management include Southwest Airlines, Costco, and Home Depot.

- *Technology development.* Competency in technology development refers to a company's ability to design new technological solutions. This competency typically leads to the strategic benefit of technological leadership. Examples of companies that have demonstrated this competency include Motorola, BASF, Google, and Intel. A competency in developing new technologies does not necessarily imply a competency in developing commercially successful products. To illustrate, Xerox and its Palo Alto Research Center (PARC) have invented numerous new technologies such as photocopying, laser printing, graphical user interface, client/server architecture, and the Ethernet, but have been slow in converting these technologies into commercial products.

- *Customer value management.* Competency in customer value management refers to expertise in understanding, creating, and managing customer value. There are three common aspects of competency in customer value management: product management, service management, and brand management. These three aspects are discussed in more detail below.

  - *Product management.* Competency in product management refers to a company's ability to develop products that deliver superior customer value. This competency typically leads to the strategic benefit of product leadership. Examples of companies with demonstrated competency in this area include Microsoft, Merck, Apple, and Palm. A competency in product management is not contingent on the company's having competency in technology management. In fact, technologically inferior products delivering need-based functionality are often more successful than technologically superior products that fail to meet customer needs. To illustrate, TiVo, the pioneer in digital video recording, exemplifies a company with competency in developing a successful product based on an existing MPEG-2 digital-encoding technology.

- *Service management.* Competency in service management refers to a company's ability to develop services that deliver superior customer value. This competency typically leads to the strategic benefit of service leadership. Examples of companies with demonstrated competency in this area include Ritz-Carlton, American Express, and Nordstrom.

- *Brand management.* Competency in brand management refers to a company's ability to build strong brands that deliver superior customer value. This competency typically leads to the strategic benefit of brand leadership. Examples of companies with demonstrated competency in this area include Harley-Davidson, Lacoste, Nike, Procter & Gamble, and PepsiCo.

The relationship between strategic assets and core competencies is dynamic. Core competencies reflect the company's expertise in specific functional areas and are a result of focused utilization of strategic assets. At the same time, a company's assets are often derived from its competencies. For example, a competency in database software development is likely to result in competency-specific assets such as business infrastructure, collaborator network, human capital, and intellectual property.

Portfolio Analysis

A company's portfolio comprises the mix of its individual strategic business units. Based on the diversity of a company's offerings, two types of portfolios can be identified: specialized and diversified. A *specialized portfolio* involves SBUs with fairly narrow assortments consisting of one or a few product lines. To illustrate, Ferrari (high-performance sports cars), Glacéau (bottled water), and TiVo (digital video recorders) have strategically limited their product mix to a fairly narrow product line. In contrast, a *diversified portfolio* involves SBUs with fairly broad assortments comprising multiple product lines. For example, companies like General Electric, Johnson & Johnson, and Unilever offer a wide variety of product lines. The primary rationale for a diversified business mix is to take advantage of growth opportunities in areas in which the company has no presence. A company's success in managing a diverse portfolio is often a function of existing synergies among individual business units. Such synergies can be related to company processes (e.g., research and development, manufacturing, and distribution) or personnel (e.g., experienced management, qualified engineers, and knowledgeable sales force).

Portfolio management focuses on two types of factors: (1) opportunities presented by a particular industry or market and (2) the company's resources, which determine its ability to take advantage of the identified opportunities (Figure 1). Here, market opportunities are typically defined in terms of overall market/industry attractiveness factors, such as its size, growth, and profitability. A company's resources, on the other hand, reflect its competitive position in the marketplace and are often measured in terms of factors such as strategic assets, core competencies, and market share.

Figure 1. The Resource–Opportunity Portfolio Matrix

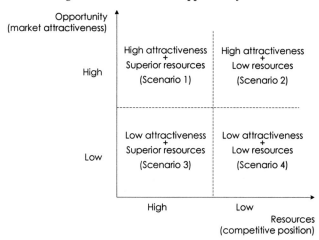

A company's market position is a function of market attractiveness and its own resources as follows.

- The *high-attractiveness/superior-resources* position (Scenario 1) refers to an attractive market that a company has the resources to exploit. Because this is the optimal scenario, companies typically invest in business units operating in these conditions.

- The *high-attractiveness/low-resources* position (Scenario 2) refers to a market that is attractive but for which the company does not have adequate resources to succeed. Because of attractive market conditions, companies selectively invest in developing the resources required to achieve success.

- The *low-attractiveness/superior-resources* position (Scenario 3) refers to a market that is relatively less attractive but for which the company has adequate resources to succeed. Because of the limited market potential, companies often reinvest part of the revenues from business units operating under these conditions in areas with greater market potential (Scenarios 1 and 2).

- The *low-attractiveness/low-resources* position (Scenario 4) refers to a relatively less attractive market for which the company does not have adequate resources. This is the least favorable scenario and companies tend to either reposition their businesses into other markets offering greater opportunities (Scenario 2) or to divest the business to companies with a better fit.

Most companies aim to position their business units in the high-attractiveness/superior-resources cell of the opportunity–resources matrix. The general strategy to achieve this is fairly intuitive. A company can move from unattractive to attractive markets (moving from Scenarios 3 and 4 to Scenarios 1 and 2) by developing offerings that will successfully compete in these markets. Similarly, a company can increase its competitive position in a given market (moving from Scenarios 2 and 4 to Scenarios 1 and 3) by developing or acquiring the resources (strategic assets and core competencies) vital for achieving success in this market.

Because the principles for making resource-allocation decisions across different business units are very similar across industries, many companies have developed generalized strategies for making such decisions. These generalized strategies are often integrated into formal portfolio models that offer guidance on how to allocate resources across multiple SBUs.

A key aspect in developing portfolio models involves identifying the metrics underlying the performance of a given business unit. Depending on the assumptions of the model, these metrics can include factors such as return on investment, market share, and industry growth rate. One of the earliest and most popular algorithms for identifying the overall performance of an SBU of a company is the DuPont model, which quantifies the profitability of a given SBU as a function of three key factors: net profit margin, asset turnover, and an equity multiplier. A detailed overview of the DuPont model is offered at the end of this chapter.

The most widely used approach to portfolio analysis that came into common use in the 1960s is the model developed by the Boston Consulting Group (BCG). This approach, commonly known as the BCG matrix, emphasizes two main criteria in evaluating a company's portfolio: market growth rate and the company's relative market share. A more comprehensive, albeit more complex, model was developed jointly by General Electric and McKinsey and is commonly known as the GE matrix. A detailed overview of the BCG and GE models is offered at the end of this chapter.

Summary

Companies often encompass multiple business units targeting distinct customer segments. Accordingly, company analysis involves two key aspects: (1) analyzing individual business units and (2) analyzing the relationships among individual units comprising a company's business portfolio.

A strategic business unit (SBU) is an operating company unit with a discrete set of offerings sold to an identifiable group of customers, in competition with a well-defined set of competitors. A key aspect of analyzing an SBU involves evaluating its strategic assets and core competencies.

Strategic assets are the company's resources that (1) are essential for the success of the company's business and (2) differentiate the company from its competitors. From a marketing standpoint, a company's strategic assets could include some or all of the following factors: business infrastructure, collaborator networks, human capital, intellectual property, brands, customer base, synergistic offerings, access to scarce resources, and access to capital.

Competencies reflect a company's ability to perform various business tasks in an efficient and effective manner. A competency is considered core if it strategically differentiates the company from its competitors. A competency that is central to a company's business operations but is not unique is generally not considered a core competency, because it does not meaningfully differentiate the company from its competitors. Thus, a core competency involves expertise in an area essential to the company's success, allowing the company to satisfy customer needs better than the competition in a way that enables the company and its collaborators to achieve their strategic goals. There are four key functional areas in which a company can establish a core competency: business management, operations management, technology development, and customer management.

A company's portfolio comprises the total mix of its individual strategic business units. Portfolio management aims to optimize the value delivered by individual strategic business units managed by the company. Managing a company's portfolio of businesses involves issues such as allocating resources among existing SBUs, deciding on the strategic direction of a company's business units, and deciding to discontinue or divest a particular business.

Portfolio management focuses on two types of factors: (1) opportunities presented by a particular industry or market and (2) the company's resources that determine its ability to take advantage of the identified opportunities. Market opportunities are typically defined in terms of overall market/industry attractiveness factors such as its size, growth, and profitability. A company's resources, on the other hand, reflect its competitive position in the marketplace and are often measured in terms of factors such as strategic assets, core competencies, and market share. These two factors comprise the Resource-Opportunity Portfolio Matrix.

Relevant Frameworks: The SWOT Framework

The SWOT framework is a relatively simple, extremely flexible, and very intuitive approach for evaluating a company's overall business condition. As implied by its name, the SWOT framework entails analyzing four key factors: the company's *strengths* and *weaknesses*, and the *opportunities* and *threats* presented to the company by the environment in which it operates. These four factors are typically organized in a 2×2 matrix based on whether they are internal or external to the company, and whether they are favorable or unfavorable from the company's standpoint. The analysis of the internal factors (strengths and weaknesses) focuses on the company, whereas the analysis of the external factors (opportunities and threats) focuses on the market in which the company operates (Figure 2).

Figure 2. The SWOT Framework

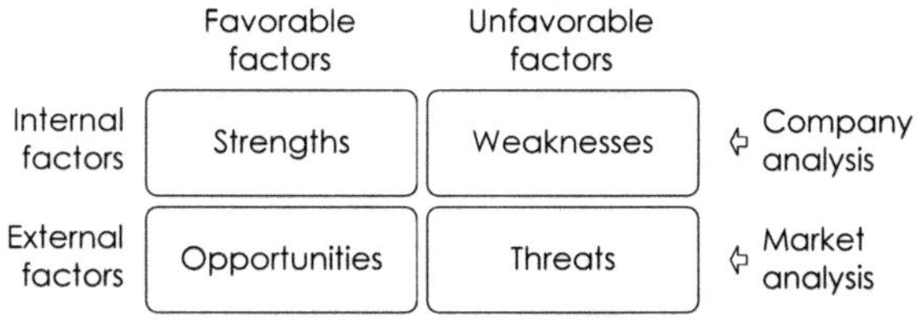

To illustrate, factors such as loyal customers, strong brand name(s), strategically important patents and trademarks, know-how, experienced personnel, and access to scarce resources are typically classified as strengths, whereas factors such as disloyal customers, diluted brand name(s), and lack of technological expertise are classified as weaknesses. Similarly, factors such as emergence of a new, underserved customer segment and a favorable economic environment are typically classified as opportunities, whereas factors such as a new competitive entry into the category, increased product commoditization, and increased buyer and/or supplier power are classified as threats.

Relevant Frameworks: The 7-S Framework

The 7-S framework identifies seven key factors crucial to the internal effectiveness and efficiency of an organization. The key aspects of the 7-S framework are outlined in Peters and Waterman's popular book *In Search of Excellence*.[1]

The 7-S framework involves analyzing seven interdependent aspects of an organization: strategy; skills (institutional capabilities such as the distinctive capabilities of personnel); shared values (culture—what the organization stands for and its central beliefs); structure (organization—the way the company's units relate to one another); staff (people—types of personnel within the organization and management training); systems (procedures—financial systems, information systems, as well as hiring, promotion and performance appraisal systems); and style (leadership style—how key managers work toward achieving the organization's goals). These seven aspects of organizational analysis are illustrated in Figure 3.

Figure 3. 7-S Framework[2]

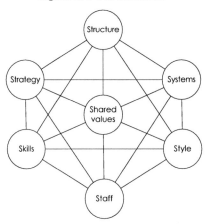

Working synergistically, these seven factors account for the effectiveness and efficiency of an organization. The 7-S framework calls for evaluating these organizational factors and analyzing the relationships among them to ensure consistency across departments and functional areas.

Relevant Frameworks: The DuPont Model

The DuPont model is based on analyzing profitability of a company using performance management tools such as return on investment and asset turnover. It was developed by F. Donaldson Brown, an engineer from the DuPont company. Its first large-scale application involved restructuring the General Motors Corporation, of which DuPont was the majority shareholder. Following General Motors' success, the model gained prominence among major U.S. corporations and remained one of the dominant forms of financial analysis until the 1970s. The popularity of the DuPont model can be attributed to its simplicity and ability to link company performance to financial results.

The DuPont model of management allows large companies to allocate resources across different business units competing for funding. The traditional DuPont model relies on three key components to calculate return on equity: net profit margin, asset turnover, and an equity multiplier.

- *Net profit margin* is the profit generated by the company relative to its revenues and is typically calculated by dividing the company's net income by its overall revenues.

- *Asset turnover* reflects the sales revenues generated by the company relative to its assets and is typically calculated by dividing the company's sales revenues by its assets. Asset turnover is used by the DuPont model to allow comparing companies that use different business models. In most cases, asset turnover is often inversely correlated with profit margins (high-margin/low-volume vs. low-margin/high-volume).

- The *equity multiplier* is a measure of a company's financial leverage and is calculated as the ratio of a company's assets to shareholders' equity. The equity multiplier is used to account for the potential impact of a company's debt when calculating its return on equity.

In this context, a company's return on equity (ROE) can be calculated as follows:

ROE = Return on assets · Equity multiplier = Net profit margin · Asset turnover · Equity multiplier

The DuPont model has several popular applications: (1) It provides managers with a basic understanding of the factors that contribute to the company's success and suggests strategies for managing the company's overall performance; (2) It provides quantifiable benchmarks that can be used for evaluating a company's performance over time; and (3) It can be used as an indicator of a company's overall performance for valuation purposes.

The DuPont model of management, and in particular the ROE metric, has provided the basis for many product-portfolio models (e.g., the BCG and GE matrixes), which depict a company's strategic business units on two dimensions: their position relative to the competition and the growth rate of the markets they serve.

Relevant Frameworks: The BCG Product-Portfolio Matrix

The BCG product-portfolio matrix is based on the notion that to be successful a company should have a portfolio of products with different market shares and different growth rates. The portfolio composition is viewed as a function of balancing cash flows between high-growth and low-growth products. In this context, the main goal of the BCG product-portfolio matrix is to guide the cash allocation decisions across different strategic business units of a company.

The BCG matrix is based on two key assumptions. The first is that profit margins are a function of market share, such that high market share leads to high margins. This assumption is derived from the experience curve effect and, in particular, from the notion that increasing the scale of production leads to a lower cost structure and, hence, to higher profit margins.[3] The second assumption is that profit margins are a function of the growth of the industry in which the company operates and that different stages of growth require different cash management strategies. In particular, high-growth businesses require cash investment, whereas low-growth businesses tend to generate cash in excess of what needs to be reinvested to maintain share. These two assumptions are reflected in the fact that market share and market growth are the two key components of evaluating the performance of a given strategic business unit.

Using the BCG matrix requires two major steps: classification and action. The *classification phase* calls for categorizing all SBUs into four types: question marks, stars, cash cows, and dogs. This categorization is based on each SBU's performance on two factors: (1) relative market share (share relative to the largest competitor) and (2) market growth. For example, a relative market share of 0.4 means that the SBU has 40% of the market leader's share, and a relative market share of 2.0 means that the SBU is the leader and has twice the share of the next largest competitor (Figure 4). For presentation purposes, the relative market share is drawn on a logarithmic scale. Market growth rate is drawn on a normal scale, with 10% annual market growth often used as the reference point. The circles depict the revenue contribution of individual SBUs, such that each circle's area is proportional to the SBU's dollar sales.

Figure 4. BCG Matrix: Step 1 (classification)[4]

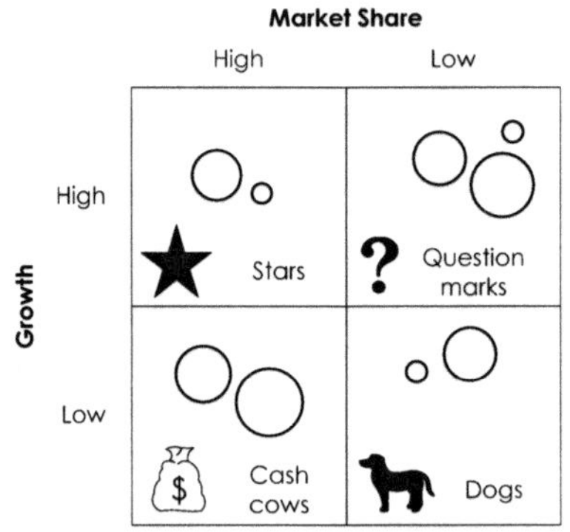

The *action phase* identifies the role to be assigned to each SBU (Figure 5). There are four basic strategies to achieve an efficient resource allocation: (1) hold (preserve market share, usually applied to stars); (2) build (increase market share and forego near-term earnings, usually applied to question marks); (3) harvest (increase cash flow and forego building market share, usually applied to cash cows); and (4) divest (sell or liquidate, usually applied to dogs).

Figure 5. BCG Matrix: Step 2 (action)[5]

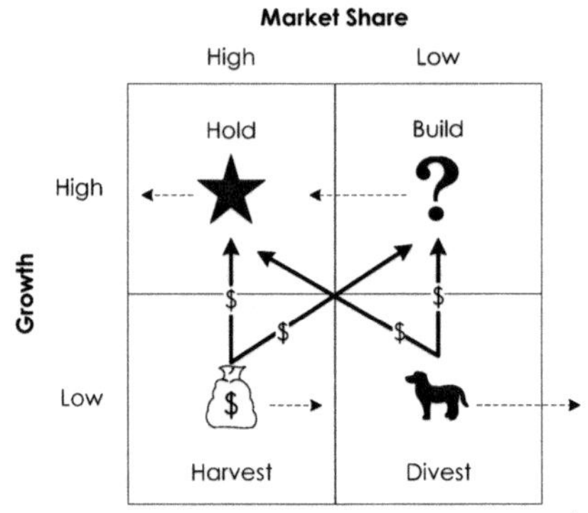

The BCG model has numerous limitations. First, its main objective is to guide a company's resource allocation across different SBUs; as a result, it is not designed to assist with strategic decisions of a single SBU. Second, it considers market share and market growth to be the only relevant cash allocation factors (factors such as cost, competitive reaction, synergies among SBUs, and various macroeconomic factors are not part of the model). Third, it assumes that higher market share means higher cash-generating ability and higher profitability from economies of scale, learning curve/experience effects, monopoly power, etc., even though these factors may not apply to all industries. Fourth, market share and market growth are ambiguous and difficult to quantify. To illustrate, the same SBU can be classified as a question mark, a star, a cash cow, or a dog when alternative operational definitions of the matrix dimensions are involved. Finally, the use of the BCG matrix can have important self-fulfilling organizational implications: Labeling an SBU as a dog will lead to minimizing the cash allocated to this unit, which is likely to decrease its performance and turn the unit into a "real" dog.

Overall, the BCG model offers a simple strategy for evaluating the relative performance of a company's strategic business units and making cash allocation recommendations. Its recommendations, however, are based on highly restrictive assumptions (e.g., market share and industry growth rate are the only relevant performance factors), and its application is subject to multiple interpretations (e.g., defining the industry in which the firm competes). While the general idea—classifying a company's SBUs based on their relative performance and the attractiveness of the industry in which they compete—is a viable approach, the use of the BCG model in its original form in today's business world is rather limited.

Relevant Frameworks: The GE Product-Portfolio Matrix

The General Electric (GE) product-portfolio matrix can be viewed as a more comprehensive version of the BCG model. Similar to the BCG matrix, it classifies business units into different categories based on their performance on two key business dimensions: market attractiveness and business strength. However, unlike the BCG matrix, in which each dimension is identified by a single factor (industry growth or market share), the GE matrix uses composite measures composed of different factors. Thus, market attractiveness is calculated as a weighted average of factors such as market size, market growth, historical profit margin, stage in the life cycle, competitive intensity (number of competitors, competitive structure, differentiation, entry barriers, and substitutes), technological requirements, inflationary vulnerability, and investment intensity. In the same vein, business position is calculated as a weighted average of factors such as market share, share growth, product differentiation, brand image, relative cost position, capacity utilization, technological and R&D performance, patents, distribution network, marketing effectiveness, access to supplies, and managerial personnel.

Because each of the two dimensions has three levels (low, medium, high), different SBUs are classified into nine different types (rather than four, as in the BCG matrix). Each SBU is denoted with a circle representing the relative size of the market and the SBU's share of that market. The recommendations derived from the GE matrix are similar to that of the BCG approach, with the four key strategies further refined to match the 3×3 design of the GE matrix (Figure 6).

The GE approach requires relatively complex analysis, which tends to limit its usability as a standardized approach. Similar to the BCG matrix, the GE approach suffers from subjectivity in evaluating different performance benchmarks (e.g., product differentiation, stage in the life cycle, and brand image) and does not incorporate multi-period competitive strategies.

Figure 6. GE Product-Portfolio Matrix

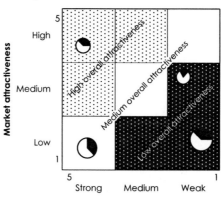

Overall, the GE model offsets many of the shortcomings of the BCG matrix, mainly its single-factor approach to identifying the key business factors that account for the overall profitability of an SBU. The comprehensiveness of the GE approach, however, comes at the expense of simplicity, which is one of the most attractive features of the BCG matrix. Because of its complexity, the GE approach is often used as a guideline for analyzing different strategic business units rather than as a quantifiable normative model.

Additional Readings

Cooper, Robert G., Scott J. Edgett, and Elko J. Kleinschmidt (2002), *Portfolio Management for New Products* (2nd ed.). Oxford: Perseus.

Prahalad, C. K. and Gary Hamel (1990), "The Core Competence of the Corporation," *Harvard Business Review*, (May–June), 79–91.

Stern, Carl W. and George Jr. Stalk (1998), *Perspectives on Strategy: From the Boston Consulting Group*. New York, NY: Wiley.

Treacy, Michael and Fred Wiersema (2006), *The Discipline of Market Leaders: Choose Your Customers, Narrow Your Focus, Dominate Your Market* (2nd ed.). London: Profile.

Notes

[1] Peters, Thomas J. and Robert H. Waterman (1982), *In Search of Excellence: Lessons from America's Best-Run Companies*. Cambridge: Harper & Row.

[2] Adapted from ibid.

[3] Stern, Carl W. and George Stalk (1998), *Perspectives on Strategy: From the Boston Consulting Group*. New York, NY: John Wiley & Sons.

[4] Adapted from ibid.

[5] Adapted from ibid.

Chapter Nine

Collaborator Analysis

Friends have all things in common.
Plato

Collaborators are entities that work with a company to design, communicate, and deliver value to target customers. Collaboration is an essential component of doing business in today's networked world. The key aspects of identifying collaborator entities and defining their functions are the focus of this chapter.

The Nature of Collaboration

Collaboration typically involves entering into a relationship with an outside entity and delegating to it a subset of the company's (typically non-core) activities. As a process, collaboration is defined by the nature of the collaborating entities and the relationships among them. These two aspects of collaboration are discussed in more detail below.

Collaborator Entities

Collaboration spans diverse functional areas, and virtually any two entities can become collaborators. Some of the most common types of collaboration are outlined below.

- *Research and development* collaborators work with the company on the development of new products and services. To illustrate, Nike, Samsung, and PepsiCo collaborate with the design company IDEO to develop innovative consumer products.

- *Manufacturing* collaborators assist the company with producing the actual product. For example, NEC provides Dell with removable media storage devices, Intel provides the processors, NVIDIA provides graphic cards, and Microsoft provides the operating system.

- *Service providers* collaborate with the company to deliver the service aspect of the company's offering. To illustrate, to gain cost-efficiency, companies like AT&T, Sprint, and Dell routinely outsource their customer support service to call centers in regions in which the production processes are more cost-efficient.

- *Advertising agencies* assist the company with promoting its offerings, managing public relations, developing communication and branding strategies, and conducting marketing research. Most advertising agencies are either subsidiaries or affiliated with larger communication services groups, such as

WPP Group, Omnicom, Interpublic, Dentsu, Havas, and Publicis, which enables them to provide a comprehensive set of communication services to large multinational clients.

- *Distributors*, such as wholesalers and retailers, collaborate with the company by facilitating the delivery of its offerings to target customers. For example, consumer packaged goods manufacturers such as Nestlé, Unilever, and Kraft make their offerings available to customers by relying on retail partners such as Carrefour, CVS, and Albertsons.

- The *sales force* collaborates with the company to promote and/or deliver its offerings to target customers. For example, Avon employs a multilevel sales force of more than **20,000** independent contractors who are paid a commission on their own sales as well as on the sales of people they recruit and train. Generally, the sales force can be viewed as a form of distribution-based collaboration. However, the function of the sales force involves promoting and selling, not necessarily delivering, the actual offering. To illustrate, pharmaceutical companies employ sales representatives to promote their products to physicians without actually selling or delivering the actual drugs (excluding samples).

- *Marketing research* entities work with the company to better understand the company's customers, collaborators, competitors, and the overall context in which the company operates. For example, consumer packaged goods manufacturers SC Johnson, Kellogg, and Heinz collaborate with marketing research companies such as The Nielsen Company and IRI in areas involving the analysis of retail data and test marketing of new products.

Collaboration Type

Depending on the relative position of the collaborating entities in the value-delivery process, two types of collaborators can be distinguished: vertical and horizontal (Figure 1).

Figure 1. Vertical and Horizontal Collaboration

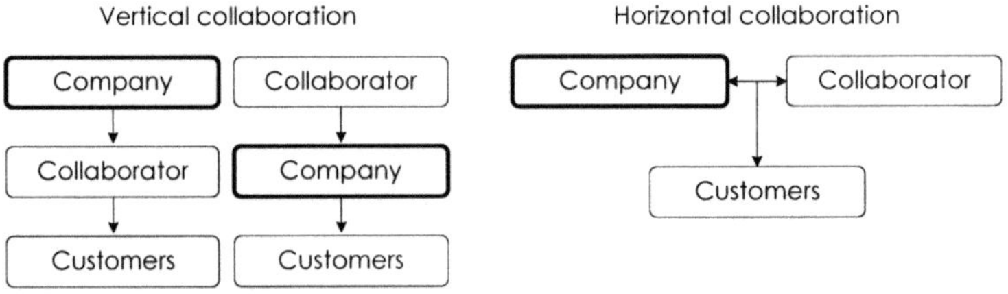

- *Vertical collaborators* are located along the value-delivery chain: supplier – manufacturer – distributor – customer. To illustrate, Intel (supplier), HP (manufacturer), and Best Buy (distributor) are vertical collaborators in delivering value to target customers. Most of the distribution partnerships between manufacturers and retailers involve vertical collaboration.

- *Horizontal collaborators* usually occupy the same level of the value-delivery chain. For example, the United Mileage credit card, which allows customers to earn frequent flyer miles on each purchase, is a result of the (horizontal) collaboration between JPMorgan Chase and United Airlines. Similarly, Nike and Apple's collaboration resulted in the popular Nike+iPod product bundle.

The relationships among collaborators can vary in the degree to which it is formalized. In particular, two types of collaboration can be identified: explicit and implicit.

- *Explicit collaboration* involves contractual relationships, such as long-term contractual agreements, joint ventures, and franchise agreements. The key advantage of explicit collaboration is that it fosters a long-term relationship among collaborating entities, which ultimately leads to greater effectiveness and cost-efficiency of their activities. Explicit collaboration has certain drawbacks, however, such as lower flexibility, greater switching costs, and the strategic risk of creating a potential competitor by sharing know-how and strategic information (e.g., pricing policies, profit margins, and cost structure).

- *Implicit collaboration* typically does not involve contractual relationships and, therefore, tends to be much more flexible than explicit collaboration. This flexibility, however, comes at the cost of inability to predict the behavior of various channel members. Another shortcoming of implicit coordination is a lower level of commitment, resulting in unwillingness to invest resources to customize the channel for a particular manufacturer. Moreover, implicit coordination is likely to lead to lower cost-efficiency (vis-à-vis explicit collaboration) resulting from a lower degree of coordination (e.g., lack of systems integration). An extreme case of implicit collaboration involves complementors—companies with complementary offerings that do not directly collaborate with one another. To illustrate, software developers often create Windows-compatible programs without directly collaborating with Microsoft, and numerous companies develop aftermarket parts and accessories for Harley-Davidson motorcycles without explicitly collaborating with Harley-Davidson.

Key Collaborator Functions

Collaboration typically involves business-to-business interactions in which a company and its collaborators work together to deliver superior value to target customers. Because value-creation involves the processes of designing, communicating, and delivering value to target customers, collaboration may occur in one or more of these areas. Thus, collaboration may involve value-design activities such as product and service development, brand building, and incentive design. In addition, it may involve value-communication activities such as advertising and public relations. Finally, collaboration might involve value-delivery activities such as product distribution, service, and incentives delivery. These three types of collaboration are illustrated in Figure 2 and are discussed in more detail in the following sections.

Figure 2. Allocating Marketing Functions across Collaborators[1]

Marketing functions

Collaborators	Design value	Communicate value	Deliver value
R&D entities	✓	✓	✓
Manufacturers	✓	✓	✓
Service providers	✓	✓	✓
Ad/PR agencies	✓	✓	✓
Suppliers	✓	✓	✓
Distributors	✓	✓	✓
Sales force	✓	✓	✓
Marketing research	✓	✓	✓

Collaboration to Design Customer Value

Collaboration to design customer value involves activities aimed at creating an offering that has the potential to deliver superior value to target customers in a way that enables the company and its collaborators to reach their strategic goals. Because the process of designing customer value involves five key aspects—product, service, brand, price, and incentives—collaboration can occur in each of these domains. These five domains of collaborating to design value are discussed in more detail below.

- *Product development.* Companies often develop products in collaboration with other entities. For example, Apple's iPhone was developed jointly with AT&T and Palm's Prē smartphone was developed jointly with Sprint.

- *Service development.* Services are often a result of the joint effort of the company and its collaborators. To illustrate, consider Dell's service delivery process. Phone-based customer support is provided by Dell's collaborators, many of which include call centers both in the United States and abroad. On-site technical support is provided by Dell's collaborators with a physical presence in the geographical areas in which Dell offers services. Finally, customer service is also available through multiple user-group sites managed by third-party entities (complementors).

- *Branding.* Similar to products and services, brands often are the result of the combined effort of the company and its collaborators. To illustrate, the Harley-Davidson brand amalgamates the efforts of the Milwaukee-based Harley-Davidson Motor Company, its dealer network, and user-based entities such as the Harley Owner Group (H.O.G.).

- *Pricing.* In most cases, pricing is a collaborative effort of the participants in the distribution channel, as well as various third-party entities. To illustrate, the suggested retail price (MSRP) set by the manufacturer is typically modified by retailers based on the volume discounts and incentives offered by the manufacturer, as well as on their own profit-maximizing strategy. The retail price may be further adjusted to include surcharges imposed by third-party entities (e.g., sales tax and usage fees).

- *Incentives.* Incentives received by the customer can be offered by the company, its collaborators, and/or third-party entities. To illustrate, incentives for purchasing a hybrid vehicle (e.g., Toyota Prius) can be offered by the manufacturer, by the dealer, and by the government offering various tax (e.g., tax credit) and usage (e.g., using carpool lanes) incentives.

Collaboration to Communicate Customer Value

Similar to designing the offering, communicating its value occurs on each of the five dimensions discussed above: product, service, brand, price, and incentives. On each of these dimensions, the company can collaborate with other entities.

- *Product.* Product benefits are often communicated by company's collaborators. For example, TiVo, the personal digital recorder, was promoted by retailers carrying the product, as well as by many of its current users.

- *Service.* Communicating service benefits can also be implemented by a company's collaborators. To illustrate, in addition to the direct communications by the film studio, awareness of a new movie is created by its direct collaborators—film distributors and movie theaters—as well as by the word of mouth generated by third-party entities, such as the media and viewers who have seen the movie.

- *Brand.* Strong brands are often built on collaborator and third-party communications. Cult brands such as Harley-Davidson, Apple, and Burton are extensively promoted by loyal users who act as brand ambassadors.

- *Price.* An offering's price is often communicated by a company's direct and indirect collaborators. To illustrate, customers might learn the price of an offering directly from the company, from retailers, or from other entities such as user groups and online search engines (e.g., froogle.com, pricegrabber.com, and pricewatch.com).

- *Incentives.* The availability of incentives is often communicated by a company's collaborators. To illustrate, the news of a temporary price reduction or a frequent-flyer bonus are often disseminated by travel agencies, as well as by third-party entities such as user-based forums (e.g., flyertalk.com).

Collaboration to Deliver Customer Value

As in the case of designing the offering and communicating its benefits, value-delivery occurs on each of the five dimensions discussed above: product, service, brand, price, and incentives. A company can collaborate with other entities on each of these dimensions.

- *Product.* Product distribution typically involves intermediaries such as wholesalers and retailers. To illustrate, Levi Strauss distributes its products through brick-and-mortar retailers such as Macy's, Target, and JCPenney, as well as through online retailers such as Amazon.com, Buy.com, and Overstock.com.

- *Service.* Similar to products, services are frequently delivered to target customers by company's collaborators. To illustrate, DirecTV outsources satellite dish setup to local installers, FedEx outsources the delivery of its ground packages to local contractors, and Sprint outsources its customer service to call centers in the Philippines.

- *Brand.* Collaborators can play an important role in delivering the brand essence to target customers. This delivery may be carried by other business entities, as in the case of Polo Ralph Lauren stores located within larger department stores, or by customers such as the case of members of the Harley Owner Group delivering the Harley-Davidson's brand essence.

- *Price.* Customer payments for the company's offerings are often collected through collaborators, such as channel members, credit card processors, and banks.

- *Incentives.* Incentives are also often distributed to customers by collaborators such as retail stores, media companies, as well as by entities specializing in distributing customer promotions.

Summary

Collaborators are entities that work with the company to design, communicate, and deliver value to target customers. Collaboration is defined by the collaborating entities and the type of collaboration, determined by the relationships among these entities.

The most common areas of collaboration include research and development, manufacturing, service delivery, communication, distribution, sales, and marketing research. Depending on the relative position of the collaborating entities in the value-delivery process, two types of collaborators can be distinguished: vertical collaborators, located along the value-delivery chain (supplier – manufacturer – distributor – customer), and horizontal collaborators, which usually occupy the same level of the value-delivery chain.

Collaboration might involve one or more of the following three areas: collaboration to design, communicate, and deliver customer value. Collaboration to design customer value involves five key aspects: product, service, brand, price, and incentives. Collaboration to communicate and deliver value to target customers also occurs on each of these five dimensions.

Additional Readings

Anderson, James C., James A. Narus, and Das Narayandas (2008), *Business Market Management: Understanding, Creating, and Delivering Value* (3rd ed.). Upper Saddle River, NJ: Prentice Hall.

Anderson, Erin, Anne T. Coughlan, Louis W. Stern, and Adel I. El-Ansary (2006), *Marketing Channels* (7th ed.). Upper Saddle River, NJ: Prentice Hall.

Young, S. David and Stephen F. O'Byrne (2000), *EVA and Value-Based Management: A Practical Guide to Implementation*. New York, NY: McGraw-Hill.

Note

[1] The checkmarks in each box indicate that each collaborator can potentially contribute to the value-creation process by designing, communicating, and delivering specific aspects of the offering's value.

Chapter Ten

Competitive Analysis

In football, everything is complicated by the presence of the other team.
Jean-Paul Sartre, French philosopher

Understanding the competitive environment in which a company operates is key to its success in the marketplace. Evaluating the competitive nature of a given market involves two key components: identifying a company's key competitors and evaluating the competitive intensity of the marketplace. These two aspects of analyzing market competitiveness are the focus of this chapter.

Identifying the Key Competitors

Competitive analysis begins with identifying the key competitors, that is, business entities with offerings positioned to satisfy the same need of the same target customers. Competitors are typically defined relative to the specific needs of a given customer segment rather than simply defined based on the industry in which the company operates. To illustrate, Kodak's film division competes not only in the 35mm film market with companies like Fuji and Agfa, but also with manufacturers of digital cameras, such as Sony and Canon, and even with manufacturers of camera-equipped mobile phones, such as Nokia and Ericsson. Starbucks competes not only with other coffee shops, such as Peet's Coffee & Tea and The Coffee Bean & Tea Leaf, but also with manufacturers of caffeinated energy drinks, such as Red Bull and Monster Energy, and even with producers of caffeinated and vitamin-enhanced water, such as Water Joe and Glacéau. Coca-Cola competes not only with other cola producers, such as Pepsi, but also with the manufacturers of other products, such as juice, bottled water, and milk, that could potentially fulfill the same customer need. In this context, juice, bottled water, and milk are cross-category competitors of Coke because they aim to satisfy the same need of the same target customers.

Because most companies have a variety of offerings targeting multiple segments, the actual competition occurs not among the companies themselves but among their offerings and the value they deliver to target customers and collaborators. In fact, companies competing for one target market might be collaborating to deliver value to another. To illustrate, Samsung and Sony compete in the flat-screen TV market but collaborate in the development and manufacturing of LCD panels. Because the competition is always market-specific, competitive analysis needs to be performed for each distinct target market.

Identifying the key competitors involves identifying not only current competitors but potential competitors as well. A company's current competitors are busi-

73

ness entities that currently target the same customers and strive to fulfill the same customer need(s). In contrast, potential competitors are business entities that currently do not target the same customers and/or aim to fulfill the same need(s), but nevertheless have the aspirations and/or the capability to satisfy the focal need(s) of the company's target customers. In this context, three groups of potential competitors can be identified.

The first type of potential competitors are companies with offerings that aim to satisfy the same need as the company's offering but, at present, target a different customer segment. Even though not currently competing with the focal company, their entry into a particular customer segment would be facilitated by their understanding of customer needs and their ability to deliver offerings that could fulfill those needs.

Another set of potential competitors are companies that currently target the same customer segment but aim to satisfy a different need. Even though these potential competitors are not directly competing with the focal company, their entry into the company's business would be facilitated by their customer expertise, defined by their understanding, access, and relationship with the target customers.

Finally, potential competitors are companies that currently satisfy a different set of needs of different customers. Even though these potential competitors are not competing directly with the focal company and have neither need-based nor customer-based expertise, they may aspire to serve the focal company's customers. They may also have some of the key resources, such as strategic assets and core competencies, that could facilitate the development of successful competitive offerings. These four types of competitors are shown in Figure 1.

Figure 1. Identifying the Key Competitors

	Same customers	Different customers
Same need	Current competitors (customer/need expertise)	Potential competitors (need expertise)
Different need	Potential competitors (customer expertise)	Potential competitors (no relevant expertise)

Competitors that target the same customers and follow similar strategies to serve the needs of these customers are often referred to as a *strategic group*. Competitors in the same strategic group often have similar products and services, similar branding strategies, similar pricing and incentive strategies, similar communications campaigns, and/or similar distribution channels. As a result, competition among companies within the same strategic group tends to be more intense than competition among companies from different strategic groups.

Evaluating the Competitive Intensity of the Market

Market competitiveness reflects the degree to which companies are trying to steal share from one another to ensure growth. Market competitiveness is a function of five factors that extend directly from the 5-C framework: customers, competitors, collaborators, company, and context. These factors are discussed in more detail below.

Customer Factors

The competitive intensity of the market is a function of customers' revenue potential and the sustainability of a company's value proposition to these customers.

The revenue potential of a given customer segment is a function of market size and profit margins. Because large markets have the potential to generate greater revenue streams, they are often associated with greater competitiveness among companies pursuing a high-volume strategy. Similarly, competition is likely to be more intense for customer segments with greater buying power because of the potential for a greater revenue stream generated from these customers.

The sustainability of a company's value proposition is a function of market competitiveness and inherent customer loyalty. Thus, market competitiveness is typically greater when market growth is low, demand is stagnant, and companies have to grow sales by stealing share from each other rather than by attracting new customers. The sustainability of a company's value proposition is also a function of inherent customer loyalty: the degree to which a particular customer segment is prone to switching brands. Competition tends to be greater in markets with low inherent loyalty, where customers can easily be induced to switch.

Competitor Factors

The competitive intensity of a given market is a function of the degree to which competitors have similar goals, core competencies, and strategic assets; the strategic importance of the market; and the rationality of the behavior of individual competitors.

Markets in which competitors have similar goals, competencies, and assets tend to be more competitive because companies tend to target the same customers with similar offerings. In addition, markets that are of strategic importance to multiple companies tend (e.g., due to synergies with other, more profitable offerings) to be more competitive.

The degree of competition is also a function of psychological factors such as the rationality of competitors' behavior. To illustrate, prior competitive history (e.g., price wars and comparative advertising campaigns) and the nature of the personal interactions among managers of competing organizations could have a significant impact on market competitiveness.

Collaborator Factors

Collaborators can influence the competitive intensity of a given market both directly and indirectly.

The direct impact of collaborators on market competitiveness reflects the likelihood that a collaborator will become a direct competitor by taking over some or all of the functions currently performed by its partners. To illustrate, a retailer may insource the manufacturing of the company's offerings, thus becoming a manufacturer's direct competitor. Similarly, a manufacturer may insource the distribution, thus becoming a retailer's direct competitor.

Collaborators' actions can also have an indirect impact on market competitiveness by influencing factors such as competitors' profit margins, which, in turn, will affect the intensity of the competition. For example, as retailers become more powerful, they are likely to squeeze manufacturers' margins, forcing them to compete more fiercely for market share to compensate for the loss of margins.

Company Factors

The competitive intensity of a given market is also a function of a company's own activities. This implies a dynamic view of the environment in which a company evaluates the competition, taking into account how its own actions affect the nature of the marketplace. For example, a company aggressively entering a particular marketplace with a low-price strategy is likely to change the competitive dynamics by influencing the overall market demand and customers' price sensitivity, and by potentially provoking a price war among the companies currently serving this market.

Context Factors

Market competitiveness can also be influenced by various economic, technological, socio-cultural, regulatory, and physical factors. Thus, context could have a direct impact on competitiveness by favoring a particular competitor or group of competitors through factors such as proprietary technology and government regulation (e.g., import quotas, licenses, and tax exemptions). In addition, context may influence competition indirectly by affecting factors such as market demand and profit margins. To illustrate, developments in the area of technology often lead to increased productivity, which in turn results in higher profit margins. Changes in technology may also lead to a shift in the strategic assets and core competencies defining the competitive advantage in a given market. For example, technological developments in digital photography and photocopying have weakened the dominant position of Kodak and Xerox in favor of companies with expertise in digital information processing, such as Sony and Canon.

Summary

Understanding the competitive environment in which a company operates is a key factor for its success in the marketplace. Competitive analysis involves identifying the key competitors and evaluating the competitive intensity of the market.

Competitive analysis begins with identifying the key competitors, that is, business entities with offerings positioned to satisfy the same need of the same target customers. Competitors are typically defined relative to the specific needs of a given customer segment rather than simply defined based on the industry in which the company operates. Identifying the key competitors involves identifying not only current competitors but also its potential competitors – business entities that currently do not target the same customers and/or aim to fulfill the same need(s) but nevertheless have the aspiration and/or the capability to satisfy the focal need(s) of the company's target customers.

The competitive intensity of a given market is a function of the different aspects of the environment in which the company operates and can be analyzed by focusing on the five factors defined by the 5-C framework. Thus, market competitiveness is a function of the relationships among the company, its customers, collaborators, and competitors, as well as the relevant context in which the company operates.

Relevant Frameworks: The Five Forces of Competition

The Five Forces framework was advanced by Michael Porter[1] as a conceptual approach for industry-based analysis of the nature of competition and is often used for strategic industry-level decisions, such as evaluating the viability of entering (or exiting) a particular industry. According to this framework, the competitiveness within an industry is determined by evaluating the following five factors: bargaining power of suppliers, bargaining power of buyers, threat of new entrants, threat of substitutes, and rivalry among extant competitors (Figure 2). The joint impact of these five factors determines the competitive environment in which a firm operates and allows the firm to anticipate competitors' actions.

Figure 2. The Five Forces of Competition[2]

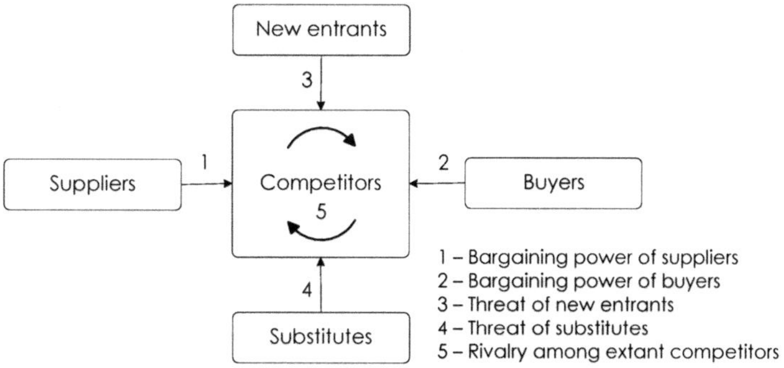

The five forces influencing the competition in an industry can be summarized as follows.

- *Bargaining power of suppliers.* A supplier is powerful when it is dominated by few companies; the product is differentiated, has switching costs, and has diverse applications (e.g., across industries); and there is a credible threat of forward integration.

- *Bargaining power of buyers.* A buyer is powerful when it has concentrated, large-volume purchases; the supplied product is undifferentiated and has no switching costs; the product represents a substantial part of buyers' costs (hence, encouraging more price shopping); the buyer's profit margins are low; the product is not crucial for the buyer; and there is a credible threat of backward integration.

- *Threat of new entrants.* The greater the threat, the greater the overall industry competitiveness. There are six common barriers to entry:

  - *Economies of scale* refer to the benefits from operating the business on a large scale (e.g., in terms of research, production, and distribution). As a general rule, large economies of scale tend to deter new entrants.

- *Product differentiation* reflects the degree to which competitive products are perceived by consumers to be different. In general, the presence of highly differentiated products is viewed as a deterrent for new entrants.

- *Capital requirements* refer to the magnitude of financial resources required to enter the industry. High capital requirements are likely to deter new entrants.

- *Cost disadvantages* (independent of size) capture factors such as experience curve effects, government subsidies, or favorable locations.

- *Access to distribution channels* refers to a new entrant's ability to ensure the availability of its products in distribution channels. In this context, limited access to distribution channels tends to serve as a deterrent for new entrants.

- *Government policy* involves factors such as government regulations, license requirements, and access to technologies (e.g., airlines, power generation, and liquor).

- *Threat of substitute products or services.* The introduction of new products tends to increase competition in an industry and limit its profitability. In general, the threat of substitutes tends to be greater in cases where the substitutes have clear advantages over existing products and/or where profit margins in the industry producing the substitute product are relatively high.

- *Rivalry among existing competitors.* Rivalry tends to be stronger in cases where existing competitors are numerous and comparable in size and power (and hence are likely to have similar goals); industry growth is slow (leading to fights for redistribution of the existing market share); the product is nondifferentiated (leading to price-based competition); fixed costs are high and/or the product is perishable; there is excess capacity; exit barriers are high; and rivals are diverse in terms of goals, strategies, and/or organizational culture.

Additional Readings

Day, George S., David J. Reibstein, and Robert E. Gunther (2004), *Wharton on Dynamic Competitive Strategy*. New York, NY: John Wiley & Sons.

Kim, W. Chan and Renée Mauborgne (2005), *Blue Ocean Strategy: How to Create Uncontested Market Space and Make the Competition Irrelevant*. Boston, MA: Harvard Business School Press.

Prahalad, C. K. and Venkatram Ramaswamy (2004), *The Future of Competition: Co-Creating Unique Value with Customers*. Boston, MA: Harvard Business School Press.

Notes

[1] Porter, Michael E. (1979), "How Competitive Forces Shape Strategy," *Harvard Business Review*, 57, (March–April), 137–145.

[2] Adapted from ibid.

Chapter Eleven

Context Analysis

All is flux; nothing stays still.
Heraclitus

Context analysis involves evaluating the relevant aspects of the environment in which a company operates. Context factors include the economic, technological, socio-cultural, regulatory, and physical environment of the marketing exchange. These five aspects of marketing context are the focus of this chapter.

Overview

To succeed, a company must understand the environment in which it operates. This environment—also referred to as the marketing context—comprises a number of factors that are likely to influence the marketing exchange among the company, its customers, collaborators, and competitors. Specifically, there are five key context factors: economic (e.g., economic growth, money supply, inflation, and interest rates); technological (e.g., the diffusion of existing technologies and the development of new ones); socio-cultural (e.g., demographic trends, value systems, and market-specific beliefs and behavior), regulatory (e.g., import/export tariffs, taxes, product specifications, pricing and advertising policies, and patent and trademark protection); and physical (e.g., natural resources, climate, and health conditions). These five context factors are illustrated in Figure 1.

Figure 1. Context Analysis: The Big Picture

Analyzing the marketing context is important when developing a new action plan, as well as when monitoring the company's progress toward implementing an already existing plan. It enables a company to better understand the environment in which it operates and tailor its actions to take advantage of the intricacies of this environment. The key aspects of the marketing context—economic, technological, socio-cultural, regulatory, and physical—are discussed in the following sections.

Economic Context

A company's ability to create value for target customers, collaborators, and shareholders is a function of the overall economic environment in which it operates. The economic environment in any given market can be characterized by a variety of factors, including the gross domestic product (GDP), economic growth, government spending, international trade, unemployment rate, level of savings and debt, commodity prices, exchange rates, inflation, interest rates, money supply, taxation, stock prices, and housing prices.

All of the above factors may influence a company's success in the marketplace. Thus, the success of a company's marketing strategy is a function of the overall level of business activity. A business model that has proven successful in times of rapid economic growth may fail during a recession. Limited money supply and credit availability may not only curb a company's expansion plans but also can threaten the company's very existence. For example, the deteriorating economic conditions and limited money supply during the financial crisis which began in 2007 resulted in a record number of bankruptcies in the United States.

Fluctuations in exchange rates also can have a significant impact on net income of companies with global exposure. For example, the depreciation of the US currency against the Euro had a positive impact on the dollar-denominated sales revenues of many U.S.-based companies that sell their products in Europe but had negative impact on the Euro-denominated revenues of many European companies that sell their products in the United States. The lower cost of borrowing money, reflected in declining interest rates, can further stimulate business, providing companies with growth opportunities and lowering the entry barriers for potential competitors. Stock market prices may influence a company's ability to expand via mergers and acquisitions, and housing prices can create a wealth effect, influencing consumers' spending behavior.

Globalization, increasing complexity, and rapid changes in the economic environment underscore the importance of understanding the importance of environmental implications on a company's business activities. Companies that are able to foresee the changes in the economic environment and manage to adjust their business models to these changes are more likely to succeed than those who fail to recognize changes and adapt to them.

Technological Context

Technological environment may influence the way companies operate in two ways: by improving a company's operations within the boundaries of its current business models and by facilitating the development of new business models. In this context, most technological innovations fall into one of two categories: incremental innovations, which lead to improvements in already existing business models, and disruptive technologies, which lead to the creation of entirely new business models.

The impact of the technology on a company's processes within the *existing business model* can be better understood in the context of value creation, delineated by the processes of designing, communicating, and delivering value. In this context, technological developments influence a company's performance in two ways: by improving the effectiveness of the value-creation processes and by improving their cost efficiency.

The improvement in *effectiveness* of a company's business activities can be attributed to the development and standardization of underlying manufacturing processes that have resulted in increasing commoditization of products in categories such as automobiles, consumer electronics, apparel, and packaged goods. In addition to constant improvement of a company's products and services, technological developments have facilitated companies' ability to effectively interact with their target customers by uncovering new means of communication and improving the effectiveness of the existing ones. Technological developments have further improved existing distribution systems by streamlining various aspects of a company's distribution channels such as product availability, transportation, and inventory.

In addition to improving the effectiveness of the company's operations, technological developments have contributed to improving the *cost-efficiency* of these operations, resulting in lower manufacturing, communication, and distribution costs. These cost savings have helped many companies improve their bottom line as well as enhance the customer and collaborator value created by their offerings.

An important way in which technology influences a company's market success is by breaking the standard industry operating mold and creating a *novel business model*. Such disruptive technologies have fundamentally changed many industries. For example, the development of the Internet revolutionized retailing (e.g., Amazon.com), auctions (e.g., eBay), mass-media communications (e.g., TiVo), social networking (e.g., Facebook), information search (e.g., Google), and movie rental (e.g., Netflix).

The current technological environment is characterized by the rapid emergence of new technologies in virtually all industries including energy, pharmaceuticals, medicine, communications, manufacturing, and education. Not only are new technologies being developed at an increasing rate but also their implementation cycle from invention to business application has been significantly shortened. This rapid adoption of new technologies is facilitated by increasing rates of global collaboration and transfer of technologies stemming from the global expansion of production, marketing, and research activities. This contributes to the ever-increasing impact of the technological context on a company's business activities.

Socio-Cultural Context

The socio-cultural environment is important to a company's success in both domestic and global markets. The key aspects of the socio-cultural environment include factors such as language, education, beliefs, attitudes, values, customs, habits, lifestyle, views of aesthetics, fashion, style, religion, spirituality, social organization, and stratification. The socio-cultural environment is further influenced by a number of demographic factors such as population size and growth, age dispersion, geographic dispersion, ethnic background, mobility, education, employment, and household composition.

An aspect of the socio-cultural context that is particularly relevant for a company's marketing activities involves the market-specific beliefs, values, and behaviors held by consumers. These factors can influence consumer reaction to different facets of a company's offering and determine its ultimate market success. For example, country of origin plays a less important role in the United States than it does in many countries around the world, where the same Gillette razor can be sold at different prices depending on where it is manufactured. In fact, in some countries, buying behavior is determined to a larger degree by the country of origin than by the offering's brand name.

The importance of understanding cross-cultural differences is often illustrated with the popular story of General Motors' Chevrolet Nova, which sold poorly in Mexico because its name translates as "doesn't go" (no va) in Spanish. Although inaccurate (it is an urban legend, not a fact), this story underscores the importance of adapting a company's marketing strategies to reflect the specifics of its target markets. Accordingly, many global companies have modified their product development, branding, pricing, incentives, communication, and distribution strategies to optimize their offerings to the cultural specifics of each individual market they compete in. For example, the iconic Marlboro symbol—the lone cowboy—is typically shown as a part of a group in many Asian countries with a collectivist culture where riding alone is associated with being an outcast rather than serving as an expression of freedom.

A company's marketing success depends not only on understanding the specifics of the socio-cultural environment in which it operates but also on a company's ability to predict the likely changes in this environment. Understanding and acting on the key socio-cultural trends enables a company to develop a successful long-term marketing strategy. Among the important socio-cultural trends is changing demographics in many countries reflected in factors such as population growth, average age, ethnic composition, and social stratification. For example, a key socio-cultural trend of global consequence is the emergence of a middle class in many newly industrialized countries, including China, India, and Brazil.

Regulatory Context

The regulatory context is defined by two types of factors: factors influencing a company's overall strategy (target customers, the company, and its collaborators and competitors) and factors influencing its tactics (product, service, brand, price, incentives, communication, and distribution). These factors are discussed in more detail below.

Regulations concerning a company's overall *strategy* fall into one of the following four key domains: (1) customer-related regulations, which include factors such as age restrictions for certain activities (e.g., driving, drinking, and smoking), place restrictions (e.g., smoking in public places), and possession restrictions (e.g., drugs, firearms); (2) company-related regulations, which include factors pertaining to relationships between the company management and its shareholders; (3) collaborator-related regulations, which seek to define the relationships among collaborating entities and protect them from potential abuse of power; and (4) competitive regulations, which seek to define the relationships among competing entities in a way that protect weaker competitors from abuse of power on the part of the stronger ones (e.g., anti-monopoly legislation) while at the same time protecting consumer interests (e.g., anti-collusion legislation).

Marketing-mix regulations concern the company's activities with respect to the seven marketing mix decisions: product, service, brand, price, incentives, communication, and distribution. For example, these regulations may involve product and service specifications, brand protection (e.g., trademark laws), regulations pertaining to pricing and price incentives (e.g., predatory pricing and price fixing), communication-specific regulations (e.g., comparative advertising), as well as regulation concerning distribution channels (e.g. antitrust laws designed to protect trade from unlawful restrictions and monopolization).

Because regulations play a pivotal role in all aspects of marketing management, a company needs to master the regulatory aspect of its business activities and understand its dynamics to effectively function in a given market. Regulatory context is market-specific and is constantly evolving in response to changes in the economic, technological, socio-cultural, and physical aspects of the marketing environment.

Physical Context

The success of a company's marketing strategy is also a function of the surrounding physical context, which includes factors such as topography, natural resources, climate, weather, and the overall health conditions. The topography tends to naturally influence the routing of goods and the choice of transportation mode as well as distribution costs, delivery schedules, and inventory management. The availability of natural resources—including energy, metals, and water—is likely to influence the technologies used by companies as well as the manufacturing and distribution costs.

Climate exerts important influence on a company's business activities. Because climate factors, such as temperature, humidity, atmospheric pressure, wind, and rainfall, tend to influence product functionality, companies often optimize their products for a particular climate. For example, motor oils are formulated to have different levels of viscosity (thickness) to ensure consistent performance in different temperatures. Special packaging is developed to safeguard products that are adversely affected by extremes in temperatures or excessive humidity changes.

A company's business activities are influenced not only by the relatively permanent regional climate conditions, but also by changes in these conditions. For example, an increase in the average annual temperatures (i.e., global warming) is likely to lead to lower yields of fruits and vegetables that thrive in cooler temperatures and higher yields of warm-climate plants. As the cold season shortens, winter sports are likely to suffer, whereas warm-weather activities are likely to grow. In addition to climate changes, which reflect the more stable weather patterns, daily weather conditions can also influence a company's business. For instance, ice cream consumption is likely to increase when it hot and decline as the weather cools down. Abnormal weather conditions can disrupt the production and delivery of a company's products.

Health conditions can influence the business activities of companies directly involved in health management (e.g., pharmaceutical companies, biotechnology companies, and health-management organizations) as well as those not directly related to heath care. For instance, the demand for a cold medicine is likely to be affected by the overall health conditions in a given market. A pandemic, such as avian influenza (H5N1) and swine flu (H1N1), can have a profound effect on all areas of business including food, tourism, hospitality, and transportation.

The physical environment not only influences a company's business model but can also shape other context factors. Understanding the relationships among the individual context factors is an important aspect of evaluating a company's economic, technological, socio-cultural and regulatory environment.

Summary

To succeed, a company must understand the environment in which it operates. This environment—also referred to as the marketing context—comprises a number of factors that are likely to influence the marketing exchange among the company, its customers, its collaborators, and its competitors. Specifically, there are five key context factors: economic (e.g., economic growth, money supply, inflation, and interest rates); technological (e.g., the diffusion of existing technologies and the development of new ones); socio-cultural (e.g., demographic trends, value systems, and market-specific beliefs and behavior); regulatory (e.g., import/export tariffs, taxes, product specifications, pricing and advertising policies, and patent and trademark protection); and physical (e.g., natural resources, climate, and health conditions).

Analyzing the marketing context is important when developing a new action plan as well as when monitoring the company's progress toward implementing an already existing plan. It enables a company to better understand the environment in which it operates and tailor its actions to take advantage of the intricacies of different environmental aspects. Failure to understand the marketing context and anticipate its dynamics hinders a company's ability to create value for its customers, collaborators, and shareholders, often leading to a failure of its marketing strategy.

Relevant Concepts

Bottom of the Pyramid: An economics term used to describe the largest and poorest socio-economic group. It was popularized by C.K. Prahalad in his seminal book *The Fortune at the Bottom of the Pyramid*, and used in reference to the four billion people who live on less than $2 per day, typically in developing countries. Also referred to as the "base of the pyramid."

Wealth Effect: An increase in spending that accompanies an actual or a perceived increase in wealth. For example, people tend to spend more as their salary, investment portfolio, and/or the value of their house increases.

Veblen Effect: A pattern of behavior named for the economist and sociologist Thorstein Veblen that refers to the acquisition of goods mainly for the purpose of attaining or maintaining social status, income, and/or wealth. Also referred to as conspicuous consumption.

Additional Readings

Cheeseman, Henry R. (2009), *Business Law*. Upper Saddle River, NJ: Prentice Hall.

Christensen, Clayton (1997), *The Innovator's Dilemma: When New Technologies Cause Great Firms to Fail*. Boston, MA: Harvard Business School Press.

Friedman, Thomas L. (2007), *The World Is Flat: A Brief History of the Twenty-First Century*. New York, NY: Picador.

Prahalad, C. K. (2006), *The Fortune at the Bottom of the Pyramid: Eradicating Poverty Through Profits*. Philadelphia, PA: Wharton School Publishing.

Part Three

Managing Customer, Company, and Collaborator Value

Introduction

Marketing is the art and science of creating and managing successful exchanges. The success of a marketing exchange is determined by its ability to create value for all relevant participants. Accordingly, an offering's success is ultimately determined by its ability to create value for target customers, the company, and its collaborators.

Optimizing the value to target customers, the company, and its collaborators is the key principle that underlies all marketing activities These three types of value comprise the 3-V framework illustrated in Figure 1. The key principle underlying the 3-V framework is that business success can be achieved only when the offering's value is optimized to all relevant participants.

Figure 1. The 3-V Value-Management Framework

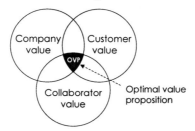

The 3-V value-management framework serves as the organizing principle for this part of the book, as follows:

- The key issues in *managing customer value* are discussed in Chapter 12, which focuses on the processes of developing a value proposition, identifying a positioning strategy, and developing a positioning statement.

- The essential aspects of *managing company value* are the focus of Chapter 13, which offers an overview of the key profit drivers and outlining a systematic approach for managing profit growth.

- The key elements of *managing collaborator value* are discussed in Chapter 14, which focuses on the antecedents and consequences of establishing successful collaboration and managing collaborator relationships.

The discussion of managing customer, company, and collaborator value logically follows the situation analysis delineated by the 5-C framework and discussed in the second part of this book. The process of identifying target markets, which is the core of the situation analysis, is typically guided by the company's ability to create value for target customers, and do so in a way that enables the company and its collaborators to achieve their strategic goals. Thus, identifying target markets and managing the value for the relevant parties in these markets is an iterative process aimed at creating a successful and sustainable value exchange.

Chapter Twelve

Managing Customer Value

There is only one boss. The customer. And he can fire everybody in the company from the chairman on down, simply by spending his money somewhere else.

Sam Walton, founder of Wal-Mart

Managing customer value is a pivotal element of a company's strategy. Because customers are the ultimate source of value for the company and its collaborators, managing customer value is essential for a company's success. The two key aspects of managing customer value—developing a value proposition and developing a positioning strategy—are the focus of this chapter.

The Big Picture

The value of an offering is a function of the degree to which it meets the needs of its target customers. Because customer needs have three key components—monetary, functional, and psychological—an offering can create customer value in three different ways: by creating functional value, by creating monetary value, and by creating psychological value (Figure 1).

Figure 1. Managing Customer Value: The Big Picture

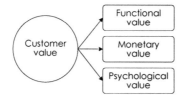

The three dimensions of customer value can be summarized as follows.

- *Functional value* reflects the benefits and costs that are directly related to an offering's performance. To illustrate, the functional value of a car involves its operational (e.g., engine power), aesthetic (e.g., visual appearance), and safety (e.g., crash-test performance) attributes.

- *Monetary value* is related to the monetary benefits and costs associated with the offering. For example, the monetary value of a car involves factors such as retail price, fees, discounts, rebates, fuel efficiency, and maintenance costs.

- *Psychological value* refers to the psychological benefits and costs associated with the offering. For example, the psychological value of a car is derived from its emotional (e.g., the joy of driving a car), social (e.g., group acceptance/social affirmation resulting from ownership of a particular brand of car), and self-expressive (e.g., using the car as a means to express one's identity) attributes.

Developing a Value Proposition

The value proposition captures all benefits and costs associated with a given offering. When developing its value proposition, a company must ensure not only that it creates value to target customers but also that it does so better than the competition. Thus, the viability of an offering's value proposition is measured by the degree to which it can deliver superior value to target customers relative to the competition. Differentiation by itself does not create value and does not constitute a competitive advantage. Competitive advantage is a company's ability to deliver greater value to target customers than the competition. The relationship between competitive advantage and customer value can be illustrated as shown in Figure 2.

Figure 2. Competitive Advantage and Customer Value

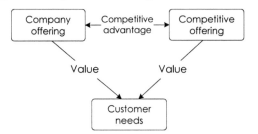

The relationship between competitive advantage and customer value, depicted in Figure 2, implies that competitive advantage can be quantified as the difference in the value delivered by the company's and competitors' offerings. Thus, competitive advantage is greatest when the benefits delivered by the company's offering perfectly fit the needs of its target customers and competitors' offerings lack any benefits relevant to these customers. This relationship can be summarized as follows:

$$\text{Competitive advantage} = \text{Customer value}_{\text{Company}} - \text{Customer value}_{\text{Competition}}$$

An offering's ability to provide superior customer value can be further analyzed on three dimensions: functional, monetary, and psychological. Because competitive advantage captures the difference in the value provided by the company's and competitors' offerings, it can also be represented as a function of the differences in the functional, monetary, and psychological value of the company's and competitors' offerings. In this context, the competitive advantage of a company's offering is a function of the differences in the customer value (denoted by Δ) delivered by the company and its competitors on each of the three dimensions (functional, monetary, and psychological).

$$\text{Competitive advantage} = \Delta\text{Functional value} + \Delta\text{Monetary value} + \Delta\text{Psychological value}$$

The essence of competitive advantage can be illustrated by examining the concepts of *differentiation* and *parity*. Thus, attributes describing a particular offering can be divided into two broad categories: (1) relevant attributes (or benefits), which create value for a particular customer segment, and (2) irrelevant attributes, which have no significant impact on the value of the offering to this customer segment. Benefits can be further divided into benefits that are shared across all offerings in the market and benefits that are unique to a particular offering. An offering's *competitive advantage* captures benefits that differentiate a particular offering from its competitors. In contrast, benefits that are shared by all offerings targeting a particular customer segment are at *competitive parity* (Figure 3). Only differences in relevant attributes create customer value; differences in irrelevant attributes rarely add value to the offering.

Figure 3. Competitive Parity and Competitive Advantage.

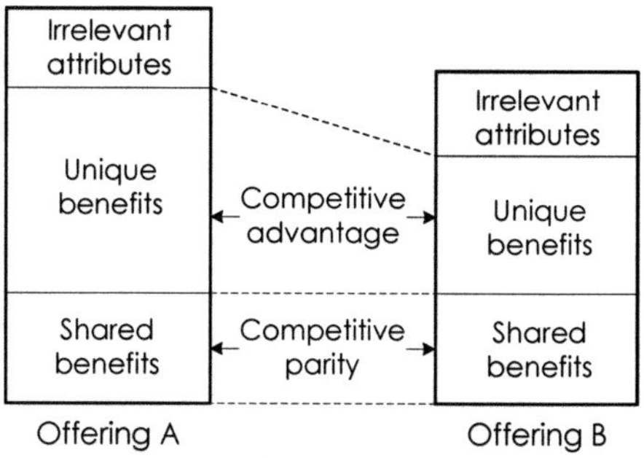

An offering's competitive advantage is determined not by the actual characteristics of the company's offerings but rather by customers' perceptions of these characteristics. It does not matter whether a particular difference is real; what matters is that it is perceived by customers as a differentiating point. To illustrate, customers might not see a difference in performance between a car with a 300-horsepower engine and one with a 310-horsepower engine, in which case the engine performance of the two cars is at parity. In contrast, attributes that are objectively at parity may be, nevertheless, differentiated in the mind of the customer, thereby creating a competitive advantage. To illustrate, Volvo is perceived to be the safest car, even though in reality this might not always be the case.

Developing a Positioning Strategy

An important aspect of managing customer value is designing a positioning strategy. Positioning reflects the company's view of how an offering should be perceived and remembered by customers;[1] it is the process of creating a distinct image of the company's offering in a customer's mind.[2,3] For example, Volvo positions its cars as the safest vehicles on the road, Toyota emphasizes reliability, and BMW focuses on the driving experience.

The concept of positioning can be better understood when compared with the concept of value proposition. Unlike value proposition, which captures *all* of the benefits and costs of an offering, positioning focuses customers' attention only on the *most important aspect(s)* of the offering's value proposition. To illustrate, the driving experience is one of the many aspects of BMW's value proposition (e.g., comfort, fuel economy, design, build quality, reliability, and safety) that the company chose to position its cars in the minds of its customers. In this context, positioning aims to present the advantages of the offering in a way that accentuates its key benefit(s) and provides customers with a compelling reason to choose and/or use the company's offering.

An offering's positioning often can be summarized in a single phrase, commonly used as a tagline in company communications. To illustrate, consider the following examples: *Fresh, hot pizza delivered in 30 minutes or less, guaranteed* (Domino's); *Better Ingredients. Better Pizza* (Papa John's); *We try harder* (Avis); *If it's got to be clean…it's got to be Tide* (Tide); *It's everywhere you want to be* (Visa); *You never actually own a Patek Philippe. You merely look after it for the next generation* (Patek Philippe men's watches); *You don't just wear a Patek Philippe. You begin an enduring love affair* (Patek Philippe ladies' watches).

Because positioning involves prioritizing the existing benefits and costs of a given offering, the same offering can often be positioned in multiple ways. Consider TiVo, the personal digital video recorder. It offers multiple benefits, such as skipping commercials, pausing live TV, recording every episode of a series through the "season pass," one-step recording, instant replay and fast-forward features, recording on two channels simultaneously, and displaying an up-to-date program guide. All of these benefits comprise TiVo's value proposition. Successful positioning requires further laddering these benefits and identifying the single most important benefit that delivers value to the customer and differentiates TiVo from the competition. For example, TiVo could be positioned as a device that allows viewers to pause live TV, as a one-step TV recording device, or as a device that allows viewers to record one channel while watching another. In this context, positioning may require ignoring some of the offering's potential benefits to bring its distinct value advantage into focus.

The term positioning can be used in two distinct contexts: desired positioning, which reflects the company's positioning goal with respect to a particular offering, and actual positioning, which reflects customers' perceptions of the offering. Indeed, despite a company's efforts to create a certain image in the minds of its target customers, these customers might have formed a very different perception of the benefits of the company's offering. Therefore, the success of a company's positioning strategy can be measured by the overlap of the company's positioning goals and customers' perceptions of the offering.

The process of developing a positioning strategy involves two key decisions: (1) identifying the primary source of the offering's value and (2) defining the reference point used to position the offering. These two aspects of developing a positioning strategy are discussed in more detail below.

Identifying the Primary Source of Value

The process of identifying the primary source of customer value involves evaluating different aspects of the offering's value proposition to select the one(s) to use to position the offering in a customer's mind. This process, often referred to as benefit laddering, aims to prioritize certain aspects of the offering's value proposition to accentuate its key aspect(s) and provide customers with a compelling reason to choose the company's offering.

There are three basic strategies to emphasize the benefits associated with an offering: single-benefit positioning, multi-benefit positioning, and holistic positioning.

The *single-benefit approach* involves identifying a single attribute and emphasizing the value delivered by the offering on this primary attribute (Figure 4). This primary attribute is the one that the company believes will most likely provide customers with a compelling reason to choose and/or use the company's offering. To illustrate, safety is the primary attribute for Volvo and reliability is the primary positioning for Maytag. Single-attribute positioning does not imply that the offering is inferior on the other, secondary attributes; it simply identifies an attribute that is likely to be of primary importance to target customers. In this context, the secondary attribute(s) enhances the value delivered by the primary attribute(s), although by themselves, they could rarely serve as a reason for choice.

Figure 4. Single-Benefit Positioning

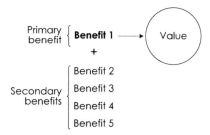

Depending on the nature of the primary benefit used to position the offering, three types of positioning strategies can be identified: functional, monetary, and psychological.

- *Positioning on functional benefits* emphasizes a particular aspect of an offering's performance. For example, Toyota emphasizes reliability and Visa emphasizes its worldwide acceptance.

- *Positioning on monetary benefits* emphasizes the monetary value associated with the offering. To illustrate, Southwest Airlines, Wal-Mart, and Priceline.com emphasize low price as a key aspect of their value proposition, and the Discover credit card emphasizes its cash-back feature as "America's number one cash rewards program."

- *Positioning on psychological benefits* emphasizes the intangible benefits associated with the offering's image. For instance, offerings such as Montblanc, Rolls-Royce, and Dom Pérignon are positioned to instill feelings of luxury, exclusivity, and prestige. An offering's positioning may also be influenced by the company's positioning as a leader in innovation (e.g., HP, Sony, and Procter & Gamble) or by its image as a socially responsible organization (e.g., Ben and Jerry's, Newman's Own, and Ecolab). Finally, an offering can be positioned by emphasizing risk-related benefits, such as reducing uncertainty and gaining peace of mind.

The *multi-benefit approach* involves emphasizing the benefits delivered by the offering on two or more primary attributes (Figure 5). To illustrate, a classic dual-benefit positioning is the one utilized by Procter & Gamble's Ivory Soap: "99 $^{44}/_{100}$ % pure; it floats." The advantage of multi-benefit positioning over a single-benefit positioning is that it captures multiple aspects of the offering's value proposition. On the downside, however, multi-benefit positioning runs the risk of diluting the offering's image in the mind of the customer and failing to establish a compelling reason for choice. As a result, positioning on more than two primary benefits is not very common.

Figure 5. Multi-Benefit Positioning (Dual-Benefit Scenario)

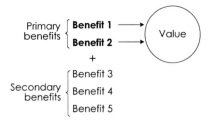

The *holistic approach* emphasizes the overall performance of an offering without identifying individual benefits (Figure 6). Unlike the single-benefit and multi-benefit approaches, the holistic approach entices customers to choose an offering based on its performance as a whole rather than on particular attributes. For example, Gillette's positioning strategy, "Gillette, the best a man can get," is designed to create a perception of superior overall performance. Colgate Total, as implied by its name, claims to offer the best overall package of category benefits. Similarly, Amoco's positioning as "America's number one premium gasoline," Tylenol's positioning as "the brand most hospitals trust," and Hertz's positioning as the "#1" car rental company in the world emphasize market leadership as a proxy for the overall performance of these offerings.

Figure 6. Holistic Positioning

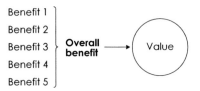

Defining the Reference Point

In defining the reference point, two types of positioning can be distinguished: noncomparative, in which the reference point is a particular customer need, and comparative, in which the reference point involves competitive offerings.

Noncomparative Positioning

Noncomparative positioning directly relates the value of the offering to customer needs without explicitly contrasting it to competitors' offerings. Here, the frame of reference for noncomparative offerings is the needs of the target customers, and the main reason for buying/using the offering is its ability to fulfill these needs.

Noncomparative positioning typically employs one of the two core strategies to relate an offering to customer needs: need-based positioning and category-based positioning.

- *Need-based positioning* directly links the benefits of the offering to an identified customer need. For example, TiVo, the pioneer in personal digital recording, was initially positioned as a device allowing viewers to have their own TV network where they could decide what to watch and when.

- *Category-based positioning* communicates the benefits of the offering by linking it to an already established product category. For example, after TiVo's initial need-based positioning strategy did not achieve the desired market impact, it was repositioned as a video recorder with a hard drive.

Comparative Positioning

Comparative positioning relates the value of the offering to customer needs by explicitly contrasting it to other offerings. The frame of reference in comparative positioning is another offering, usually a competitor's. The main reason for buying/using the company's offering is its ability to fulfill customer needs better than the referent offering. The referent offering can be explicitly identified, or it can be broadly described without identifying a particular brand (e.g., "It's not delivery. It's DiGiorno.").

Comparative positioning typically employs one of two core strategies: differentiation-based positioning and similarity-based positioning.

- *Differentiation-based positioning* is by far the prevalent approach, reflecting the belief that differentiation is the key source of the offering's sustainable competitive advantage. The goal here is to establish a single point or multiple points of *differentiation* and steal share from the referent offering by demonstrating the superiority of the company's offering.

- *Similarity-based positioning*, also referred to as "me-too" positioning, aims to show lack of differentiation between the company's offering and other offerings. The goal here is to establish multiple points of *parity* and steal share from the referent company, typically the market leader, because of customer indifference between the two products. For example, Unilever's cosmetic brand Suave claims to "work just as hard as expensive brands."

As a general rule, comparative positioning is usually employed by smaller share offerings trying to steal share from the market leader. It is rarely used by the market leader because by comparing its offering with one with a smaller share, the market leader often ends up implicitly promoting the referent offering. Note, however, that this principle does not hold for offerings in different price tiers that do not directly compete for the same customers; in this case, a larger share brand could actually benefit by comparing itself with a smaller share upscale brand (e.g., comparing Volkswagen to Porsche).

Developing a Positioning Statement

The positioning statement is an internal document that presents a succinct summary of an offering's targeting and positioning strategy. This statement is used by various divisions within the company (e.g., research and development, sales, and accounting), as well as in a company's communications with its collaborators (e.g., advertising agencies, public relations agencies, and distributors) to ensure that their actions are consistent with the offering's strategy.

The positioning statement identifies three main aspects of an offering's strategy:

- Target customers
- Frame of reference (the reference point used by customers to evaluate the offering)
- The primary reason for buying/using the offering (the key source of value)

The scope of the positioning statement is broader than just summarizing the offering's positioning. In addition to identifying the two key aspects of the offering's positioning (the frame of reference and the key benefit), it also identifies the customer segment targeted by the offering.

Depending on the frame of reference, two types of positioning statements can be distinguished: noncomparative and comparative. The noncomparative statement defines the key benefit of the offering relative to customer needs without explicitly comparing the offering to the other offerings in the market. The structure of a typical noncomparative positioning statement is illustrated in Figure 7.

Figure 7. Noncomparative Positioning Statement

.... is the best ....
              (offering)   (product category)

for ....
                                    (target customers)

because ....
                                    (primary reason)

To illustrate, consider the following noncomparative positioning statements:

Mountain Dew is the soft drink that gives young, active consumers who have little time for sleep the energy they need because it has a very high level of caffeine.

Gatorade is a smart choice for athletes because it rehydrates, replenishes, and refuels.

Palm Pilot is an electronic organizer that allows busy professionals to back up files on their PC easily and reliably.

For the tradesman who uses power tools to make a living and cannot afford downtime on the job, DeWalt offers dependable professional tools that are engineered to the highest standards and are backed by a guarantee for repair and replacement within 48 hours.

In contrast, the comparative statement defines the offering's key benefit by explicitly relating it to other market offerings. The structure of a typical comparative positioning statement is illustrated in Figure 8.

Figure 8. Comparative Positioning Statement

```
.................................... is a better ....................................
            (offering)                           (product category)


than ..............................................................................
                          (competitive offering)



for ..............................................................................
                          (target customers)



because ..............................................................................
                          (primary reason)
```

To illustrate, consider the following comparative positioning statements:

Mountain Dew is the soft drink that gives young, active consumers who have little time for sleep more energy than any other brand because it has the highest level of caffeine.

Gatorade is a smart choice for athletes because it rehydrates, replenishes, and refuels in ways water can't.

Palm Pilot is an electronic organizer that allows busy professionals to back up files on their PC more easily and reliably than competitive products.

For the tradesman who uses power tools to make a living and cannot afford downtime on the job, DeWalt offers professional tools that are more dependable than other brands because they are engineered to higher standards and are backed by a guarantee for repair and replacement within 48 hours.

Summary

Because customers ultimately create value for the company, managing customer value is essential for a company's success. The two key aspects of managing customer value involve developing a value proposition and developing a positioning strategy.

The value proposition reflects all benefits and costs associated with a particular offering. The success of an offering is determined by the degree to which its value proposition can fulfill customer needs better than the competition. In this context, an offering's competitive advantage is determined by its ability to deliver superior customer value on each of the three value dimensions: functional, monetary, and psychological.

Positioning reflects the company's view of how the offering should be perceived and remembered by the customer; it is the process of creating a distinct image of the company's offering in a customer's mind. Unlike value proposition, which captures *all* of the benefits and costs of an offering, positioning focuses customers' attention only on the most important aspect(s) of the offering's value proposition. Because positioning involves prioritizing the existing benefits and costs of a given offering, the same offering can often be positioned in multiple ways.

The process of developing a positioning strategy involves two key decisions: identifying the primary source of the offering's value and defining the reference point used to position the offering. Identifying the primary source of customer value involves evaluating different aspects of the offering's value proposition to select the one(s) to use to position the offering in a customer's mind. There are three common strategies to position an offering: single-benefit, multi-benefit, and holistic. With respect to defining the reference point, two types of positioning can be distinguished: noncomparative, in which the reference point is a particular customer need, and comparative, in which the reference point involves competitive offerings.

The customer value proposition is summarized in an offering's positioning statement, which identifies three main aspects of the offering's strategy: target customers, frame of reference, and the primary reason for buying/using the offering. Depending on the frame of reference, two types of positioning statements can be distinguished: noncomparative and comparative. The noncomparative statement defines the key benefit of the offering relative to customer needs without explicitly comparing the offering to the other offerings in the market.

Relevant Concepts: Attribute-Value Maps

Attribute-value maps (also referred to as value curves) capture customer evaluations of an offering's performance on key attributes and relate them to the attribute performance of competitive offerings (Figure 9). Here, higher levels of customer value associated with a particular benefit correspond to higher levels of an offering's performance on that attribute, and the competitive advantage of a company's offering is defined by the differences in its customer value vis-à-vis competitors. By capturing an offering's performance on all relevant attributes in a competitive context, attribute-value maps enable the company to better understand the drivers of its unique value proposition to target customers.

Figure 9. Attribute-Value Map

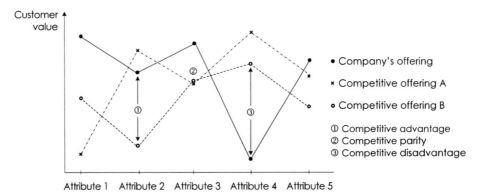

A potential shortcoming of attribute-value maps is that they do not take into account the relative importance of each attribute; as a result, they offer little guidance as to which attributes are likely to have greater impact on the overall attractiveness of an offering. To address this limitation, the relative importance of each attribute (typically given as percentages totaling 100) is often incorporated into attribute-value maps.

Relevant Concepts: Positioning Maps

Positioning maps reflect buyers' perception of an offering's performance relative to that of the competition. Similar to attribute-value maps, positioning maps are derived from customer evaluations of the various aspects of the offerings available to target customers. Unlike attribute-value maps, which reflect performance on all relevant attributes, positioning maps reflect perceived performance only on the most relevant factor(s). These factors may be individual attributes, such as those used in the attribute-value map or, alternatively, they may reflect holistic evaluations of different aspects of the offerings (e.g., benefits and costs). In addition to plotting the available offerings, perceptual maps can also display consumers' ideal points (or ideal vectors), which reflect customers' ideal combinations of different aspects of the offering.

Perceptual maps can have any number of dimensions, although two-dimensional maps are the most common because they are the easiest to interpret (Figure 10). To illustrate, in the case of headache remedies, a perceptual map can illustrate the relative performance of different drugs on factors such as effectiveness and duration, such that the most effective and longest lasting drugs will occupy the upper right quadrant of the chart and the least effective and shortest duration drugs will occupy the lower left quadrant.

Figure 10. Positioning Map

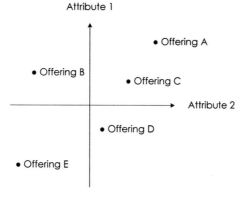

Positioning maps can be derived by asking respondents to rate an option's performance on a set of predefined attributes (as in deriving an attribute-value map) and then aggregating these attribute-based evaluations into a few (usually two) more general factors. Alternatively, positioning maps can be derived based on customers' similarity-based evaluations of the offerings relative to one another to derive the underlying dimensions and plot the offerings onto a two-dimensional space.

Positioning maps offer two main advantages over attribute-value maps. First, by using only a few composite dimensions instead of many individual attributes, positioning maps offer a holistic view of an offering as it is perceived by customers. Second, unlike attribute-value maps, which typically depict an offering's intrinsic value, positioning maps illustrate the offering's value relative to the other offerings in the market. At the same time, a major shortcoming of positioning maps is that they do not capture the impact of individual attributes on an offering's overall attractiveness. The complementary nature of the advantages and shortcomings of attribute-value and positioning maps reflects the fact that these two tools reflect different aspects of the value-creation process and, therefore, should be used jointly in marketing analysis.

Additional Readings

Barwise, Patrick and Sean Meehan (2004), *Simply Better: Winning and Keeping Customers by Delivering What Matters Most*. Boston, MA: Harvard Business School Press.

Gupta, Sunil and Donald R. Lehmann (2005), *Managing Customers as Investments: The Strategic Value of Customers in the Long Run*. Upper Saddle River, NJ: Wharton School Publishing.

Keller, Kevin Lane (2007*), Strategic Brand Management: Building, Measuring, and Managing Brand Equity* (3rd ed.). Upper Saddle River, NJ: Prentice Hall.

Ries, Al and Jack Trout (2001), *Positioning: The Battle for Your Mind* (20th ed.). New York, NY: McGraw-Hill.

Tybout, Alice M. and Tim Calkins (2005), *Kellogg on Branding*. Hoboken, NJ: John Wiley & Sons.

Notes

[1] A broader view of positioning involves creating a distinct image of the offering not only in the minds of customers but also in the minds of the company's employees, stakeholders, and collaborators.

[2] Kotler, Philip (1984), *Marketing Management: Analysis, Planning, and Control* (5th ed.). Englewood Cliffs, NJ: Prentice-Hall.

[3] Ries, Al and Jack Trout (2001), *Positioning: The Battle for Your Mind* (20th ed.). New York, NY: McGraw-Hill.

Chapter Thirteen

Managing Company Value

The business enterprise has two—and only two—basic functions: marketing and innovation. Marketing and innovation produce results; all the rest are costs.

Peter Drucker

A company is a business entity established for the purpose of creating value for its stakeholders. Accordingly, managing company value is an essential aspect of a company' strategy, concerning the very existence of the company as a business enterprise. The key aspects of creating and managing company value are the focus of this chapter.

The Big Picture

The value of an offering to the company is a function of the degree to which its benefits meet the company's goals. Because a company's goal may involve one or more of the following three domains—monetary, functional, and psychological—an offering can create value to the company in three different ways: by creating monetary value, by delivering functional value, and by creating psychological value (Figure 1).

Figure 1. Managing Company Value: The Big Picture

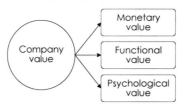

The three dimensions on which an offering can create value the company can be summarized as follows.

- *Monetary value* is a function of the degree to which the monetary benefits of the offering meet the monetary goals of company. Monetary value is directly linked to a company's desired financial performance and is typically represented in metrics such as net income, profit margins, sales revenue, earnings per share, and return on investment.

- *Functional value* is determined by the degree to which the offering can help the company achieve certain functional goals. Thus, an offering can create value by facilitating other strategically important and more profitable offerings. For example, a low-margin entry-level car can help a car manufacturer gain market share among younger customers so that they are more likely to upgrade to this manufacturer's more profitable models, and a free software program can provide a company with a technological platform for distributing revenue-generating offerings.

- *Psychological value* is determined by the ability of an offering to create outcomes of psychological importance to the company employees and/or stakeholders. For example, a company's stakeholders may derive value from socially responsible acts, such as improving social welfare, preserving the environment, and supporting various social causes.

Because maximizing monetary value is the primary goal for most companies, the rest of this chapter focuses on understanding the key factors influencing profitability and identifying strategies for effectively managing profit growth.

Managing Profit Gtrowth

The most relevant measure of monetary value is a company's net income. Because net income is a function of revenues and costs, income growth can be achieved by increasing revenues (top-line growth) and/or reducing costs.

Costs can be reduced by lowering one of the following three types of expenses: cost of goods sold (COGS), marketing costs, and other costs such as research and development costs, cost of capital, and general and administrative expenses. Revenue growth, on the other hand, can be achieved by an increase in sales volume and/or a change in per-unit price. Sales volume, then, can be increased by either attracting new customers or by increasing sales to the company's current customers. Sales volume to new customers, in turn, can be increased by either growing the size of the entire market (i.e., by attracting customers who are new to the particular product category) or by attracting competitors' customers (i.e., by stealing customers from direct competitors). The relationships among different factors driving a company's net income are illustrated in Figure 2.

Figure 2. Managing Company Value: Profit-Growth Analysis

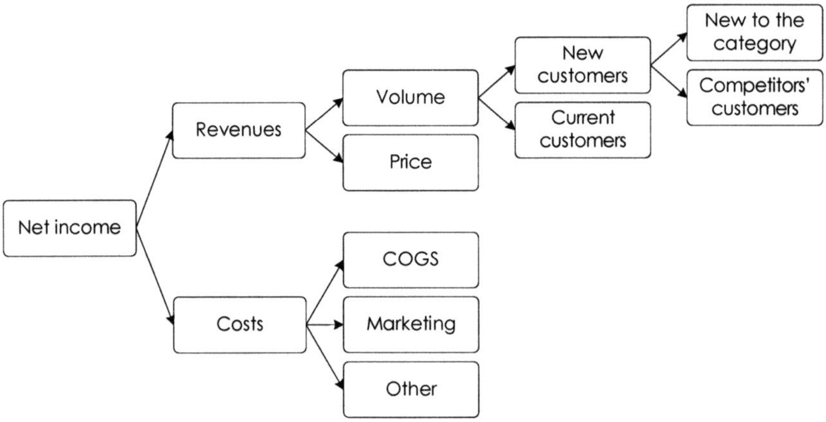

The most effective strategy to achieve profit growth varies depending on a company's goals and the specific market conditions. In some cases, it might involve lowering marketing expenses and/or the costs of goods sold. In other scenarios, profitability can best be achieved by increasing sales volume, for example, by generating incremental volume from current customers. Different strategies for achieving profit growth are outlined in more detail in the following sections.

Managing Profit Growth by Increasing Sales Revenues

Sales revenues are a function of two main factors: sales volume and unit price. These two aspects of managing sales revenues are discussed below.

Increasing Sales Revenues by Growing Sales Volume

The development of a sales-volume strategy begins by identifying market opportunities that the company can capitalize on to increase its net income. A popular approach for identifying viable market opportunities is given by the product-market growth framework (also referred to as the Ansoff matrix).[1] This framework can be represented by a 2×2 matrix in which one of the factors is the type of offering (existing vs. new) and the other factor is the type of customers (current vs. new). The resulting four product-market strategies are commonly referred to as market penetration, market development, product development, and diversification (Figure 3).

Figure 3. Product-Market Growth Matrix[2]

These four sales growth strategies can be summarized as follows:

- *Market-penetration* strategies aim to increase sales of an existing offering to a company's current customers. A common market-penetration strategy involves increasing usage rate. To illustrate, airlines stimulate demand from current customers by adopting frequent-flyer programs; packaged goods manufacturers enclose repurchase coupons as part of their product offerings; orange juice manufacturers promote drinking orange juice throughout the day rather than only for breakfast.

- *Market-development* strategies aim to grow sales by introducing an existing offering to new customers. In this case, the company builds on the success of its offerings to attract new customers. The two most common market-development strategies involve targeting a new customer segment in an existing geographic area and introducing the offering to a different geographic area (e.g., exporting products to a new country). Market-development strategies aimed at attracting new customers include price promotions (e.g., price reductions, coupons, and rebates), new distribution channels, and communication strategies focused on different customer segment(s).

- *Product-development* strategies endeavor to grow sales by developing new (to the company) offerings for existing customers. In this case, the company builds on its current customer base by offering new products. The two most common product-development strategies include developing entirely new offerings or extending the current product line by modifying existing offerings.

- *Diversification strategies* aim to grow sales by introducing new offerings to new customers. Because both the offering and the customers are new to the company, this strategy tends to be riskier than the other product-market strategies. The primary rationale for diversification is to take advantage of growth opportunities in areas in which the company has no presence.

The four strategies identified above are not mutually exclusive: A company can pursue multiple sales growth strategies. However, the company needs to prioritize these strategies based on their market potential and then select the one(s) that will enable it to achieve its long-term goals.

Strategies for managing a company's current offerings are delineated in more detail in Chapter 22, which identifies two basic strategies to increase sales volume: increasing the *rate of adoption* of its offerings (market development) and increasing the *usage rate* of its offerings (market penetration).

Increasing Sales Revenues by Modifying Price

Setting prices is a key component in managing a company's profitability. The impact of pricing on profitability is two-pronged. On one hand, raising prices can have a positive impact on profitability: If the sales volume remains steady or rises, higher prices lead to higher profits. On the other hand, higher prices can have a negative impact on profitability because they frequently lead to a decline in sales volume and, hence, erode overall profits. Thus, the impact of price on sales volume is a function of customers' price elasticity, which represents the percentage change in quantity sold relative to the percentage change in an offering's price. When customers' price elasticity is low, raising prices often does not have a significant impact on sales volume; in contrast, when price elasticity is high, raising prices typically leads to a significant decline in sales volume.[3]

Given the nature of the relationships among an offering's price, sales volume, and profitability, setting a price requires optimizing the impact of its various aspects on profitability. Thus, in cases where the decrease in sales volume caused by a price increase can be offset by the increase in revenues attributed to the higher price, raising the price of an offering can lead to an increase in sales revenues. In contrast, when the lost revenues from a price cut can be offset by an increase in sales volume, lowering the price can lead to an increase in sales revenues.

Two issues in managing price merit attention. First, because in most cases the company's offerings are delivered to its customers by a third party (e.g., retailers), the price paid by customers is typically higher than the price the company charges its channel partners. In this context, the (manufacturer) price the company charges its channel partners, rather than the retail price that customers pay, is the key driver of a company's profitability at a given level of an offering's sales volume. Following the same logic, the impact of price on sales volume is a function of the retail price paid by customers rather than the manufacturer price invoiced by the company.

Second, the term "price" in the above discussion reflects not only the "list" price of an offering but also all other monetary aspects of the transaction between the company and its customers and collaborators. These include price reductions, coupons, rebates (in the case of customer transactions), and trade discounts such as volume discounts and allowances (in the case of collaborator transactions). This is an important consideration given the ever-increasing amount of sales promotions in today's marketplace. A more detailed discussion of price and incentives management is offered in Chapters 17 and 18.

Managing Profit Growth by Lowering Costs

An offering's costs can be divided into three broad categories: (1) cost of goods sold, (2) marketing costs, and (3) other costs such as research and development costs, cost of capital, and general and administrative costs. These three types of costs are discussed in more detail below.

Managing the Cost of Goods Sold

There are two basic strategies to lower the cost of goods sold. The first is to lower the costs of *inputs*, which involve factors such as the raw materials, labor, and inbound logistics used in developing the company's offering. Lowering the costs of inputs can be achieved by outsourcing, switching suppliers, and adopting alternative technologies that use more cost-effective inputs. The second approach to managing the cost of goods sold is to lower the costs associated with the *processes* that transform the inputs into the end product, such as optimizing operations and adopting alternative technologies that use more cost-effective processes.

Managing Marketing Costs

Marketing costs can be grouped into four categories: communication costs, costs of incentives, distribution costs, and other marketing costs.

- *Communications costs* comprise advertising expenditures (e.g., television, radio, print, outdoor, point-of-purchase, and event advertising); public relations expenditures (e.g., press coverage, product placement); and personal selling (e.g., sales force and detailers). Most mass media communication expenditures (e.g., television, radio, print, and outdoor) are fixed costs; they do not depend on the number of units sold.[4]

- The *cost of (consumer) incentives* involves consumer-focused promotions such as price reductions, coupons, rebates, contests, sweepstakes, and premiums. Because most incentives (e.g., price reductions, coupons, rebates, and premiums) are variable costs, increasing sales volume does not lower the per-unit cost of the incentives.

- *Distribution costs* are a function of the margins received by distributors, cost of the sales force, and trade incentives such as trade allowances, volume discounts, and co-op advertising allowances.

- *Other marketing costs* reflect the costs of factors such as marketing research and marketing overhead.

Managing Other Costs

In addition to the cost of goods sold and marketing expenses, factors such as research and development costs, various administrative costs, legal costs, and cost of capital contribute to a company's overall expenses. Because the nature of these costs is beyond the scope of this book, they are not further discussed here.

Managing Profit Growth via Mergers and Acquisitions

So far, the discussion focused on strategies to manage profit growth using internal resources (an approach commonly referred to as "organic growth"). A popular alternative to organic growth is growth through mergers and acquisitions. Mergers and acquisitions describe business activities that lead to combining two (or sometimes more) entities into a single one. In the case of an acquisition, one company (the acquirer) takes over another company. In contrast, in the case of a merger, two companies, typically similar in size, agree to go forward as a single new company in which they are more or less equally represented.

Companies tend to pursue mergers and acquisitions when they believe that external opportunities present a better opportunity to achieve their goals than the internally available options. Mergers and acquisitions are typically aimed at (1) increasing sales volume by gaining access to new markets and/or gaining a competitive advantage in existing markets and (2) lowering costs by achieving economies of scale and/or scope.[5] These factors are discussed in more detail below.

Increasing Sales Volume via Mergers and Acquisitions

Mergers and acquisitions can facilitate sales volume growth by (1) providing access to new markets as well as by (2) strengthening the company's competitive advantage in existing markets.

Increasing Sales Volume by Gaining Access to New Markets

Mergers and acquisitions can be used to gain access to untapped domestic markets and to establish global presence, as follows.

- *Gaining access to domestic markets.* Mergers and acquisitions are often motivated by a company's desire to gain access to new markets. For example, the largest banks in the United States—Citigroup, JPMorgan Chase, Bank of America, and Wells Fargo—have historically relied on acquisitions to achieve sustainable growth. Combining companies with complementary products (e.g., banking and brokerage services) also creates opportunities for reaching new markets for each of the companies.

- *Establishing a global presence.* Mergers and acquisitions are a common strategy to gain access to international markets. For example, hotel chains InterContinental Hotels Group, Hilton Hotels Corporation, and Starwood Hotels & Resorts Worldwide have established their worldwide presence by acquiring existing hotels in different parts of the globe.

Increasing Sales Volume by Gaining Competitive Advantage

Two common ways for a company to gain competitive advantage using mergers and acquisitions involve eliminating key competitors and acquiring strategic resources in short supply.

- *Eliminating key competitors.* By merging with or acquiring a key competitor, a company can effectively eliminate some of its strategically important competition. For example, with the acquisition of Siebel Systems' leading CRM (customer relationship management) solutions in 2006, Oracle effectively eliminated one of its key competitors in the customer-centric applications market.

- *Acquiring scarce resources.* Mergers and acquisitions can provide unique access to resources in short supply, such as scarce raw materials, proprietary technologies, and skilled personnel. Thus, to stay on top of technological developments, medical, pharmaceutical, and high-tech companies often merge with or acquire firms with proprietary technologies. For example, the pharmaceutical giant Johnson & Johnson acquired (in 2009) a stake in Elan Corporation to gain rights to use its research on treatment of Alzheimer's.

Lowering Costs via Mergers and Acquisitions

In addition to increasing sales volume, mergers and acquisitions can lower a company's costs. The two most common ways in which mergers/acquisitions can lower costs are through economies of scale and economies of scope.

Lowering Costs by Achieving Economies of Scale

The general idea is that combining two companies will result in greater operational efficiencies due to the increased size of the combined assets and operations. Economies of scale typically can be achieved in several areas:

- *Lower operation costs.* Combining the operations (e.g. manufacturing and supply-chain management) of two companies often leads to greater efficiency stemming from the larger scale and better coordination. Consequently, mergers and acquisitions often lead to workforce reduction due to elimination of duplicate functions.

- *Greater collaborator power.* Another reason companies favor mergers and acquisitions is to gain power over the other entities in the value-delivery chain. For example, the consolidation in the retail space that resulted in a market dominated by a few large retailers such as Wal-Mart, Costco, and Home Depot significantly strengthened their power over manufacturers, subsequently leading to better trade margins, promotional allowances, and inventory management.

- *Lower financial costs.* Combining two companies can also lead to a reduction in financial costs because larger firms often have an easier time raising capital and tend to have lower cost of capital than smaller companies.

Lowering Costs by Achieving Economies of Scope

Economies of scope arise from synergies among the combined companies. The general idea here is that combining two companies will result in greater operational efficiencies due to the complementarity of their assets and competencies. Economies of scope typically can be achieved in two main areas:

- *Gaining operation synergies.* Combining companies can create operational efficiencies by optimizing complementary resources and processes. For example, mergers and acquisitions leading to a vertical integration of entities in the value-delivery chain (e.g., a manufacturer acquiring a supplier) can lead to cost savings from optimizing joint operations, such as production logistics, delivery schedules, and resource allocation.

- *Optimizing financial performance.* Mergers and acquisitions can be used to diversify a company's product line to hedge a company's financial performance in case of an economic downturn. In addition, combining the resources of the two diverse entities can facilitate access to capital and/or lower the cost of capital, as well as offer certain tax advantages.

Summary

A company is a business entity established for the purpose of creating value for its stakeholders. Accordingly, managing company value is an essential aspect of a company' strategy, affecting the very existence of the company as a business enterprise.

The value of an offering to the company is a function of the degree to which its benefits meet the company's goals. Because a company's goal may involve one or more of the following three domains—monetary, functional, and psychological—an offering can create value to the company in three different ways: by creating monetary value, by delivering functional value, and by creating psychological value.

Achieving sustainable profit growth is the ultimate goal for most companies. Managing profit growth can be achieved by increasing sales revenues and/or reducing costs. Increasing sales revenues can be achieved by managing price and/or by increasing sales volume, which in turn can be achieved by one of four strategies defining the product-market growth matrix: market penetration, market development, product development, and diversification. Managing costs involves decreasing costs of goods sold, optimizing marketing costs, as well as lowering various other costs (e.g., research and development costs, administrative costs, and cost of capital).

In addition to managing profit growth using internal resources, a company can grow profits through mergers and acquisitions. Companies tend to pursue mergers and acquisitions when they believe that external opportunities present a better opportunity to achieve their goals than the internally available options. In this context, mergers and acquisitions are typically aimed at (1) increasing sales volume by gaining access to new markets and/or gaining a competitive advantage in existing markets and (2) lowering costs by achieving economies of scale and/or scope.

Relevant Formulas

Net income can be formally represented as a function of sales volume, unit price, and costs. Sales volume, in turn, is a function of two factors: the unit share of the company's offering relative to competitors and the overall market size. The resulting profit equation is shown below.

$$\text{Net income} = \underbrace{\text{Market share}_{\text{Unit}} \cdot \text{Market size}_{\text{Unit}}}_{\text{Sales volume}} \cdot \text{Price}_{\text{Unit}} - \text{Costs}$$

In addition to being represented as a function of sales volume, unit price, and total costs, net income can be viewed as a function of sales volume, unit margins, and fixed costs. Unit margins can be expressed in monetary terms as the difference between an offering's unit price and its unit variable costs; or as a percentage, as the difference between an offering's unit price and its unit variable costs, which is then divided by the offering's unit price. In this context, profitability can be linked to margins as shown in the following equation. This equation implies three basic strategies for growing net income: increasing sales volume, increasing margins, and lowering fixed costs.

$$\text{Net income} = \text{Sales volume} \cdot \underbrace{(\text{Price}_{\text{Unit}} - \text{Variable cost}_{\text{Unit}})}_{\text{Margin}_{\text{Unit}}} - \text{Fixed costs}$$

Relevant Concepts

Economies of Scale: Cost savings arising from greater manufacturing and/or sales volume. Economies of scale occur in cases when marginal production costs decrease with an increase in production output. In cases where marginal manufacturing/sales costs do not vary as a function of the output volume, there are no economies of scale. Typically, as the output volume increases, marginal costs initially decrease (economies of scale) until they reach a certain point at which they begin to increase (diseconomies of scale).

Economies of Scope: Cost savings arising from synergies among different offerings. Economies of scope are conceptually similar to economies of scale in that an increase in size typically leads to lower costs. Unlike economies of scale, however, where cost savings stem from increasing the scale of production of a single offering, economies of scope refer to cost savings resulting from synergies among different offerings in a company's portfolio.

Learning Curve: The curve describing how costs of production decline as cumulative output increases over time. The logic behind this concept is that labor hours per unit decline on repetitive tasks. The term learning curve is often used interchangeably with the concept of experience curve.[6]

Six Sigma: Introduced by Motorola and later adopted by General Electric, Six Sigma[7] is a methodology for managing process variations that cause defects. The Six Sigma approach builds on the notion that to ensure an offering's consistency with specifications, the underlying processes should be set to ensure that the difference between the actual and the desired outcomes does not exceed six standard deviations. In this context, a widely accepted definition of a six sigma process is one that reduces defect levels below 3.4 defective items per million outcomes. Over time, the term "six sigma" has evolved beyond its literal definition as a metric (i.e., 3.4 defects per one million opportunities) and is often used in reference to a more general methodology of improving business processes that focuses on understanding customer needs and aligning the business processes to fulfill these needs with minimal variation.

Additional Readings

Aaker, David A. (2007), *Strategic Market Management* (8th ed.). New York, NY: John Wiley & Sons.

Best, Roger J. (2008), *Market-Based Management: Strategies for Growing Customer Value and Profitability* (5th ed.). Upper Saddle River, NJ: Prentice Hall.

Kumar, Nirmalya (2004), *Marketing as Strategy: Understanding the CEO's Agenda for Driving Growth and Innovation*. Boston, MA: Harvard Business School Press.

Notes

[1] Ansoff, H. Igor (1979), *Strategic Management*. New York, NY: John Wiley & Sons.

[2] Adapted from ibid.

[3] For an in-depth discussion of price elasticity see Chapter 17.

[4] Even though their absolute size remains unchanged regardless of the output volume, these expenditures become progressively smaller per unit of output as volume increases (because the fixed costs are allocated over a larger number of output units).

[5] Mergers and acquisitions can also be driven by management-specific factors such as management compensation (e.g., merging with or acquiring a company with a higher scale of compensation is likely to benefit the managers paid at the lower scale) or power (e.g., managing a larger company).

[6] Henderson, Bruce, D. (1974), "The Experience Curve Reviewed: Why Does It Work?," in *Perspectives on Strategy: From the Boston Consulting Group* (1998), W. S. Carl and J. George Stalk, Eds. New York, NY: John Wiley & Sons.

[7] Sigma refers to the Greek letter σ commonly used in statistics to represent the standard deviation (a measure of the degree of variance) in a given population.

Chapter Fourteen

Managing Collaborator Value

Get not your friends by bare compliments, but by giving them sensible tokens of your love.
Socrates

Collaboration is an essential aspect of all business relationships. Because successful relationships are based on a mutually-beneficial value exchange, a company needs to ensure that its offerings deliver superior value to its collaborators. The process of managing collaborator value is the focus of this chapter.

The Big Picture

Because a company's collaborators most often are other business entities, they tend to operate on the same principles as the company itself. Accordingly, an offering's value to a company's collaborators is a function of the degree to which this offering enables these collaborators to reach their goals. In particular, an offering can create value for a company's collaborators in three different ways: monetary, functional, and psychological (Figure 1).

Figure 1. Managing Collaborator Value: The Big Picture

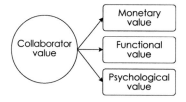

The three dimensions on which an offering can create value to collaborators can be summarized as follows.

- *Monetary value* is a function of the degree to which the monetary aspects (benefits and costs) of the offering meet a collaborator's monetary goals (e.g. maximizing the net income, profit margins, and sales revenues). For example, in the case of vertical collaboration (e.g., manufacturer–retailer–consumer), monetary value is often defined by the margins collected by the channel partners for distributing the company's offering.

- *Functional value* is determined by the degree to which the offering can help collaborators achieve certain functional goals (e.g., gain a competitive advantage, facilitate the sales of a strategically important offering, and strengthen its image to target customers). For example, carrying an unprofitable but popular item can help a retailer build store traffic, exclusive collaboration can create a competitive advantage (e.g., Apple's collaboration with AT&T), and the availability of an up-scale item can strengthen a retailer's image (e.g., Dom Pérignon Champagne, Tumi luggage, and Cartier watches at Costco).

- *Psychological value* is determined by the ability of an offering to create outcomes of psychological importance to the company's collaborators. For example, collaborators may derive value from championing various social causes, such as fighting poverty, fostering education, and promoting human rights.

Because most collaborators are for-profit entities, the monetary aspect of value management is of utmost importance. The basic principles of managing profit margins and profit growth are the same as those discussed in Chapter 8. Therefore, the rest of this chapter focuses on value-management issues that are pertinent to collaboration.

Understanding Collaborator Value

To succeed, collaboration must create value for all participants. Therefore, to successfully manage the relationship with its collaborators, a company must have a clear understanding of the value that its partners derive from the collaboration and ensure that this value is optimized with respect to the alternative options available to its collaborators. The key factors defining collaborator value and alternatives to collaboration are discussed in more detail in the following sections.

The Benefits and Costs of Collaboration

The value a company derives from collaborating with another entity is a function of the benefits and costs resulting from their interaction. Although these benefits and costs are situation-specific, there are several common benefits sought by most collaborating entities. These benefits include greater effectiveness, cost-efficiency, flexibility, and time-to-market.

- *Effectiveness.* Collaboration enables companies to specialize in a particular aspect of the value-delivery process (e.g., research and development, manufacturing, and distribution). Collaboration enables each party to take advantage of the expertise of the other entity, which in turn provides both entities with a competitive advantage.

- *Cost-efficiency.* In addition to facilitating the effectiveness of the value-delivery process, collaboration can also make it more cost-efficient. By specializing in a given function, each collaborator can achieve greater cost-efficiency through economies of scale and experience. Specialization might also encourage a company to invest in cost-efficient solutions (e.g., inventory-management system) that it would not invest in if it lacked scale of operations.

- *Flexibility.* Relative to developing the necessary expertise in-house, collaboration requires a lesser commitment of resources and, hence, offers much greater flexibility in terms of switching technologies, entering new markets and/or exiting existing ones. For example, the development of a new distribution channel requires substantial resources and hence calls for a long-term commitment, whereas using an already existing distribution channel (i.e., renting rather than buying the shelf space) offers much more flexibility in terms of a company's commitment to the project.

- *Time-to-market.* Collaboration enables a company to achieve the desired results much faster than building in-house expertise. For example, a manufacturer can gain access to target markets virtually overnight using an existing distribution chain, whereas launching its own distribution channel will take considerably longer.

Despite its numerous advantages, collaboration also has a number of important *drawbacks*, including loss of control, loss of competencies, and the danger of empowering the competition.

- *Loss of control.* Delegating certain aspects of a company's activities to an external entity often leads to loss of control over the value-delivery process. For example, outsourcing manufacturing operations often hinders the company's ability to monitor production processes and product quality. Outsourcing also diminishes the company's ability to monitor the financial aspects of the value-delivery process.

- *Loss of competencies.* Outsourcing key activities tends to weaken a company's core competencies. For example, outsourcing research and development activities over time tends to diminish a company's ability to drive innovation.

- *Empowering the competition.* Outsourcing key activities also may enable collaborating entities to develop a set of strategic competencies thus becoming a company's potential competitor.

When the benefits from collaboration outweigh the corresponding costs for each of the relevant parties, the collaboration tends to be sustainable. In contrast, when collaboration fails to create superior value for (at least) one of the parties, collaborators might pursue alternative options such as acquiring the other entity or terminating the collaboration relationship.

Alternatives to Collaboration

A common alternative to collaboration involves insourcing the activities performed by collaborators by launching a new, company-controlled entity, or by acquiring (or merging with) an existing entity. Such insourcing is commonly referred to as integration. Depending on the relative position of the entities in the value-creation process, there are two types of integration: vertical and horizontal. These two types of integration are discussed in more detail below.

Vertical Integration

Vertical integration typically involves the acquisition of (or a merger with) an entity occupying a different level in the value-delivery chain[1]. Depending on the relative position of the entities, there are two common types of vertical integration: forward and backward. Extending ownership upstream (toward suppliers) is referred to as backward integration, while extending ownership of activities downstream (toward buyers) is referred to as forward integration (Figure 2). For example, a manufacturer acquiring a retailer to establish its own distribution system is a form of forward integration, whereas a retailer acquiring a wholesaler and/or a manufacturer is a form of backward integration.

Figure 2. Vertical Integration

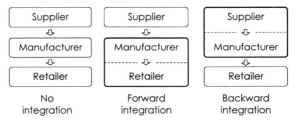

Vertical integration tends to be favored by companies seeking to control the key aspects of the value-delivery process. For example, ExxonMobil engages in oil and gas exploration, production, supply, and transportation worldwide. Starbucks directly manages all aspects of its business including sourcing, roasting, distributing, and serving the coffee. American Express directly markets to customers, issues its cards, processes the payments through its own network, and directly acquires the merchant relationships.

Horizontal Integration

Horizontal integration involves acquiring (or merging with) a business entity at the same level of the value-delivery chain (Figure 3). For example, a retailer acquiring another retailer or a manufacturer merging with another manufacturer constitutes horizontal integration. Horizontal integration may occur among entities with similar core competencies—a common scenario for companies seeking economies of scale through consolidation, as well as for companies seeking economies of scope through diversification.

Figure 3. Horizontal Integration

Horizontal integration tends to be favored by companies for a variety of reasons, including gaining access to new markets, acquiring the rights to a proprietary research and/or technology, reducing the competition in strategically important markets, and/or gaining power over the other entities in the value-delivery chain.

Managing Collaborator Relationships

Despite a company's efforts to optimize the value of its offering(s) to collaborators, often the company's and collaborators' goals are not perfectly aligned. As a result, collaborator relationships often face tensions resulting from different goal-optimization strategies pursued by collaborating entities. Such tensions are often facilitated by the power imbalance of the collaborating entities and frequently lead to explicit conflicts. The issues of collaborator power and collaborator conflicts are discussed in more detail in the following sections.

Collaborator Power

Collaborator power refers to the ability of a given company to exert influence over another entity. This influence often leads to an imbalance in the value exchange in favor of the more powerful entity and often leads to market outcomes such as higher prices, margins, discounts, and/or allowances; preferential access to scarce resources; and premier shelf space and product-delivery schedules.

Power in collaborator relationships is a function of a number of factors, including the differentiation of collaborator offerings, collaborator size, strategic importance of the collaboration to each entity, and their switching costs.

- *Offering differentiation.* Companies with differentiated offerings in high demand are likely to have more power over their collaborators than companies with commoditized offerings. For example, companies with strong brands such as Coca-Cola, Adidas, and Samsung have more power dealing with their distribution partners than companies with lesser-known brands.

- *Size.* Consolidated entities—both manufacturers and distributors—are likely to have more power over fragmented ones. For example, large consumer packaged goods manufacturers, such as Procter & Gamble, Unilever, and Nestlé, often receive preferential treatment (e.g., better shelf space, lower volume discounts, and lower promotional allowances) from retailers compared to smaller manufacturers. Similarly, relative to smaller retail stores, retail giants Wal-Mart, Carrefour, and Home Depot often receive various monetary and non-monetary benefits from manufacturers, such as preferential volume discounts, greater promotional allowances, and customized product-delivery schedules.

- *Strategic importance.* An entity tends to have more power when it accounts for a significant portion of its' collaborators' profits. For example, Wal-Mart is in the position of power when negotiating with small manufacturers because their individual net contribution to Wal-Mart's net income is low, whereas for many of them Wal-Mart accounts for a substantial part of profits.

- *Switching costs.* An entity is likely to have more power when the switching costs of its collaborators are high and its own switching costs are low. Such switching costs may result from a variety of factors, including a high level of systems integration between a company and its collaborator(s), long-term contractual obligations, and the learning curve associated with collaborating with a new entity.

Collaborator Conflicts

Collaborator conflict describes tensions among collaborators, often caused by the differences in their profit-optimization strategies. Based on the nature of the collaborator relationship, there are two types of collaborator conflicts: vertical and horizontal.

Conflicts in Vertical Collaboration

Vertical conflicts typically depict tensions among entities occupying different levels in the value-delivery chain. The most common type of vertical conflict is that between a manufacturer and a retailer. Depending on the nature of the tension, there are two types of channel conflicts: vertical and horizontal. These two types of conflict are illustrated in Figure 4 (black arrows indicate the areas of conflict) and are described in more detail below.

Figure 4. Conflicts in Vertical Collaboration

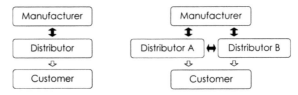

A. Vertical channel conflict   B. Horizontal channel conflict

- *Vertical channel conflict* depicts tensions between entities in a single distribution channel (e.g. a manufacturer and a retailer). For example, vertical conflict might involve tensions between a manufacturer and a retailer regarding the size and composition of the manufacturer's product line carried by the retailer. The conflict here stems from the gap between a manufacturer's desire that a retailer carry its entire product line and a retailer's desire to carry only the most profitable, noncompeting offerings from individual manufacturers. Vertical conflict can also occur when collaborating entities exercise their power in the relationship to achieve their strategic goals (e.g., the supplier of a component in high demand raises the price, negatively affecting the manufacturer's margins).

- *Horizontal channel conflict* involves tensions among entities in multiple distribution channels (e.g., a manufacturer and two different retailers). Horizontal conflicts occur when a manufacturer targets the same customers utilizing multiple distribution channels with different cost structures and profit margins. Consider a manufacturer that makes a product available through a high-margin full-service retail store as well as through a low-margin category-killer. This manufacturer is likely to create channel conflict when the two retailers try to sell the same product at different price points to the same customer. To address such conflicts, manufacturers often develop different versions of the same product that vary on minor attributes (e.g., color, packaging, and optional features) so that their offerings in different distribution channels are not readily comparable.

Conflicts in Horizontal Collaboration

Horizontal conflicts typically depict tensions between entities occupying the same level in the value-delivery chain (Figure 5). For example, horizontal conflicts may occur between a manufacturer and a research-and-development company collaborating to develop a new product, between two entities collaborating to manufacture the product, and between a manufacturer and a service provider collaborating to offer post-purchase customer service.

Figure 5. Conflicts in Horizontal Collaboration

The tension between collaborating entities in this case can be caused by issues such as profit sharing, access to proprietary technologies, ownership of jointly developed intellectual property, and sharing core competencies and strategic assets. These tensions are often exacerbated when entities collaborating in one domain are competing in another.

Summary

Collaboration is essential aspect of all business relationships. Because successful relationships are based on a mutually beneficial value exchange, a company must ensure that its offerings deliver superior value to its collaborators.

A company's collaborators tend to operate on the same principles as the company itself. Accordingly, an offering's value for a company's collaborators is a function of the degree to which this offering enables these collaborators to reach their goals. In particular, an offering can create value to a company's collaborators in three different ways: monetary, functional, and psychological.

To successfully manage the relationship with its collaborators, a company must understand the value that its partners derive from the collaboration and ensure that this value is optimized with respect to the alternative options available to its collaborators. Collaborator benefits include greater effectiveness, cost-efficiency, flexibility, and time-to-market. Despite its numerous advantages, collaboration also has a number of important *drawbacks*, including the loss of control, loss of competencies, and the possibility of strengthening the competition.

A common alternative to collaboration involves insourcing the activities performed by collaborators, by acquiring or merging with an existing entity. Such insourcing is commonly referred to as integration. Depending on the relative position of the entities in the value-creation process, there are two types of integration: vertical and horizontal.

Despite a company's efforts to optimize the value of its offering(s) to collaborators, frequently the company's and collaborators' goals are not perfectly aligned. As a result, collaborator relationships often face tensions resulting from different goal-optimization strategies pursued by collaborating entities. Such tensions are often facilitated by the imbalance in power of the collaborating entities and often lead to explicit conflicts.

Collaborator power refers to the ability of a given company to exert influence over another entity. This influence often leads to an imbalance in the value exchange in favor of the more powerful entity and is often displayed in market behaviors such as higher prices, margins, discounts, and/or allowances; preferential access to scarce resources; and premier shelf space and product-delivery schedules. Power in collaborator relationships is a function of a number of factors, including the differentiation of collaborator offerings, collaborator's size, the strategic importance of the collaboration to each entity, and their switching costs.

Collaborator conflict describes tensions among collaborators, often caused by the differences in their profit-optimization strategies. In distribution channels, there are two common types of conflicts: vertical conflicts, which involve different levels of the same channel (e.g., a manufacturer and a retailer), and horizontal conflicts, which involve members within the same channel level (e.g., two retailers).

Additional Readings

Anderson, James C., James A. Narus, and Das Narayandas (2008), *Business Market Management: Understanding, Creating, and Delivering Value* (3rd ed.). Upper Saddle River, NJ: Prentice Hall.

Anderson, Erin, Anne T. Coughlan, Louis W. Stern, and Adel I. El-Ansary (2006), *Marketing Channels* (7th ed.). Upper Saddle River, NJ: Prentice Hall.

Young, S. David and Stephen F. O'Byrne (2000), *EVA and Value-Based Management: A Practical Guide to Implementation*. New York, NY: McGraw-Hill.

Note

[1] Instead of acquiring (or merging with) an existing entity, vertical integration may involve the launch of a new entity. For example, Apple launched its own chain of retail stores rather than acquiring an existing retail outlet.

Part Four

Managing the Marketing Mix

Introduction

The marketing mix outlines a set of specific activities employed to execute a given strategy. The marketing mix is composed of seven elements: product, service, brand, price, incentives, communication, and distribution.

- The *product* and *service* aspects of the offering depict its functional characteristics. The key decisions involved in crating and managing the product and service aspects of an offering are discussed in Chapter 15.

- The *brand* serves to identify the company's offering, to differentiate it from the competition, and to create value that goes beyond its product and service attributes. The main aspects of creating and managing brand are the focus of Chapter 16.

- The *price* reflects the monetary aspect of the offering; it refers to the amount of money the company charges for an offering's benefits. The essential elements of pricing are outlined in Chapter 17.

- *Incentives* offer solutions, typically short-term, aimed at enhancing the value of the offering by providing additional benefits and/or reducing costs. Managing incentives is discussed in Chapter 18.

- *Communication* aims to inform target customers about the availability of the offering and highlight its particular characteristics. The essential decisions involved in managing communications are discussed in Chapter 19.

- *Distribution* depicts the channel through which the offering is delivered to target customers. Managing distribution is the focus of Chapter 20.

The elements of an offering's marketing mix—product, service, brand, price, incentives, communication, and distribution—can be represented by the processes of *designing, communicating,* and *delivering* value. These processes incorporate the seven marketing mix variables, such that the product, service, brand, price, and incentives comprise the value-design aspect of the offering; communication captures its value-communication aspect; and distribution reflects its value-delivery component (Figure 1).

Figure 1. The D-C-D Marketing Mix Framework

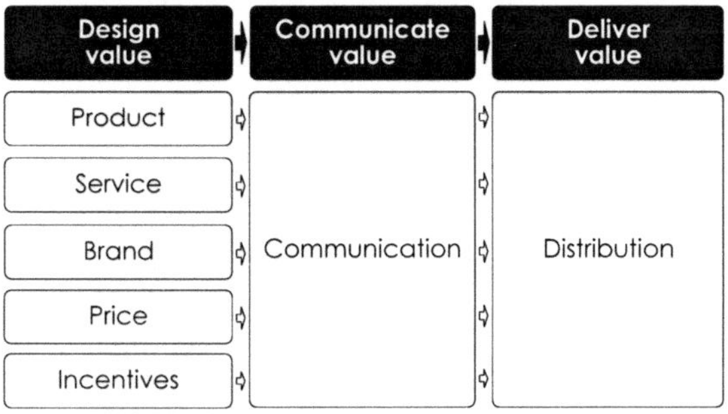

The organization of the marketing mix depicted in Figure 1 reflects the relationships among its individual elements. Thus, the process of designing an offering's value involves the first five marketing mix elements (product, service, brand, price, and incentives). Communication, in turn, involves informing target customers about *each* of the value-design elements. For example, a company may promote the benefits of a product or service, communicate the meaning of its brand, publicize its price, and inform customers about its current incentives. Finally, distribution involves delivering *each* of the value-design elements to target customers. Thus, a company may deliver its products and services, enable customers experience its brand, facilitate the price-related monetary transactions, and distribute offering-related incentives.

Chapter Fifteen

Managing Products and Services

Quality in a product or service is not what the supplier puts in.
It is what the customer gets out and is willing to pay for.

Peter Drucker

Product and service management aim to optimize the value that product and service aspects of the offering to deliver to target customers, the company, and its collaborators. The main decisions involved in creating and managing the product and service aspects of the offering are the focus of this chapter.

Overview

The product and service aspects of an offering capture its key functional characteristics. Products typically change ownership during purchase; once created, they can be physically separated from the manufacturer and distributed to end users via multiple channels. Based on their consumption pattern, products can be classified into one of two categories: durable or nondurable. Durable goods are consumed over multiple occasions and over an extended period (e.g., cars, household appliances, and machinery). In contrast, nondurable goods are typically consumed on a single occasion and/or over a short period (e.g., food, disposable items, and cosmetics).

The service aspect of the offering is in many respects similar to the product aspect, with two main exceptions: change of ownership and inseparability. Unlike products, which typically change ownership during purchase, services do not necessarily imply a change in ownership; instead, the customer acquires the right to use the service within a given time frame. Furthermore, unlike products, which can be physically separated from the manufacturer, services are usually delivered and consumed at the same time.

Because services are created and delivered at the same time, they are difficult to standardize, and their quality varies as a function of the interaction between the service provider and the customer. To illustrate, a customer may experience different levels of service from the same service provider at different times and/or in different locations, and the same service provider may have different interactions with different customers depending on customers' behavior. The inseparability of creating and delivering value also makes services perishable in the sense that they cannot be inventoried—an important consideration in industries where companies with a fixed service capacity face fluctuating customer demand (e.g., airlines, hotels, and call centers).

Based on the level of uncertainty, product and service characteristics can be classified into one of three categories: search, experience, and credence.[1] *Search characteris-*

tics are associated with the least amount of uncertainty and are typically identifiable through inspection before purchase. *Experience characteristics* carry greater uncertainty and are revealed only through consumption. *Credence characteristics* have the greatest amount of uncertainty and are not identifiable even from ex-post observations; as a result, consumers never can be certain of the quality and value of credence attributes even after experiencing the product/service. For example, in the case of toothpaste, size is a search attribute, taste is an experience attribute, and cavity prevention is a credence attribute. The boundaries among these categories are fuzzy, and search–experience–credence categories represent regions in a continuum. In general, search attributes are more common for tangible offerings, whereas credence attributes are more typical for intangible offerings. Because services have more intangible properties relative to products, they are heavy on experience and credence attributes; in contrast, search attributes are more typical for products than services.

A Framework for Managing Products and Services

Managing products and services involves two types of decisions: (1) strategic decisions, which aim to optimize products and services as a function of the offering's target market, and (2) tactical decisions, which aim to optimize products and services as a function of the other marketing mix variables. These two types of decisions are outlined in more detail below.

Product and Service Management: Strategy

From a strategic standpoint, product and service decisions are a function of the offering's target market, defined by the 5-C framework: customers, company, collaborators, competition, and context. These five factors are illustrated in Figure 1 and outlined in more detail below.

Figure 1. Product and Service Management as a Function of the Target Market

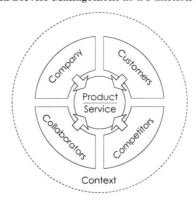

- *Customers.* An offering's product and service strategy is influenced by the characteristics of its target customers. To illustrate, when launching a product/service based on a new technology, a company targeting tech-savvy early adopters is likely to introduce a more advanced, feature-rich, and more expensive version, whereas a company targeting the mainstream market will be more successful introducing a less expensive option that offers only basic features and functionality.

- *Company.* A company's goals, strategic assets, and core competencies are important factors in determining an offering's product and service strategy. For example, a company can manage supply by outsourcing part of its product/service operations, optimizing its logistics to use just-in-time manufacturing, and/or offering flexible workforce scheduling (e.g., to address the seasonality of demand, as in the travel, hospitality, and shipping industries). Similarly, to ensure the consistency of the product/service benefits across units and over time, a company can optimize the effectiveness of its operations by employing quality management programs (e.g., Total Quality Management and Six Sigma).

- *Collaborators.* An offering's product and service strategy is also a function of the company's relationship with collaborators. For instance, to increase the benefits to its channel partners, a company can design the product to facilitate inventory management (e.g., by optimizing product nomenclature and labeling), extend the shelf life of perishable products, and optimize the channel's inventory costs (e.g., by creating space-efficient packaging).

- *Competitors.* An offering's product and service strategy is influenced by its competitors' products and services. Thus, when designing their products and services, most companies strive to deliver superior value relative to that of competitive offerings. In this context, competitors' offerings, especially those that have achieved market success, often serve as benchmarks for designing new products and services.

- *Context.* Product and service design is also influenced by various economic, technological, socio-cultural, regulatory, and physical aspects of the environment in which the company operates. To illustrate, most offerings must comply with product/service specifications and standards imposed by various government and nongovernment agencies (e.g., FCC and IEEE).[2]

Product and Service Management: Tactics

From a tactical standpoint, product and service aspects of the offering need to be coordinated with the other marketing mix variables (i.e., brand, price, incentives, communication, and distribution). The key aspects of product and service decisions are illustrated in Figure 2 and outlined in more detail below.

Figure 2. Product Management as a Function of the Marketing Mix[3]

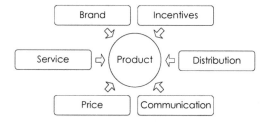

- *Product and service.* To optimize their customer value proposition, companies often strive to balance the product and service aspects of their offerings. For example, commoditized products are often differentiated by adding services, whereas the intangibility of services often benefits from being enhanced with a tangible product component.

- *Brand.* An offering's product and service design is a function of its brand. Thus, the product and service design should be consistent with the essence of the brand. To illustrate, Gillette constantly strives to ensure that all products in its product line are aligned with its image of delivering "the best a man can get."

- *Price.* An offering's product and service design is often contingent on its price. For example, the viability of introducing a new product/service feature is a function of the price premium that the company is able to charge its target customers.

- *Incentives.* Because incentives are, in most cases, added to the offering after the product/service has already been created, their impact is typically not a key factor in product/service design. Nevertheless, by incurring additional expenses, incentives may influence the resources available for developing the product/service aspects of the offering.

- *Communication.* The product and service aspects of an offering are also a function of its communication strategy. To illustrate, product design, packaging, and labeling can familiarize target customers with the key aspects of the offering. These aspects can identify the product, brand, and country of origin, describe the product, its contents, and recommended usage; as well as provide customers with reasons to buy the product.

- *Distribution.* An offering's product and service design is influenced by its distribution. Thus, product design can facilitate its transportation and storage (by both channel members and customers), as well as extend the shelf life of perishable products. For example, Coca-Cola introduced refrigerator-size packaging to facilitate the storage of its products (and in the process ensure that consumers always have a cold drink when they want one). Similarly, containers for products such as ketchup and mustard facilitate the use of the product (e.g., plastic upside-down containers designed to improve the ease of dispensing the product).

Product and Service Decisions

Creating and managing products and services involves a series of specific decisions concerning factors such as performance, consistency, reliability, durability, compatibility, ease-of-use, technological design, degree of customization, form, style, and packaging. These factors are described in more detail below.

- *Performance.* Performance is typically defined in terms of an offering's features and its performance on relevant attributes. Features describe the discrete (most often binary) characteristics of a given product or service (e.g., heated steering wheel, anti-lock brakes, and sunroof). In contrast, attributes describe dimensions on which options can perform at different levels (e.g., engine power, acceleration, and fuel efficiency). The key principle when deciding on the level of performance of a given product or service is that it should deliver superior value to target customers while enabling the company and its collaborators to achieve their strategic goals. In cases when a given offering is a part of a product line, its performance also needs to be coordinated with the other offerings comprising this product line (see Chapter 24 for more detail).

- *Consistency.* An important aspect of designing an offering is ensuring that all individual products and services are identical and consistent with specifications. Because variability is a key characteristic of the service aspect of an offering, consistency is especially important in the case of service delivery and is one of the key contributors to the success of companies like McDonald's and Ritz-Carlton. A popular approach to managing product consistency is the Six Sigma method described in more detail at the end of this chapter.

- *Reliability.* Reliability refers to the probability that the product/service will operate according to its specifications and will not malfunction for the duration of its projected life cycle. An important characteristic of the product/service aspect of the offering, reliability is often used as a differentiating point to create a unique positioning of a company's offering. For example, FedEx promises "absolutely, positively overnight" next-day delivery service, the discount brokerage TD Ameritrade guarantees that certain trades will be executed within five seconds, and Verizon claims to be the most reliable wireless network in the United States with a call-completion rate of more than 99.9%.

- *Durability.* Another important consideration in product design involves deciding on the expected length of the offering's life cycle. Because in many categories durability is an important consideration in buyers' decision processes, products that are perceived to be more durable tend to be preferred by customers. At the same time, while durable products help companies attract new customers and build loyalty among existing customers, durability tends to have a negative impact on the frequency of repeat purchases since users are often reluctant to replace fully functioning products with new ones. As a result, manufacturers have to invest in research and development to design superior models that will encourage customers to upgrade their existing products. When designing new models, car manufacturers often use styling to make previous models obsolete, thus encouraging customers to upgrade. This process of designing new products in a way that makes prior generations inferior on key attributes is often referred to as planned obsolescence (see Chapter 23 for more details).

- *Compatibility.* Compatibility refers to the degree to which the product/service is consistent with certain already existing standards and/or complementary products. Compatibility can be used strategically by companies to create barriers to entry by ensuring that offerings are uniquely compatible with customers' existing systems and processes. Product compatibility is also an effective strategy in networked environments, where it forces users to adhere to a certain standard. To illustrate, the popularity of Microsoft Office products is to a great degree a function of the need for compatibility when sharing information. Compatibility is also a key consideration in multipart pricing, where a company charges a relatively low price for the first part (e.g., razors, printers) and higher prices for the complementary parts (e.g., blades, cartridges). In this case unique compatibility is essential so that only parts manufactured by the same company can work together (e.g., only Gillette-manufactured blades will fit a Gillette razor).

- *Ease-of-use.* An important and often overlooked characteristic of many products and services is their ease of use. It reflects customers' experience with the company's offering and is a result of the functionality afforded by the offering and customers' ability to utilize this functionality. There is a common misconception that the relationship between functionality (e.g., number of product features) and customer satisfaction is linear, such that greater functionality inevitably leads to greater satisfaction. In reality, however, this is not the case. Adding functionality in cases when customers lack the knowledge necessary to utilize it can backfire. To illustrate, in an attempt to incorporate the latest technology in its newly redesigned 7-series, BMW introduced iDrive, an over-engineered computer system used to control most secondary functions of a car, including the audio system, climate, and navigation. Designed to manage more than 700 functions with a single knob, the iDrive had a steep learning curve and quickly became the most controversial feature of the 7-series.

- *Technological design.* An important factor in product design is technology used to create the product, as well as the technology used by the product. Depending on the novelty of the product/service, two product-development methods can be identified: product innovation and product variation. The product-innovation approach involves technology-based innovations and innovative use of existing technology to design new offerings. Unlike the product-innovation strategy, which leads to substantive functional differences among offerings, the product-variation approach leads to offerings characterized by relatively minor variations in their functionality, such as adding different colors, flavors, tastes, sizes, designs, or packaging variations.

- *Degree of customization.* When designing the product and service aspects of its offerings, a company needs to decide on the degree to which these offerings will be customized to target customers. At one extreme, a company may decide to pursue a mass-production strategy, offering the same product/service to all customers. At the other extreme, the company might pursue a one-to-one customization in which the company's products and services are customized for each individual customer. A compromise between the mass-production approach and the one-to-one customization approach is segment-based customization. By developing offerings for groups of customers with similar needs, segment-based customization allows companies to develop fewer offerings while ensuring that these offerings fit customer needs. To illustrate, Dell offers more than a hundred options from which customers can choose to customize their computer; Porsche offers nearly a thousand customization options for its flagship 911 Carrera; and Nike offers more than 10,000 different design/color sport-shoe customization options through its website nikeid.com.

- *Form.* Product design typically involves decisions concerning the physical structure of the offering, such as product size and shape, in order to optimize the value of the offering to the customer, the company, and its collaborators. Design has an effect on the value derived from manufacturing, transporting, storing, inventorying, and consuming the product. Because people vary in their purchase-quantity and consumption preferences, many consumer packaged goods are offered in a variety of sizes and shapes. Thus, Johnson & Johnson's pain relief medicine Tylenol is available in more than fifty different SKU forms: regular, extra strength, and children's dosages; normal and extended relief; tablets, caplets, gelcaps, geltabs, and liquid—all in a variety of sizes.

- *Style.* An important aspect of product design involves its look and feel. Styling is particularly important for products that have a primarily hedonic (e.g., a sports car) and/or self-expressive (e.g., fashion apparel) function and tends to be less relevant in the case of products used for utilitarian purposes (e.g., manufacturing equipment). Because product styling can create value above and beyond the functional characteristics of the product, it is used by companies to differentiate their offerings from the competition. For example, Apple revolutionized the personal computer industry by offering computers designed to deliver hedonic value and serve as a means of self-expression. Another example of style-based differentiation is Method Products, a home and personal cleaning products company, which differentiates its products through innovative, futuristic-styled styling of the containers.

- *Packaging.* Packaging aims to prepare the product for transporting, storing, inventorying, promoting, selling, and consumption. Packaging serves several key functions: (1) protecting the product during transportation and storage; (2) physically containing liquid, powder, and granular goods; (3) agglomerating small items into larger packages; (4) preventing tampering, counterfeit, and theft; (5) providing convenience in transportation, handling, storing, display, sale, and consumption; (6) offering information on how to transport, store, use, and dispose of the product; and (7) promoting the product to potential buyers by providing them with reasons to purchase/use the product. Packaging can also be used to create value above and beyond the value created by the underlying product. To illustrate, Tiffany's signature blue box creates value for customers by highlighting the exclusivity of the offering while at the same time strengthening its brand image and helping differentiate it from competitors' offerings.

In addition to deciding on the characteristics of the individual products and services, companies often must decide how to differentiate them from the other products/services comprising their product lines and how to manage these products and services over their life cycles. A more detailed discussion of managing product/service lifecycle and product line management is offered in Chapters 23 and 24.

Summary

Product and service management aims to optimize the value of the product and service aspects of the company's offering to deliver superior value to target customers, the company, and its collaborators. Products typically change ownership during purchase; once created, they can be physically separated from the manufacturer and distributed to end users via multiple channels. In contrast, services imply a right of use (rather than a change in ownership) and are typically delivered and consumed at the same time.

Managing products and services involves two types of decisions: (1) strategic decisions, which are a function of the offering's target market defined by the 5-C framework (customers, company, collaborators, competition, and context), and (2) tactical decisions, which are a function of the other marketing mix variables (product/service, brand, price, incentives, communication, and distribution).

Product and service management involves deciding on factors such as performance, consistency, reliability, durability, compatibility, ease of use, technological design, degree of customization, form, style, and packaging. In addition to deciding on the characteristics of the individual products and services, companies often have to decide on how to differentiate them from the other products/services composing their product lines.

Relevant Concepts

Consumer Packaged Goods (CPG): A term used to describe consumer products packaged in portable containers, such as food, beverages, health and beauty aids, tobacco, and cleaning supplies.

Six Sigma: Introduced by Motorola and later adopted by General Electric, Six Sigma[4] is a methodology for managing process variations that cause defects. The Six Sigma approach builds on the notion that to ensure an offering's consistency with specifications, the underlying processes should be set to ensure that the difference between the actual and the desired outcomes does not exceed six standard deviations. In this context, a widely accepted definition of a six sigma process is one that reduces defect levels below 3.4 defective items per million outcomes. Over time the term "six sigma" has evolved beyond its literal definition as a metric (i.e., 3.4 defects per one million opportunities) and is often used in reference to a more general methodology of improving business processes that focuses on understanding customer needs and aligning the business processes to fulfill these needs with minimal variation.

Stock Keeping Unit (SKU): A unique identifier assigned to each distinct product or service.

Additional Readings

Berry, Leonard L. (2004), *Marketing Services Competing through Quality*. New York, NY: Free Press.

Lehmann, Donald R. and Russell S. Winer (2005), *Product Management* (4th ed.). Boston, MA: McGraw-Hill/Irwin.

McGrath, Michael E. (2001), *Product Strategy for High Technology Companies: Accelerating Your Business to Web Speed* (2nd ed.). New York, NY: McGraw-Hill.

Zeithaml, Valarie A., Mary Jo Bitner, and Dwayne D. Gremler (2006), *Services Marketing: Integrating Customer Focus Across the Firm* (4th ed.). Boston, MA: McGraw-Hill/Irwin.

Notes

[1] Nelson, Phillip (1970), "Information and Consumer Behavior," *Journal of Political Economy*, 78 (March–April), 311–29.

[2] The Federal Communication Comission (FCC) is an independent agency of the U.S. government that regulates radio, television, wire, cable, and satellite communications. The Institute of Electrical and Electronics Engineers (IEEE) is a developer of voluntary, consensus-based industry standards in a broad range of industries, including energy, healthcare, and information technology.

[3] Figure 2 illustrates the impact of marketing mix analysis on product design; the analysis of the impact of the marketing mix on services is conceptually identical, with the exception that the concepts of product and service are switched.

[4] Sigma refers to the Greek letter σ commonly used in statistics to represent the standard deviation (a measure of the degree of variance) in a given population.

——————————— Chapter Sixteen ———————————

Managing Brands

Any fool can put on a deal, but it takes genius, faith, and perseverance to create a brand.
David Ogilvy, founder of Ogilvy and Mather advertising agency

Brands are marketing tools used to identify a company's offering, differentiate it from the competition, and create value that goes beyond its product and service characteristics. The key aspects of creating and managing brands are the focus of this chapter.

Overview

A brand is a marketing tool created with the purpose of differentiating a company's offering from the competition and creating value for customers, the company, and its collaborators. A brand has two key aspects: (1) brand identity, which includes identifying characteristics such as name, sign, symbol, character, and/or design, and (2) brand meaning, which reflects a set of offering-related associations in the mind of the buyer. To illustrate, the identity of BMW is captured by elements such as its distinct name and logo, whereas its meaning—"the ultimate driving machine"—reflects the mental associations that target customers make with the brand. The key aspects of the identity and the meaning of a brand are delineated in more detail below.

- *Brand identity* is typically achieved through attributes such as brand name, logo, symbol, character, slogan, jingle, product design, and packaging. The key criteria for deciding on brand identity elements are that they should be unique, memorable, likeable, and consistent with the other brand elements and with the meaning of the brand. Brand elements should also be flexible and adaptable to changes in the market environment (e.g., to accommodate shifts in consumer preferences) and the company's product-line strategy (e.g., to be extendable to other product categories). Furthermore, the company should be able to protect the uniqueness of its brand elements against infringement by competitors.

- *Brand meaning* reflects the brand-related perceptions and beliefs held by the brand's current and potential customers; it reflects customers' understanding of this brand's value proposition, often referred to as a brand's promise. The meaning of the brand has dual impact on customers' perceptions of value: (1) it signals the quality of the products and services associated with the brand and (2) it adds value above and beyond the one provided by the underlying product or service. This added value can involve factors such as emotional

benefits (e.g., the satisfaction from using and owning the brand), social benefits (e.g., group acceptance resulting from ownership of a particular brand),
and self-expressive benefits (e.g., using the brand as a means to express one's
identity).

The primary function of brand identity is to identify the company's offering and differentiate it from the competition. In contrast, brand meaning aims to create value (for
customers, the company, and its collaborators) that goes beyond the product and service
characteristics of the offering. A brand's identity can exist independently from its target
customers; in contrast, a brand's meaning exists primarily in the minds of the buyers.

A Framework for Managing Brands

Managing brands involves two types of decisions: (1) strategic decisions, aimed
at optimizing brands as a function of the offering's target market, and (2) tactical
analysis, aimed at optimizing brands as a function of the other marketing mix variables. These two types of decisions are outlined in more detail below.

Managing Brands: Strategy

From a strategic standpoint, branding decisions are a function of the offering's target
market, defined by the 5-C framework: customers, company, collaborators, competition,
and context. These factors are illustrated in Figure 1 and outlined in more detail below.

Figure 1. Brand Management as a Function of the Target Market

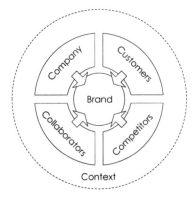

- *Customers.* Because one of the primary functions of any brand is to create
  value for its target customers, understanding these customers' needs is essential for building and managing successful brands. In this context, changes
  in customer preferences often lead to repositioning the brand in a way that
  maximizes its value to customers.

- *Company.* An offering's branding strategy is influenced by the existing
  brands in the company's brand portfolio. To illustrate, a company with a
  portfolio of strong brands can build on these brands for its new offerings.

- *Collaborators.* An offering's branding can be influenced by the branding strategies of its collaborators. For example, collaboration in the area of branding often leads to the development of long-term co-branding strategies (e.g., co-branding between Microsoft and Intel, between Coca-Cola and Splenda, and among Citibank, American Airlines, and MasterCard). In this context, understanding a collaborator's branding strategy is essential for developing and managing a company's own brands.

- *Competitors.* Competitors' branding strategies can have a significant impact on designing and managing an offering's brand. Indeed, because one of the primary goals of brands is to differentiate a company's offering from the competition, competitive differentiation is essential for successful brand management. Of particular relevance here are the concepts of points of parity (associations shared by competing brands) and points of difference (associations that are unique to a particular brand), which are used by companies to position their brands vis-à-vis those of their competitors.

- *Context.* An offering's branding strategy is also influenced by the economic, technological, socio-cultural, regulatory, and physical aspects of the environment in which it operates. For instance, the protectability of a brand name is a function of the degree to which it has been adopted by the population and has become synonymous with the associated category. Thus, because of their common use as a generic term, brands such as Aspirin, Thermos, and Escalator have lost their legal trademark-protected status.

Managing Brands: Tactics

From a tactical standpoint, branding needs to be coordinated with the other marketing mix variables (i.e., product, service, price, incentives, communication, and distribution). The key aspects of branding decisions are illustrated in Figure 2 and outlined in more detail below.

Figure 2. Brand Management as a Function of the Marketing Mix

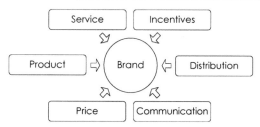

- *Product and service.* An offering's brand is directly linked to the product and service characteristics of the offering. Thus, the more commoditized a company's product or service is and the less observable its benefits are, the greater the importance of branding in differentiating the offering. For instance, brand characters are typically used to differentiate commoditized products with benefits that are not readily observable, such as the Michelin Man (tires), Green Giant (processed vegetables), Tony the Tiger (cereal), and Mr. Clean (cleaning products). An offering's brand can also be enhanced by its packaging. For example, the swirl design of Coca-Cola's bottle, the frosty design of the Grey Goose vodka bottle, and the signature blue Tiffany box are important brand elements that create value in the minds of customers above and beyond that of the actual product.

- *Price*. An offering's pricing is an important factor in developing and managing its brand. Low prices can hurt the image of an upscale brand just as high prices are inconsistent with the image of a value brand.

- *Incentives*. An offering's brand is a function of the nature of its incentives. Because monetary incentives emphasize the importance of price, they typically tend to erode the strength of the brand. In contrast, nonmonetary incentives and promotions that are consistent with the brand image (e.g., toys and games involving the brand's character) can ultimately strengthen the brand.

- *Communication*. The impact of an offering's communications on branding is a function of the nature of the communicated message. For example, brand-related communications tend to strengthen the brand, whereas communications focused on price and monetary incentives typically have the opposite effect and erode the brand image.[1]

- *Distribution*. An offering's brand is a function of its distribution strategy. For example, the increasing role of online and warehouse retail formats decreases the role of personal selling in branding in favor of point-of-sales branding through packaging and in-store communications. An offering's distribution channels can also become a vehicle for brand delivery. For instance, Disney World theme parks and Niketown retail stores function as channels delivering Disney and Nike brands.

Brand Hierarchy

Brand hierarchy (also referred to as brand architecture) reflects the relationship among different brands in a company's portfolio. There are several popular approaches to managing multiple brands:

- *Individual branding* involves creating a separate brand for each product or product line. To illustrate, Tide, Cheer, Bold, and Era are individual brands of laundry detergents created by Procter & Gamble. Chevrolet, Buick, Cadillac, and GMC are individual brands of General Motors. Campbell Soup Company uses Campbell's for soups, Pepperidge Farm for baked goods, and V8 for juices. Sears uses Kenmore for appliances, Craftsman for tools, and Die-Hard for batteries. In some cases, the brand names for different products may even have the same origin: Nescafé, Nesquik, Nestea, and Nespresso are used by Nestlé to brand different beverages.

- *Umbrella branding* involves using a single brand for all of a company's products. For example, General Electric, Heinz, Virgin, and Costco (Kirkland Signature) use a single brand for nearly all of their products. The main advantage to using umbrella branding is that it leverages the equity of an existing brand, benefiting from the instant recognition of the core brand while avoiding the costs associated with building a new brand. A drawback to using umbrella branding is that poor performance by any particular product carrying the brand name can easily hurt the reputation of the entire brand. Using a single brand may also limit the company's ability to attach a specific meaning to the brand across different product categories.

- *Sub-branding* involves combining two or more brand names, one of which typically is the umbrella brand. For instance, Courtyard by Marriott, Residence Inn by Marriott, Fairfield Inn by Marriott, and SpringHill Suites by Marriott exemplify using sub-brands in the context of umbrella branding. Similarly, Porsche uses sub-branding for the different offerings in its product line: Carrera, Boxster, Cayenne, and Cayman. Using this strategy enables the company to leverage an existing brand name while minimizing the spillover risk of potential negative associations to the parent brand.

- *Co-branding* involves combining two or more brands, typically from different product categories, such as United Airlines–JPMorgan Chase–Visa credit cards, Lexus "Coach edition" sport utility vehicles, and HP–iPod MP3 players. A form of co-branding involves ingredient branding in which an ingredient or component of a product has its own brand identity, such as Teflon surface protector, Gore-Tex fabrics, NutraSweet and Splenda sweeteners, and Intel microprocessors.

Companies with multiple product lines may also employ hybrid brand structures that involve a variety of individual, umbrella-branding, and sub-branding strategies. To illustrate, Chevrolet and Cadillac are individual brands of General Motors; at the same time, each one serves as an umbrella brand for its sub-brands (Camaro, Impala, Corvette, Malibu, Monte Carlo, and Blazer are Chevrolet sub-brands, and CTS, STS, XLR, and Escalade are Cadillac sub-brands).

Brand Dynamics

Once created, brands evolve over time. There are two common types of changes in an offering's branding strategy: (1) brand repositioning, which involves changes to an existing brand, most often to make the brand more relevant to its target customers, and (2) brand extensions, which involve broadening the set of underlying product categories to which the brand is applied. These two types of brand dynamics are discussed in the following sections.

Brand Repositioning

Brand repositioning involves changing an essential aspect of a brand's identity and/or image. There are several common reasons to reposition an existing brand, including (1) in response to a change in target customers, (2) when reaching a new target market, and (3) in reaction to a change in the positioning of a competitor's brand. These reasons are illustrated in more detail below.

- *Reacting to a change in the target customers.* One of the most common reasons for repositioning a brand is to ensure that it remains relevant to the changing needs of its target customers. For example, to reflect the changing values and lifestyles of women, General Mills has consistently refined the image of Betty Crocker, a fictitious character designed to offer cooking advice to consumers. Over the years, she has had eight different "looks," from the first stern, gray-haired, older woman in 1936 to today's olive-skinned, dark-haired Betty. Similarly, to increase its appeal to younger customers, Procter & Gamble repositioned its half-century-old beauty brand, Oil of Olay. The key changes introduced in 2000 included changing the name to Olay (to avoid associations equating oil to "greasy"), streamlining its logo, replacing the woman's image (which resembled a nun) on the label with a younger one, and cleaning up the packaging design. In response to customers' concerns over fried food, Kentucky Fried Chicken abbreviated its name to KFC to project a healthier image.

- *Reaching a new target market.* Companies often reposition their brands when entering new markets to allow the brand image to reflect the specifics of that market and better resonates with the needs and values of target customers. For example, Philip Morris' Marlboro brand was originally introduced in 1924 as a women's cigarette, tagged "Mild as May"; in 1954 it was repositioned using the rugged cowboy image of the Marlboro Man, which was more likely to appeal to male smokers. Procter & Gamble's cleaning product Mr. Clean was introduced as Mr. Proper in Germany, Flash in the United Kingdom, Monsieur Propre in France, Mastro Lindo in Italy, Don Limpio in Spain (from *limpiar*—"to clean"), and Maestro Limpio in Mexico.

- *Reacting to a change in a competitor's positioning.* Because companies strive to create superior customer value relative to that of other offerings in the marketplace, a change in the positioning of a competitor's offering often induces the company to reposition its brand to preserve and/or enhance its competitive advantage. To illustrate, the popularity of the Energizer Bunny in the United States forced Duracell to discontinue the use of its brand mascot—the Duracell Bunny—now used to brand Duracell batteries only outside of North America.

Brand Extensions

Brand extension refers to the strategy of using the same brand name in a different context, such as a different product category or a different price tier. For example, Montblanc—which over a century built a reputation for producing the finest quality pens—extended its brand to include items such as luxury watches, sunglasses, cufflinks, wallets, briefcases, and even fragrances. In a similar manner, Oakley extended its brand from eyewear to other domains such as apparel, footwear, bags, and watches.

Brand extensions can be better understood when considered in the context of product line extensions. Product line extensions involve adding a new offering to a company's existing product line. In contrast to product line extensions, brand extensions involve the development of a branding strategy for an existing product line extension. To illustrate, consider the decisions of Toyota and Volkswagen to enter the luxury car market. Both companies decided to extend their product line upscale but chose different branding strategies. Believing that its existing brand name could not convey the luxury image required to successfully compete with Mercedes S-class and BMW 7-series, Toyota launched a new brand—Lexus—rather than trying to extend its existing brand. In contrast, Volkswagen launched its upscale extension branded as Volkswagen Phaeton, prominently featuring the VW logo on the front and the back of the car. Thus, in Volkswagen's case, the product line extension went hand in hand with a brand extension, whereas in Toyota's case the product line extension involved launching a new, freestanding brand.

The primary reason for extending an existing brand is to leverage its equity by applying it to a new offering. The popularity of brand extensions stems from the fact that building new brands is a costly and time-consuming task. As a result, when entering a new product category, companies often choose to leverage the equity of their existing brands rather than invest in creating new ones.

Based on their breadth, there are two main types of brand extensions: within-category extensions and cross-category extensions. In within-category brand extensions, the same brand name is applied to several products within the same product category. In contrast, in cross-category brand extensions, the same brand name is applied to products in different categories. To illustrate, extending the Starbucks name to different coffee flavors is typically referred to as a within-category brand extension, whereas extending it to ice cream is considered a cross-category brand extension.

Based on their relation to the offering's pricing, two types of brand extensions are commonly distinguished: vertical and horizontal.

- *Vertical brand extensions* stretch the brand to a product or service in a different price tier. Depending on the direction in which the original offering is being extended, two types of vertical brand extensions can be distinguished: upscale and downscale.

  Examples of *upscale brand extensions* include Gallo's entry into the premium wine segment with Gallo Family Vineyards Estate Series, Volkswagen's (unsuccessful) extension into the luxury car segment with the VW Phaeton, and Levi Strauss' (unsuccessful) entry into the designer suit category in the 1980s. Because the image of the core brand generally hurts rather than helps the upscale extension, launching a successful upscale brand extension is a challenging task.

  Examples of *downscale brand extensions* include the BMW 1-series, Porsche's Boxster, and Armani Exchange. Because they leverage the image of the core brand, downscale extensions tend to be more successful than upscale ones. The key shortcoming for downscale brand extensions is the potential dilution of the brand's image. To illustrate, the brand image of Lotus Cars (English manufacturer of sports and racing cars) was negatively influenced by the introduction of Lotus Elise – a downscale extension featuring a Toyota-sourced engine that has been used in several Toyota models, including Celica and Corolla.

- *Horizontal brand extensions* involve applying the brand to a different product category in the same price tier. For example, Ralph Lauren successfully extended its Polo brand from clothing to home furnishings like bedding and towels, Timberland extended its brand from boots to outerwear and travel gear, and Porsche extended its brand from sport cars to sport utility vehicles. A potential downside of horizontal brand extensions is brand dilution, which is likely to occur when a brand is extended to diverse product categories that are inconsistent with its essence. To illustrate, Costco's strategy to use a single brand—Kirkland Signature—for all its store-branded products, from food and wine to appliances and clothes, limits its ability to attach a specific meaning to its brand.

Brand Equity

The term brand equity refers to the financial value of the brand; it is the net present value of the financial benefits derived from the brand. Thus, brand equity reflects the financial outcome from brand ownership and determines the premium that should be placed on a company's valuation because of brand ownership.

The key component of a brand's equity is the brand's strength. Brand strength (also referred to as brand power or customer-based brand equity[2]) reflects the brand's ability to differentiate the offering from the competition and create customer value through meaningful associations. Unlike brand equity, which reflects the value of the brand to the company, brand strength reflects the value of the brand among current and potential customers.

Brand equity is a function of brand strength, as well as a number of additional factors reflecting the company's utilization of the strength of its brand (e.g., sales revenues). Thus, a stronger brand does not necessarily imply greater brand equity. For example, although the Armani, Möet & Chandon, Audi, and Lexus brands are considered stronger than the Gap, McDonald's, Volkswagen, and Toyota brands, respectively (as measured by the greater price premium they command over identical unbranded products), the equity of the latter set of brands is estimated to be higher than that of the former (e.g., the brand equity of Toyota is higher than the brand equity of Lexus).[3]

Brand strength can be defined as the differential impact of brand knowledge on consumer response to an offering's marketing efforts.[4] Thus, a brand has greater strength when customers react more favorably to the various aspects of an offering (product, service, price, incentives, communication, and distribution) when the brand is identified relative to when it is not identified. To illustrate, one of the benefits of brand strength is the price premium customers are willing to pay for the branded (as opposed to the identical unbranded) product. In addition to the price premium, other dimensions of brand strength include greater loyalty; enhanced perceptions of product performance; greater licensing, merchandising, and brand extension opportunities; less vulnerability to service inconsistencies and marketing crises; more elastic response to price decreases and more inelastic response to price increases; greater communications effectiveness; and increased channel power.

Measuring Brand Equity

Knowing the monetary value of a company's brand(s) is essential for company valuation (e.g., for mergers and acquisitions, sale of assets, licensing, financing, and estimating benefits or damages to the brand). Despite the importance of brand equity, there is no commonly agreed-upon methodology for its calculation; instead, there are several alternative methods, each placing emphasis on different aspects of brand equity. The three most common approaches to brand equity measurement are outlined below.

- *Cost-based approach* involves calculating brand equity based on the costs involved (e.g., marketing research, advertising, and legal costs) if the brand needs to be created from scratch at the time of valuation.

- *Market-based approach* involves calculating brand equity based on the difference in the cash flows generated from the branded product and a functionally equivalent but nonbranded product, adjusted for the costs of creating the brand. The market-based approach can be summarized in the following equation:

$$\text{Brand equity} = \text{Sales revenues}_{\text{Brand}} - \text{Sales revenues}_{\text{Generic}} - \text{Branding costs}$$

- *Financial approach* involves calculating brand equity based on the net present value of the cash flows derived from the brand's future earnings. This approach typically involves three key steps: (1) estimating the company's future cash flows, (2) estimating the contribution of the brand to these cash flows, and (3) adjusting these cash flows using a risk factor that reflects the volatility of the earnings attributed to the brand. The financial approach can be summarized in the following equation:

$$\text{Brand equity} = \text{NPV of future cash flows} \cdot \text{Brand contribution factor} \cdot \text{Risk factor}$$

The financial approach to estimating brand equity can be illustrated using Interbrand's methodology, which is the basis for *Business Week's* annual ranking of the top 100 brands. Interbrand's method involves three steps. The first step consists of estimating the percentage of the overall revenues that can be attributed to the brand. Based on reports from analysts at JPMorgan Chase, Citigroup, and Morgan Stanley, Interbrand projects five years of earnings and sales for the products and services associated with the brand. Interbrand then deducts the estimated earnings that can be attributed to tangible assets, on the assumption that the income generated beyond that point is the result of intangible assets. The next step involves stripping out the nonbrand intangibles such as patents, trademarks, technological know-how, and management strength to determine the portion of the company's income generated by intangible assets that can be attributed to the brand. The final step involves assessing the risk profile of these projected earnings based on a variety of factors such as market leadership, stability, market growth, global reach, trend, support (e.g., investment in the brand), and protection. The discount rate resulting from this risk analysis is applied to brand-related earnings to produce the net present value of the brand.

Summary

A brand is a marketing tool created for the purpose of differentiating a company's offering from the competition and creating value for customers, the company, and its collaborators. A brand has two key aspects: (1) brand identity, which includes identifying characteristics such as name, sign, symbol, character, and/or design, and (2) brand meaning, which reflects a set of offering-related associations in the mind of the buyer. Brand identity aims to *identify* the company's offering and *differentiate* it from the competition. In contrast, brand meaning aims to *create value* (for customers, the company, and its collaborators) that goes beyond the product and service characteristics of the offering.

Managing brands involves two types of decisions: (1) strategic decisions, which are a function of the offering's target market defined by the 5-C framework (customers, company, collaborators, competition, and context) and (2) tactical decisions, which are a function of the other marketing mix variables (product, service, price, incentives, communication, and distribution).

Two important branding decisions involve managing the brand hierarchy and managing the brand dynamics. Brand hierarchy reflects the relationships among different brands in a company's portfolio. Popular approaches to managing multiple brands include individual branding, umbrella branding, sub-branding, and co-branding. Brand dynamics reflect the brand evolution over time. The two common types of brand dynamics are brand repositioning, which involves changes to an existing brand, most often to make the brand more relevant to its target customers, and brand extension, which involves broadening the set of underlying product categories to which the brand is applied.

Brand equity is the net present value of the financial benefits derived from the brand. Brand equity is a function of brand power, as well as a number of additional factors reflecting the company's utilization of the strength of its brand. Brand power reflects the brand's ability to differentiate the offering from the competition and create customer value through meaningful associations. Unlike brand equity, which reflects the value of the brand to the company, brand power reflects the value of the brand among current and potential customers. The three most popular approaches to measuring brand equity are cost-based (the cost of recreating the brand), market-based (the difference in the cost-adjusted cash flows of a branded and nonbranded product), and financial (the net present value of the cash flows of the offering's future earnings that are attributed to the brand).

Relevant Concepts

Brand Audit: A comprehensive analysis of a brand, most often to determine the sources of brand equity.

Brand Essence: The fundamental nature of the brand, also referred to as "brand promise." Brand essence distills the meaning of the brand into one key aspect—the positioning of the brand. One way to think about brand essence is to think of the "ness" of the brand, such as "BMW-ness," "Apple-ness," and "Microsoft-ness."

Copyright: A legal term describing rights given to creators for their literary and artistic works. The types of works covered by copyright include literary works such as novels, poems, plays, reference works, newspapers, and computer programs; databases; films, musical compositions, and choreography; artistic works such as paintings, drawings, photographs, and sculpture; architecture; and advertisements, maps, and technical drawings.

Fighting Brand: A downscale (lower-priced) brand introduced to shield a major brand from low-priced competitors.

Generification: Colloquialized use of brand names (e.g., in reference to the products they are associated with). The use of a brand name as a generic term can lead to the loss of a company's right to the exclusive use of that brand name. To illustrate, Trampoline, Brazier, Escalator, Thermos, Yo-Yo, and Aspirin lost their trademark-protected status because of popular use; Xerox, Rollerblade, Velcro, and Google are considered to be at risk of following them.

Global Brand: A brand with a comprehensive international distribution system, such as Coca-Cola, Pepsi, and Sony.

Industrial Property: A type of intellectual property that involves (1) inventions (patents), (2) industrial designs, and (3) identity marks such as trademarks, service marks, commercial names, and designations, including indications of source and appellations of origin. An invention is a product or process that provides a new way of doing something or offers new solutions to technical problems; a patent is an exclusive right granted for an invention. An industrial design is the aesthetic aspect of a product and may consist of three-dimensional features, such as shape or surface, or two-dimensional features such as patterns, lines, or color. Industrial design is primarily of an aesthetic nature and does not protect any technical aspects of the product to which it is applied. Identity marks, such as trademarks, service marks, commercial names, and designations, are designed to identify an offering or a company and protect it from the competition. Thus, a trademark (or service mark in the case of services) is a distinctive sign that identifies certain goods or services as those produced or provided by a specific entity. A geographical indication is a sign used on goods that have a specific geographical origin and possess qualities or a reputation that stem from the place of origin. Geographical indications may be used for a wide variety of agricultural products, such as "Tuscany" for olive oil produced in Tuscany, Italy, or "Roquefort" for cheese produced in the Roquefort area of France.

Intellectual Property: The legal entitlement attached to the expressed form of an idea, or to some other intangible subject matter. Intellectual property is divided into two categories: (1) *industrial property*, which encompasses inventions, industrial designs, and identity marks such as trademarks, service marks, commercial names, and designations, including indications of source and appellations of origin, and (2) *copyright*, which includes literary and artistic works such as novels, poems and plays, films, musical works; artistic works such as drawings, paintings, photographs and sculptures; and architectural designs.

National Brand: A brand available nationwide.

Private Label: Branding strategy in which an offering is branded by the retailer (e.g., Kirkland Signature, Costco's private brand; Kenmore, Sears' brand for home appliances; White Cloud, Wal-Mart's private label for laundry detergents). Private labels (also referred to as store brands) are often contrasted with national brands, which are branded by the manufacturer or a third party rather than by the retailer (e.g., Coca-Cola, IBM, and Nike). Typically, private labels tend to be less expensive than national brands, although there are many exceptions, such as private labels offered by upscale retailers (e.g., Nordstrom, Marks & Spencer).

Regional Brand: A brand available only in a particular geographic region.

Store Brand: See *private label*.

Additional Readings

Aaker, David A. (1996), *Building Strong Brands*. New York, NY: Free Press.

Aaker, David A. (2004), *Brand Portfolio Strategy: Creating Relevance, Differentiation, Energy, Leverage, and Clarity*. New York, NY: Free Press.

Keller, Kevin Lane (2007), *Strategic Brand Management: Building, Measuring, and Managing Brand Equity* (3rd ed.). Upper Saddle River, NJ: Prentice Hall.

Kapferer, Jean-Noël (2008), *The New Strategic Brand Management: Creating and Sustaining Brand Equity Long Term* (4th ed.). Sterling, VA: Kogan Page.

Kumar, Nirmalya and Jan-Benedict E. M. Steenkamp (2007), *Private Label Strategy: How to Meet the Store Brand Challenge*. Boston, MA: Harvard Business School Press.

Lamons, Bob (2005), *The Case for B2B Branding: Pulling Away from the Business to Business Pack* (1st ed.). Mason, OH: Thomson/South-Western.

Tybout, Alice M. and Tim Calkins (2005), *Kellogg on Branding*. Hoboken, NJ: John Wiley & Sons.

Notes

[1] With the exception of companies such as Wal-Mart, Home Depot, and Priceline.com, where low prices are directly related to the essence of the brand.

[2] Keller, Kevin Lane (2007), *Strategic Brand Management: Building, Measuring and Managing Brand Equity* (3rd ed.). Upper Saddle River, NJ: Prentice Hall.

[3] *Business Week* (2008), "The 100 Top Brands." September 29.

[4] Keller, Kevin Lane (2007), *Strategic Brand Management: Building, Measuring, and Managing Brand Equity* (3rd ed.). Upper Saddle River, NJ: Prentice Hall.

Chapter Seventeen

Managing Price

Price is what you pay. Value is what you get.
Warren Buffett

Setting and managing an offering's price is one of the key factors in setting the value of the offering to customers, the company, and its collaborators. Moreover, of all marketing mix variables, price is the only one that produces revenue for the company; all the others are costs. The main aspects of price management are the focus of this chapter.

Overview

There are three popular approaches to determine an offering's price. The first approach involves setting the price based on the company's costs. In the most extreme case, referred to as *cost-plus pricing* (or *markup pricing)*, the offering's final price is determined by adding a fixed markup to the cost of the offering. Another approach, often referred to as *competitive-parity pricing*, involves setting the offering's price in a way that puts the offering's value at parity with that of competitors. The third approach, often referred to as *customer-value pricing*, focuses on customer demand, determined by customers' willingness to pay for the benefits afforded by the company's offering. While each of these approaches has its advantages, they miss the point that the pricing decision is not an isolated decision but a key component of the offering's strategy and tactics.

The key to determining the optimal price is to consider its implications on an offering's value to customers, collaborators, and the company in a broad context that involves all other aspects of the company's strategy and tactics. Setting the price is really a decision about value, not just price. Thus, the "optimal" price is a price that, in combination with the other marketing mix variables (product, service, brand, incentives, communication, and distribution), delivers superior value to target customers, the company, and collaborators. This approach is outlined in more detail in the following sections.

A Framework for Managing Price

Managing price involves two types of decisions: (1) strategic decisions, which aim to optimize price as a function of the offering's target market, and (2) tactical decisions, which aim to optimize price as a function of the other marketing mix variables. These two types of decisions are outlined in more detail below.

Managing Price: Strategy

From a strategic standpoint, pricing is a function of the offering's target market, defined by the 5-C framework: customers, company, collaborators, competition, and context. These five factors are illustrated in Figure 1 and are outlined in more detail next.

Figure 1. Price Management as a Function of the Target Market

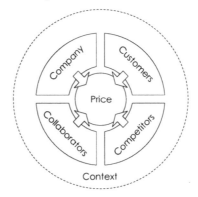

- *Customers.* An offering's pricing is a function of customers' willingness to pay for the benefits it offers, such that greater willingness to pay is typically associated with higher price. Pricing based entirely on customers' willingness to pay is often referred to as demand pricing.

- *Company.* Pricing is a function of the strategic assets and core competencies of the company, which determine its cost structure. To illustrate, a lower cost structure provides the company with the strategic option to lower its price without incurring a loss. Pricing based entirely on the company's costs is often referred to as cost-based pricing.

- *Collaborators.* Pricing is also influenced by the goals and resources of company collaborators (e.g., channel partners). For example, the price of offerings sold though consolidated distribution channels such as Wal-Mart is likely to be influenced by the profit optimization strategies of these channels.

- *Competitors.* Prices of competitive offerings have a direct impact on an offering's price. For instance, based on its strategic goals, a company may set the price of its offering at par, below, or above that of competitors. Pricing based entirely on competitors' prices is often referred to as competitive pricing.

- *Context.* Pricing is also a function of various economic, technological, sociocultural, regulatory, and physical factors describing the environment in which the company operates. To illustrate, the price of travel services is influenced by seasons; the price of high-tech products is a function of the availability of superior technologies; and the price of gasoline, tobacco, and alcohol products is a function of government regulations and taxation.

Managing Price: Tactics

From a tactical standpoint, pricing needs to be coordinated with the other marketing mix variables (i.e., product, service, brand, incentives, communication, and distribution). The key aspects of pricing decisions are illustrated in Figure 2 and outlined in more detail next.

Figure 2. Price Management as a Function of the Marketing Mix

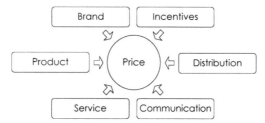

- *Product and service.* Product and service characteristics of an offering are key drivers of the offering's price. Thus, price is a function of the monetary value that target customers are willing to pay for the benefits provided by the company's products and services. Typically, a company can set higher prices for highly differentiated products and services than for commoditized offerings.

- *Brand.* In addition to the product and service characteristics of the offering, its brand has a significant impact on pricing. To illustrate, strong brands command substantial price premiums over weaker brands and nonbranded offerings. In fact, the price premium associated with a given brand is also used to measure the strength of this brand.

- *Incentives.* Incentives are typically used to make further adjustments to the offering's price to better meet the needs of target customers, collaborators, and the company. As a result, incentives have become an integral component of a company's pricing strategy, such that an offering's price is typically augmented by some form of monetary incentive offered to channel members (e.g., volume discounts and promotional allowances) and/or customers (e.g., price reductions and coupons).

- *Communications.* Pricing decisions are also influenced by the offering's communication strategy. For example, an offering may be priced 50% less than the market leader to more effectively communicate its benefits ("half-price").

- *Distribution.* An offering's price is also a function of its distribution system, such as channel structure (e.g., direct, indirect, or hybrid), channel ownership (e.g., ownership-based, contractual, or implied), channel type (e.g., specialized vs. broad), and channel coverage (e.g., limited vs. extensive). To illustrate, a company selling through indirect channels typically cannot directly set retail prices; it can only suggest the price at which the offering should be sold to customers (manufacturer's suggested retail price, or MSRP).

Psychological Pricing

Successful pricing strategies take into account the fact that people do not always perceive pricing information objectively; instead, price perception is often a function of factors such as the availability of other prices and the price format. The psychological aspects of pricing have an important impact on people's perception of an offering's value. Many of these effects are also very robust and tend to hold even when buyers are made aware of their implications. The four most common effects—reference-price effects, price–quantity effects, price-tier effects, and price-ending effects—are outlined below.

- *Reference-price effects.* To assess the price of a given offering, people typically evaluate it relative to another price, which serves as a reference point. This reference price can be either internal (e.g., a remembered price from a prior purchase occasion or advertising) or external (e.g., a competitor's price or the MSRP). Understanding the reference prices that buyers use when evaluating the offering can provide the company with valuable information that may be relevant for setting the offering's price. Furthermore, by strategically choosing the reference price, a company can frame the price of its offering in a way that makes it more attractive (e.g., by comparing it to a more expensive competitive offering).

- *Price–quantity effects.* People tend to be more sensitive to changes in price than to changes in quantity. To illustrate, the sales volume of a ten-pack of hotdogs priced at $2.49 is likely to decline further following a $.50 price increase (a ten-pack for $2.99) than following a two-item reduction in unit volume (an eight-pack for $2.49), even though on a per-item base, the eight-pack is more expensive than the ten-pack.

- *Price-tier effects.* People tend to encode prices in tiers, such that an item priced at $1.99 is typically encoded into "$1+" price tier, whereas an item priced at $2.00 is typically classified into "$2+" price tier. This tiered price encoding leads to the somewhat paradoxical perception that the difference between items priced at $1.99 and $2.00 is one dollar rather than one cent.

- *Price-ending effects.* In many cases, prices ending in "9" tend to create the perception of a discount, whereas prices ending on "0" tend to create perception of quality.

Pricing Dynamics

Price is one of the more dynamic marketing mix variables. Indeed, changing the price, either directly or by offering price incentives, is often much easier to conceive and implement than changing the product and service characteristics of the offering or repositioning its brand. As a result, competition typically occurs in the domain of pricing. Because companies increasingly rely on monetary incentives as a tool for managing the dynamic aspect of pricing, the following discussion examines the joint impact of price and monetary incentives. In particular, the focus is on two key aspects of price dynamics: the impact of price changes on customer demand and the use of pricing as a competitive tool. These two aspects of price dynamics are discussed in more detail in the following sections.

Customer Reaction to Changes in Price

In most cases, because sales volume is a function of price, the company has to determine the price level at which it is most likely to achieve its goals. Typically, sales volume is inversely related to price: Lowering the price results in an increase in the sales volume, and vice versa. The impact of changes in price on sales volume is a function of customers' price sensitivity. Lowering the price to increase volume is most effective in cases where demand is elastic, meaning that a small change in price leads to a large change in sales volume. In contrast, in cases where demand is inelastic, profits may be increased by raising the price since the decrease in sales volume resulting from the change in price is likely to be relatively small.

The price–quantity relationship is quantified through an offering's price elasticity. Price elasticity represents the percentage change in quantity sold ($\Delta Q\%$) relative to the percentage change in price ($\Delta P\%$) for a given product or service. Because the quantity demanded decreases when the price increases, this ratio is negative; however, for practical purposes, the absolute value of the ratio is used, and price elasticity is often reported as a positive number.

$$E_p = \frac{\Delta Q\%}{\Delta P\%} = \frac{\Delta Q \cdot P}{\Delta P \cdot Q}$$

To illustrate, price elasticity of –2 means that a 5% price increase will result in a 10% decrease in the quantity sold. In cases where price elasticity is greater than one ($|E_p| > 1$), demand is said to be elastic in the sense that a change in price causes an even larger change in quantity demanded. In contrast, when price elasticity is less than one ($|E_p| < 1$), demand is said to be inelastic, meaning that a change in price results in a smaller change in quantity demanded. When price elasticity is equal to one ($|E_p| = 1$), demand is said to be unitary, meaning that a change in price results in an equal change in quantity demanded.

Because price elasticity reflects proportional changes, it does not depend on the units in which the price and quantity are expressed. Note also that because price elasticity is a function of the initial values, the same absolute changes in price can lead to different price elasticity values. For example, the impact of lowering the price by five cents will vary based on the initial price: it is 5% of an initial price of $1.00 but only 1% of an initial price of $5.00.

Competitive Reaction to Price Dynamics: Managing Price Wars

Price wars do not necessarily involve direct price reductions on the part of manufacturers. They may be a result of a change in different aspects of an offering's value proposition to customers and/or collaborators. To illustrate, an increase in a manufacturer's incentives (e.g., volume discounts and allowances) may prompt retailers to lower the offering's prices, thus provoking a price war. Because price wars often stem from a change in the value proposition of a particular offering, it is also possible that a price war may be caused by increasing the level of benefits while holding price constant. In this case, to preserve their market share, competitors may decide to lower their prices rather than match the increased level of benefits, thus initiating a price war.

In most cases, price wars start when a company is willing to sacrifice margins to gain market share. Not every price cut, however, leads to a price war. Price wars are more likely to occur in the following cases:

- Offerings are undifferentiated and can be easily substituted.

- Significant economies of scale can be achieved by increasing volume.

- Markets are mature, and to grow sales, a company has to steal share from its direct competitors.

- Customers' price sensitivity is high and switching costs are low.

Price cuts, the forerunner of price wars, are popular among managers for several reasons:

- Price cuts are easy to implement and typically produce fast results.

- Price cuts are an effective tool to increase sales volume. Thus, even though most price cuts ultimately result in loss of profits, companies focused on sales volume can achieve their sales-volume goals by lowering price.

- Unlike most of the other marketing mix variables, changes in price can be easily reversed or further modified based on market response.

- Lowering the price to match or beat a competitor's price is consistent with the competitive-focus mentality among many managers who focus on competitors' behavior instead of on developing strategies to better serve the needs of their customers in a way that is profitable to the company.

Price wars are easy to initiate but costly to win. Indeed, winning a price war often comes at the expense of significant loss of profits, making it more of a Pyrrhic victory than a true success. Price wars are detrimental to a company's profitability for several reasons:

- Price reductions have an exponential impact on profitability. To illustrate, reducing the price of an offering with a 10% profit margin by 1% will result in a 10% decrease in operating income unless there is a significant increase in sales volume.

- Because in most cases price reductions can be easily implemented by the key competitors, they rarely lead to a sustainable competitive advantage. Firms with similar cost structures can quickly lower their prices in response to a competitor's action.

- Price wars often result in a shift in customers' future price expectations, such that the lowered prices become the reference points against which all future prices are judged.

- Emphasis on price tends to erode brand strength. This effect is exacerbated by the heavy price-focused communication campaigns that tend to accompany most price wars. Indeed, to justify lowering the price of an offering, a company needs to promote the low price so that the lost profits resulting from the decrease in price can be offset by the incremental profits achieved by generating new sales.

Price wars rarely enable companies to achieve their strategic goals, and in most cases, the only true beneficiaries of a price war are the companies' customers. Quite often, the best strategy for a company to win a potential price war is to avoid it.

Even if a company is not seeking a price war, it may end up being confronted with a scenario in which a competitor initiates a price cut. There are many strategies to handle such situations. A three-step approach for developing a strategic response to a competitor's price cut is outlined below.

The first step is to verify the validity of the threat of a price war. Price wars are often caused by miscommunication of pricing information or misinterpretation of a competitor's strategic goals. Thus, when competitive prices are not readily available (e.g., in contract bidding), a company may perceive that a particular competitor has significantly lowered its price without this actually being the case. It is also possible that a competitor's price decrease is driven by internal factors (e.g., clearing the inventory prior to introducing a new model) rather than by an intention to initiate a price war.

The second step involves identifying customers most likely to be affected by competitors' price cuts and prioritizing these customers based on their value to the company and their price sensitivity. Thus, based on their value to the company and price sensitivity, customers may be classified into one of four categories: high-value/loyal customers, high-value/price-sensitive customers, low-value/loyal customers, and low-value/price-sensitive customers (Figure 3). Identifying which of these customers are likely to be affected by a competitor's price cut and the impact of this price cut on a company's profitability aids the development of a segment-specific response strategy.

Figure 3. Customer Loyalty Matrix

The third step involves developing segment-specific strategies to address the competitive threat. There are three basic strategies to respond to a potential price war: (1) doing nothing, (2) repositioning its existing offering (e.g., by increasing benefits and/or decreasing costs), and (3) adding new offerings.

- *Doing nothing.* The decision to ignore a competitor's price cut reflects a company's belief that the price cut will not have a significant impact on the company's market position, that the price cut is not sustainable and will dissipate by itself, or that serving the customer segment targeted by the price cut is no longer viable (e.g., low-value, price-sensitive customers).

- *Repositioning the existing offering.* The most common practice (although not necessarily the best) of responding to a competitor's price cut is a corresponding price reduction. This reduction in price can be accomplished either on a permanent basis by lowering the actual price or as a temporary solution by offering price incentives (e.g., discounts, coupons, and rebates).

- *Adding new offerings.* A common response to low-priced competitors involves launching a downscale extension, commonly referred to as a fighting brand. Using a fighting brand enables the company to compete for price-sensitive customers without discounting its premium offering. Alternative strategies for responding to low-priced competitors are discussed in more detail in Chapter 21.

Summary

The key to determining the optimal price is to consider its implications on an offering's value to customers, collaborators, and the company in a broad context that involves all other aspects of the company's strategy and tactics. Setting the price is really a decision about value, not just price. Thus, the optimal price is one that, in combination with the other marketing mix variables (product, service, brand, incentives, communication, and distribution), delivers superior value to target customers, the company, and collaborators.

Managing price involves two types of decisions: (1) strategic decisions, which are a function of the offering's target market defined by the 5-C framework (customers, company, collaborators, competition, and context), and (2) tactical decisions, which are a function of the other marketing mix variables (product, service, brand, incentives, communication, and distribution).

Successful pricing strategies take into account that people do not always perceive pricing information objectively; instead, price perception is often a function of a variety of psychological effects such as reference-price effects, price–quantity effects, price-tier effects, and price-ending effects.

Competing on price often results in price wars, which typically start when companies are willing to sacrifice margins to gain market share. Price wars are likely to occur in the following cases: when offerings are undifferentiated, when capacity utilization is low, when significant economies of scale can be achieved by increasing volume, when markets are mature and a company has to steal share from its direct competitors to grow sales, and when customers' price sensitivity is high and switching costs are low. An effective approach for developing a strategic response to a competitor's price cut involves the following three steps: (1) verifying the validity of the threat of a price war, (2) prioritizing customers that are most likely to be affected by the competitors' price cut based on their value to the company and price sensitivity, and (3) developing segment-specific strategies to address the competitive threat (i.e., do nothing, repositioning the existing offering, and/or adding new offerings).

Relevant Concepts

Captive Pricing: See *complementary pricing*.

Complementary Pricing: Pricing strategy applicable to uniquely compatible, multipart offerings, whereby a company charges a low (relative to its cost) introductory price on the first part and higher prices for the other parts. Classic examples include razors and blades, printers and cartridges, and cell phones and cell phone service. The unique compatibility is crucial to the success of complementary pricing: Only the printer manufacturer should be able to sell cartridges that fit its printers.

Cost-Plus Pricing: A pricing method in which the final price is determined by adding a fixed markup to the cost of the product. It is easy to calculate and is commonly used in industries where profit margins are relatively stable. Its key drawback is that it does not take into account customer demand and competitive pricing.

Cross-Price Elasticity: The percentage change in quantity sold of a given offering caused by a percentage change in the price of another offering.

Deceptive Pricing: The practice of presenting an offering's price to the buyer in a way that is deliberately misleading. Deceptive pricing is illegal in the United States.

Everyday Low Pricing (EDLP): Pricing strategy in which a retailer maintains low prices without frequent price promotions.

Experience Curve Pricing: Pricing strategy based on an anticipated future lower cost structure resulting from scale economies and experience curve effects.

High-Low Pricing: Pricing strategy in which a retailer's prices fluctuate over time, typically a result of heavy reliance on sales promotions.

Horizontal Price Fixing: A practice in which competitors explicitly or implicitly collaborate to set prices. Price fixing is illegal in the United States.

Image Pricing: See *price signaling*.

Loss Leadership: Pricing strategy that involves setting a low price (often at or below cost) in an attempt to increase the sales of other products and services (e.g., a retailer sets a low price for a popular item in an attempt to build store traffic, thus increasing the sales of other, more profitable items).

Penetration Pricing: Pricing strategy aimed at rapidly gaining market share. This strategy often leads to higher sales volume, albeit at lower margins.

Predatory Pricing: A strategy that involves selling below cost with the intent of driving competitors out of business. In most cases, predatory pricing is illegal in the United States.

Prestige Pricing: Pricing strategy whereby the price is set at a relatively high level for the purpose of creating an exclusive image of the offering.

Price Discrimination: A strategy that involves charging different buyers different prices for goods of equal grade and quality.

Price Fixing: A practice in which companies conspire to set prices for a given product and/or service. Price fixing is illegal in the United States.

Price Segmentation: See *price discrimination*.

Price Signaling: (1) Pricing strategy that aims to capitalize on price-quality inferences (i.e., higher priced products are also likely to be higher quality). Primarily used when the actual product benefits are not readily observable (also known as prestige pricing); (2) Indirect communication (direct price collusion is prohibited by law) between companies, aimed at indicating their intentions with respect to their pricing strategy.

Price Skimming: Pricing strategy in which a firm sets a high initial price to maximize profit margins, usually at the expense of market share.

Product-Line Pricing: Pricing strategy in which the price of each individual offering is determined as a function of the offering's place in the relevant product line (e.g., the price of BMW's 3-series models is a function of the prices of its 5- and 7-series models).

Second Market Discounting: Pricing strategy in which a company charges a lower price for the products/services it offers in more competitive markets (e.g., exports for developing countries).

Two-Part Pricing: See *complementary pricing.*

Vertical Price Fixing: The practice whereby channel partners (e.g., a manufacturer and a retailer) explicitly or implicitly collaborate to set prices. Price fixing is illegal in the United States.

Yield-Management Pricing: Pricing strategy whereby the price is set to maximize revenue for a set amount of capacity at a given time (typically used by airlines and hotels).

Additional Readings

Baker, Ronald J. (2006), *Pricing on Purpose: Creating and Capturing Value.* Hoboken, NJ: John Wiley & Sons.

Marn, Michael V., Eric V. Roegner, and Craig C. Zawada (2004), *The Price Advantage.* Hoboken, NJ: John Wiley & Sons.

Nagle, Thomas T. and John E. Hogan (2006), *The Strategy and Tactics of Pricing: A Guide to Growing More Profitably* (4th ed.). Upper Saddle River, NJ: Pearson/Prentice Hall.

——————————— **Chapter Eighteen** ———————————

Managing Incentives

But wait, there's more!
Ron Popeil, inventor and infomercial salesman

Incentives offer solutions, typically short-term, aimed at enhancing the value of the offering by providing additional benefits and/or reducing costs. Because they typically lead to an increase in sales volume, incentives are often referred to as sales promotions. The key aspects of managing incentives are the focus of this chapter.

Overview

Most incentives fall into one of three categories: incentives given to customers (e.g., coupons, loyalty programs, sweepstakes, contests, and premiums), incentives given to the company's collaborators, most often channel partners (e.g., price cuts, volume discounts, allowances, and co-op advertising), and incentives given to the company's employees (e.g., bonuses, rewards, and contests).

Incentives can be further divided into two categories: monetary, such as volume discounts, price reductions, coupons, and rebates; and nonmonetary, such as premiums, contests, and rewards. In contrast to monetary incentives, which typically aim to reduce an offering's costs, nonmonetary incentives often aim to enhance the offering's benefits. The most popular incentives, organized by their target (customers, collaborators, and company) and type (price and nonprice), are given in Table 1.

Table 1. Incentive Types

	Price incentives	Nonprice incentives
Customer incentives	Coupons, rebates, price reductions, volume discounts	Premiums, rewards, sweepstakes
Collaborator incentives	Advertising, slotting, stocking, display, and market-development allowances; spiffs; volume discounts; volume rebates; off-invoice incentives	Contests, bonus merchandise, buy-back guarantees, sales support and training
Company incentives	Performance bonuses, monetary prizes, spiffs	Contests, recognition awards, free goods, vacation and travel incentives

Deciding on the optimal mix of these various incentives can be facilitated using a systematic approach, outlined in more detail in the following sections.

A Framework for Managing Incentives

Managing incentives involves two types of decisions: (1) strategic decisions, which aim to optimize incentives as a function of the offering's target market, and (2) tactical decisions, which aim to optimize incentives as a function of the other marketing mix variables. These two types of decisions are outlined in more detail below.

Managing Incentives: Strategy

From a strategic standpoint, incentive decisions are a function of the offering's target market, defined by the 5-C framework: customers, company, collaborators, competition, and context. These five aspects of incentive analysis are illustrated in Figure 1 and outlined in more detail below.

Figure 1. Incentives Management as a Function of the Target Market

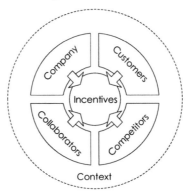

- *Customers.* An offering's incentive strategy is a function of customer factors, such as their needs, price sensitivity, and product knowledge. In general, companies are more likely to rely on incentives in cases where buyers understand the commodity nature of many products; when the relative importance of brands is declining at the expense of the importance of price; and when customers become more deal oriented and accustomed to buying only in the presence of a sales promotion.

- *Company.* An offering's incentive strategy is also influenced by the company's goal, strategic assets, and core competencies. To illustrate, the use of incentives is often driven by a company's desire to achieve certain performance benchmarks within a specified time frame (e.g., sales revenues by the end of the fiscal year). Because of their immediate impact on sales, a company can increase sales volume in a very short period, thus allowing managers to time the offering's market performance. Although not optimal from a long-term perspective, this use of incentives often results from pressure by the company's shareholders and business analysts concerned with quarterly accountability of sales-related (rather than profit-based) benchmarks.

- *Collaborators.* A company's collaborators, and in particular its channel partners, have a major impact on its incentive strategy. For example, the increased reliance on trade incentives is the result of pressure from channel partners, who are gaining power because of consolidation of many retail chains, concentrated buying, stagnant shelf space, and the growth of private labels.

- *Competitors.* Companies often offer incentives in response to pressure from competitors that use incentives as a universal offensive and defensive tool. This widespread use of incentives often contributes to the escalation of the promotional expenditures of most companies in a given market.

- *Context.* The use of incentives is also a function of context factors, such as overall economic conditions and advances in technology. Thus, adverse economic conditions can lead to greater reliance on incentives to stimulate demand. Technological advancements can facilitate the use of incentives by making the process of identifying target customers and delivering incentives to these customers more effective and cost-efficient.

Managing Incentives: Tactics

From a tactical standpoint, incentives need to be coordinated with the other marketing mix variables (i.e., product, service, brand, price, communication, and distribution). The key aspects of an offering's incentives as a function of the marketing mix are illustrated in Figure 2 and outlined in more detail below.

Figure 2. Incentives as a Function of the Marketing Mix

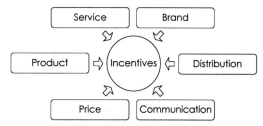

- *Product and service.* A company's use of incentives is a function of the characteristics of the product and service aspects of the offering. To illustrate, the increased standardization and commoditization of products and services resulting from technology developments and outsourcing make it more difficult to differentiate offerings based on functional benefits, which, in turn, leads to increased reliance on incentives.

- *Brand.* The use of incentives is a function of the strength of the offering's brand. Thus, a decline in a brand's strength (e.g., resulting from brand proliferation and/or commoditization of the underlying products) forces many companies to rely on incentives as a means of differentiating their offerings. In contrast, incentives are not the key differentiator for strong brands such as Apple, Lacoste, and Porsche. The nature of the brand and its elements can be also used as the basis for developing incentives (e.g., using Tony the Tiger, the cartoon character associated with Kellogg's Frosted Flakes cereal, to launch a contest, game, or sweepstakes).

- *Price.* An offering's pricing strategy plays a key role in its use of incentives. Thus, certain pricing strategies (e.g., everyday low pricing) imply limited use of incentives, whereas others (e.g., high-low pricing) heavily rely on incentives. As an integral part of an offering's pricing strategy, incentives offer greater flexibility in managing increasingly complex pricing structures.

- *Communications.* An offering's incentives are a function of its communication strategy. Thus, companies relying on direct-to-customer communications (pull strategy) are also more likely to utilize customer incentives to promote their offering to customers, whereas companies with limited or no direct-to-customer communications (push strategy) are more likely to rely on trade incentives to induce channel members to promote the offering to customers.

- *Distribution.* An offering's distribution can have an important impact on incentives as well. To illustrate, a distribution strategy that involves using consolidated, powerful channels (e.g., Albertsons, Target, and Macy's) is typically associated with greater reliance on trade incentives.

Customer Incentives

Customer incentives vary based on the entity creating and delivering the incentive. Thus, customer incentives can be created by either the manufacturer (manufacturer incentives) or the channel member (retailer incentives). Manufacturer incentives can then be delivered either directly by the manufacturer or indirectly by the retailer. In the latter case, because the incentives are created by the manufacturer and then given to retailers to distribute to target customers, they are often referred to as pass-through incentives.

Most customer incentives serve one of two goals: (1) temporarily increasing sales volume by enhancing the value of the offering, thus giving target customers additional reasons to buy the offering and (2) serving as a segmentation tool by selectively enhancing the value of the company's offering to target customers. For example, sales-focused incentives designed to stimulate sales volume within a given time frame are typically driven by company, competitor, and channel-related factors (e.g., meeting quarterly sales goals, responding to a competitor's promotion, or reducing inventory). In contrast, segment-focused incentives serve as a segmentation tool by making the offering attractive to a particular customer segment. An incentive can combine both sales-focused and segment-focused functions by selectively increasing sales from a particular segment.

Based on the type of reward, customer incentives can be divided into two groups: monetary and nonmonetary. Monetary incentives aim to reduce an offering's costs by providing customers with a monetary inducement to purchase the offering. The most common forms of *monetary* incentives are coupons, rebates, price reductions, and volume discounts.

- *Coupons* entitle the buyer to receive a price reduction for a given product or service at the time of purchase.

- *Rebates* involve cash refunds that are fulfilled after the purchase has been made.

- *Price reductions* involve straightforward price discounts that do not require any action from customers.

- *Volume discounts* involve price reduction offers conditional upon the purchase of multiple items.

The most common forms of *nonmonetary* incentives are premiums, prizes, contests, sweepstakes, games, and loyalty programs.

- *Premiums* involve bonus products or services offered for free or at deeply discounted prices as an incentive for purchasing a particular offering. Premiums can be delivered instantly with the purchase (e.g., packaged with the product) or may require the customer to send in a proof of purchase to receive the premium.

- *Prizes* offer customers the opportunity to win an award as an incentive for purchasing a particular offering. Unlike premiums, where the reward (bonus products or services) is given with every purchase, in the case of prizes, the actual reward is given to a relatively small number of participants. Prizes can be both monetary and nonmonetary.

- *Contests, sweepstakes,* and *games* involve prizes that typically require customers to submit some form of entry and are usually not contingent on customers purchasing the offering. Winners are selected by a panel of judges (e.g., in the case of contests), by drawing (e.g., in the case of sweepstakes), or by an objective criterion, such as points collected (e.g., in the case of games).

- *Loyalty programs* involve rewards related to the frequency, volume, and type of products and services purchased. Loyalty programs can be both monetary (e.g., cash-back credit cards offering a reward based on purchase volume) and nonmonetary (e.g., frequent-flyer awards).

Based on their reach (whether they are available to all customers or target a particular subset of customers), customer incentives can be organized into three categories: (1) widespread incentives, readily available to all target customers (e.g., temporary price reductions), (2) widespread conditional incentives that require a certain action on the part of potential buyers (e.g., possession of a coupon or completion of a survey), and (3) targeted incentives available to a particular subset of customers (e.g., senior citizens, students, repeat buyers, or high-volume buyers). Most conditional incentives are used as a tool for price segmentation, because price-sensitive buyers who are willing to expend time and effort to receive a discount are more likely to take advantage of the incentive.

Collaborator Incentives

The most common form of collaborator incentives are those offered to members of the distribution channel. These incentives, also referred to as trade incentives, can have multiple objectives, such as gaining distribution through a particular channel, (2) encouraging channel members to stock the offering at certain inventory levels (e.g., to avoid stock-outs or to transfer the inventory from the manufacturer to intermediaries and customers), and encouraging channel members to promote the company's offering. Similar to customer incentives, trade incentives can be divided into two main types: monetary and nonmonetary.

Monetary incentives involve payments or price discounts given as encouragement to purchase the product or as an inducement to promote the product to customers. Typical monetary incentives include the following.

- *Slotting allowance*: an incentive paid to a distributor to allocate shelf space for a new product.

- *Stocking allowance*: an incentive paid to a distributor to carry extra inventory in anticipation of an increase in demand.

- *Cooperative advertising allowance*: an incentive paid by the manufacturer to a distributor in return for featuring its offerings in a retailer's advertisements. The magnitude of the allowance can be determined as a percentage of the distributor's advertising costs or as a fixed dollar amount per unit.

- *Market-development allowance*: an incentive for achieving certain sales volume in a specific customer segment.

- *Display allowance*: an incentive paid by the manufacturer to a distributor in return for prominently displaying its products and/or services.

- *Spiffs*: incentives such as cash premiums, prizes, or additional commissions given directly to the salesperson (rather than the distributor) as a reward for selling a particular item.[1] Because they encourage the retailer's sales personnel to "push" the product to customers, spiffs are often referred to as "push money."

- *Volume discount*: price reductions determined based on purchase volume.

- *Volume rebate* (also referred to as volume bonus): an incentive paid by the manufacturer to a distributor as a reward for achieving certain purchase-volume benchmarks (e.g., selling 1,000 units per quarter).

- *Off-invoice incentive*: any temporary price discounts offered by manufacturers to distributors.

- *Cash discount*: price reductions for payments made instantly or within a short time frame.

- *Inventory financing* (also referred to as floor planning): loans provided to a distributor for acquiring manufacturers' goods.

Nonmonetary incentives involve nonmonetary inducements designed to encourage channel support for a particular offering. Typical nonmonetary incentives include the following.

- *Contests*: performance-based rewards (e.g., vacation trips, cars, and monetary compensation) given to the best achievers.

- *Bonus merchandise*: free goods offered as a reward for purchasing a particular item.

- *Buyback guarantees*: an agreement that the manufacturer will buy back from the distributor product quantities not sold within a certain time frame.

- *Sales support* and *training*: various forms of aid offered to distributors that are designed to familiarize the distributor with the offering and facilitate sales.

Company Incentives

In addition to incentives focused on target customers and collaborators, companies often develop incentives designed to motivate and reward their own personnel. Company-focused incentives typically aim to motivate employees to achieve better performance.

Company incentives commonly involve rewards for employees who meet certain performance benchmarks. Typical company incentives include performance-based awards such as contests, monetary bonuses, employee recognition awards, free goods and services, vacation and travel incentives, prizes, sweepstakes, and games. Some sales force incentives, such as spiffs, may be applied at the company level as well.

Summary

Incentives offer solutions, typically short term, aimed at enhancing the value of the offering by providing additional benefits and/or reducing costs. Most incentives fall into one of three categories: incentives given to customers (e.g., coupons, loyalty programs, sweepstakes, contests, and premiums); incentives given to the company's collaborators, most often channel partners (e.g., price cuts, volume discounts, allowances, and co-op advertising), and incentives given to the company's employees (e.g., bonuses, rewards, and contests).

Managing incentives involves two types of decisions: (1) strategic decisions, which are a function of the offering's target market defined by the 5-C framework (customers, company, collaborators, competition, and context) and (2) tactical decisions, which are a function of the other marketing mix variables (product, service, brand, price, communication, and distribution).

Most customer incentives serve one of two goals: (1) temporarily increasing sales volume by enhancing the value of the offering, thus giving target customers additional reasons to buy the offering, or (2) serving as a segmentation tool by selectively enhancing the value of the company's offering to target customers. Customer incentives can be divided into two categories: monetary incentives that typically aim to reduce an offering's costs (e.g., coupons, rebates, price reductions, and volume discounts), and nonmonetary incentives, which often aim to enhance the offering's benefits (e.g., premiums, prizes, contests, and loyalty programs).

Most collaborator incentives are offered to members of the distribution channel. Also referred to as trade incentives, they can have multiple objectives: (1) to gain distribution through a particular channel, (2) to encourage channel members to stock the offering at certain inventory levels (e.g., to avoid stock-outs or to transfer the inventory from the manufacturer to distributors), and (3) to encourage channel members to promote the company's offering. Similar to customer incentives, trade incentives can be divided into two main types: monetary incentives (e.g., discounts and allowances), and nonmonetary incentives (e.g., contests and bonus merchandise).

Relevant Concepts

Free Standing Inserts (FSI): Leaflets or coupons inserted into newspapers.

Incentives Ratio: Percentage of sales that involves an incentive relative to the company's total sales.

$$\text{Incentives ratio} = \frac{\text{Sales revenues with incentives}}{\text{Total sales revenues}}$$

Pass-through Incentives Ratio: Percentage of the incentives provided to customers by a channel member (e.g., a retailer) relative to the incentives provided to that channel member (e.g., by a manufacturer).

$$\text{Pass-through incentives ratio} = \frac{\text{Incentives provided to customers by a channel member}}{\text{Incentives provided to the channel member}}$$

Push and Pull Promotions: Based on the flow of promotions (i.e., incentives and communications) from the manufacturer to target customers, two core promotion strategies can be identified: pull and push. Pull strategy refers to the practice of creating demand for a company's offering by promoting the offering directly to end users, who in turn demand the offering from intermediaries, ultimately "pulling" the offering through the channel (Figure 3). To illustrate, the manufacturer may extensively advertise its products and services to end users and/or promote its offerings using means such as direct mail, coupons, contests, etc.

In contrast, push strategy refers to the practice of creating demand for a company's offering by incentivizing channel members, who in turn push the product downstream to end users. For example, the manufacturer may offer high margins on its products and services so that retailers have a vested interest in selling them. The manufacturer may also educate a retailer's sales force about the benefits of its offerings and provide the retailer with promotional materials, thus facilitating the sales process.

Figure 3. Pull and Push Promotion Strategies

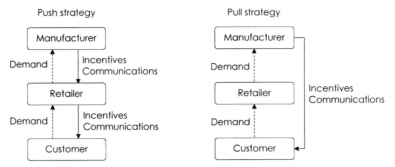

Run-of-Press Coupons: Coupons that appear in the actual pages of a newspaper (rather than being inserted as a separate page). Sometimes run-of-press coupons are part of an advertisement promoting the same offering.

Slippage: The percentage of customers who fail to redeem a promotional offer made with the purchase.

Trade Allowance: A broad range of trade incentives (e.g., slotting allowance, stocking allowance, and advertising allowance) offered as a reward for conducting promotional activities on behalf of the manufacturer. Trade allowances are typically implemented as a discount from the wholesale price rather than as a separate promotional payment. From an accounting standpoint, they are often considered as a discount to the channel rather than as a separate marketing expense.

Additional Readings

Blattberg, Robert C. and Scott A. Neslin (1990), *Sales Promotion: Concepts, Methods, and Strategies*. Englewood Cliffs, NJ: Prentice Hall.

Neslin, Scott A. (2002), *Sales Promotion*. Cambridge, MA: Marketing Science Institute.

Schultz, Don E., William A. Robinson, and Lisa Petrison (1998), *Sales Promotion Essentials* (3rd ed.). Lincolnwood, IL: NTC Business Books.

Note

[1] The origin of the term *spiff* is connected with the use of the word in the middle of the nineteenth century in reference to somebody smartly dressed (hence *to spiff up*—to improve the appearance of a place, a product, or a person). An alternative interpretation of the term *spiff* is as an acronym—Sales Promotion Incentive Fund.

—————————— Chapter Nineteen ——————————

Managing Communications

The single biggest problem in communication is the illusion that it has taken place.

George Bernard Shaw

The communication aspect of the marketing mix involves the process of informing relevant market entities about the specifics of the company's offering. The main aspects of managing communications are the focus of this chapter.

A Framework for Managing Communications

Managing communications involves two types of decisions: (1) strategic decisions, which aim to optimize communications as a function of the offering's target market, and (2) tactical decisions, which aim to optimize communications as a function of the other marketing mix variables. These two types of decisions are outlined in more detail below.

Managing Communications: Strategy

From a strategic standpoint, communications are a function of the offering's target market, defined by the 5-C framework: customers, company, collaborators, competition, and context. These five factors are illustrated in Figure 1 and outlined in more detail below.

Figure 1. Communication Management as a Function of the Target Market

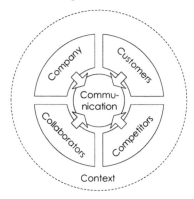

- *Customers.* An offering's communication strategy is a function of the characteristics of its target customers. To illustrate, customers' familiarity and attitudes toward the offering play an essential role in determining the goals of the communication campaign. For customers unaware of the company's offering, a key communication goal is to create awareness, whereas for customers who are already familiar with the offering, the communication campaign may focus on strengthening their preference for the offering, forming an intent to purchase the offering, and/or acting on their already formed purchase intent.

- *Company.* The nature of the communication campaign is often influenced by company-specific factors, such as the company's overall strategic goals and available resources. For instance, the scale of the communications campaign (i.e., budget) and the media selection (e.g., television, radio, print, and/or online) are often a function of the resources available to the company, as well as of its budgeting and media policies.

- *Collaborators.* An offering's communication strategy is often coordinated and sometimes even developed jointly with the company's collaborators. For example, companies collaborating in the area of product development, services, and branding often choose to develop a joint communication campaign. In addition, particular aspects of a company's communication campaign are often implemented by its collaborators (e.g., point-of-sale promotions and co-op advertising implemented by distribution channels).

- *Competitors.* Competitors' communications often have a major influence on a company's own communication strategy. To illustrate, an increase in competitive spending frequently leads to a corresponding increase in the company's own communication budget (a strategy referred to as competitive parity budgeting). In the same vein, the nature of a competitor's message can directly influence the company's own message (e.g., comparative advertising often evokes a competitive response).

- *Context.* An offering's communication campaign is also a function of the economic, technological, socio-cultural, regulatory, and physical environment in which the company operates. For instance, by enabling companies to reach their target customers in a more effective and cost-efficient manner, recent technological developments are changing the traditional media strategies in favor of targeted one-on-one communication strategies. An offering's communication campaign is also contingent on the existing regulations concerning specific products and services (e.g., tobacco, alcohol, and pharmaceuticals), as well as the use of specific communication strategies (e.g., comparative and benefit-specific claims).

Managing Communications: Tactics

From a tactical standpoint, an offering's communications need to be coordinated with the other marketing mix variables (i.e., product, service, brand, price, incentives, communication, and distribution). The main aspects of deciding on an offering's communications are illustrated in Figure 2 and outlined in more detail below.

Figure 2. Communication Management as a Function of the Marketing Mix

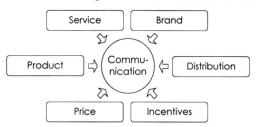

- *Product and service.* An offering's communications are a function of the nature of the attributes describing the offering. To illustrate, communications depend on the balance between the tangible and intangible characteristics of the offering. Thus, in the case of offerings with predominantly intangible characteristics (e.g., service-based offerings), communications often aim to highlight their tangible characteristics (e.g., creating tangible symbols such as the Rock of Gibraltar for Prudential). In the same vein, to better differentiate offerings with predominantly tangible attributes (e.g., product-based offerings), communications often strive to highlight their intangible characteristics (e.g., emphasizing the service, reliability, and durability aspects of the offering).

- *Brand.* Communications also depend on the identity and meaning of the offering's brand. For instance, brands with mass appeal (e.g., Coca-Cola) are more likely to rely on communications utilizing mass media, whereas non-mainstream brands appealing to a specific market segment (e.g., Harley-Davidson, Burton, and Red Bull) often rely on nontraditional communication strategies focused on user-based communities.

- *Price.* An offering's communications are also a function of its price. For example, to minimize potential price–quality inferences in the case of low-priced offerings, pricing information is sometimes communicated by distributors rather than manufacturers, so that the cause of the low price is attributed to the cost-efficiency of the distributor rather than the quality of the offering.

- *Incentives.* An offering's incentives often have a direct impact on communications. Indeed, because incentives often aim to increase revenues by generating new sales that would not have occurred in their absence (e.g., by attracting new customers or by inducing current customers to make incremental purchases), informing target customers about these incentives is a crucial factor for ensuring their success (i.e., without promoting the incentive, the only buyers who would take advantage of the incentive are those who would have purchased the offering anyway).

- *Distribution.* An offering's communications are also influenced by its distribution strategy. For example, the popularity of the self-serve retail format and the growth of online commerce has diminished the role of personal selling in favor of product-based (e.g., packaging) and in-store communication formats (e.g., flyers, promotional displays, and shelf talkers). In addition, the increasing power of retailers has resulted in a shift of the promotional budget in favor of channel-based communications and incentives rather than traditional mass media communications.

The Communication Process

Managing the communication aspect of an offering involves six key decisions: setting the goal, developing the message, selecting the media, developing the creative solution, implementing the communication campaign, and evaluating the campaign results. The key steps are illustrated in Figure 3 and are briefly outlined below.

Figure 3. Planning a Communication Campaign

```
┌─────────────────────┐
│        Goal         │
└─────────────────────┘
          ⇩
┌─────────────────────┐
│      Message        │
└─────────────────────┘
          ⇩
┌─────────────────────┐
│       Media         │
└─────────────────────┘
          ⇩
┌─────────────────────┐
│  Creative solution  │
└─────────────────────┘
          ⇩
┌─────────────────────┐
│   Implementation    │
└─────────────────────┘
          ⇩
┌─────────────────────┐
│      Control        │
└─────────────────────┘
```

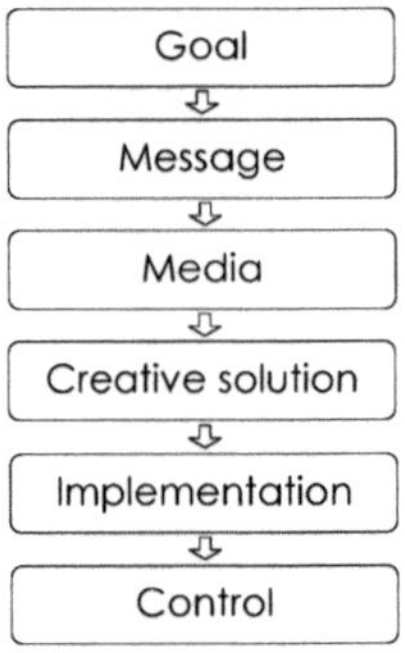

- The *goal* identifies the criteria to be achieved by the communication campaign within a given time frame.

- The *message* identifies the information to be communicated to target customers. The message can focus on one or several of the five value-design marketing mix variables: product, service, brand, price, and incentives. To illustrate, a company can choose to promote the benefits of its product and service, communicate the meaning of its brand, publicize its price, and inform customers about its current incentives.

- The *media* describes the means used by the company to convey its message. The media decision involves three aspects: budget, media type, and scheduling.

- The *creative solution* involves the execution of the company's message in a given media. Among the key aspects of the creative solution are appeal type (e.g., information-based or emotion-based) and execution style (e.g., text, format, and layout).

- The *implementation* aspect of marketing communications identifies the logistics and the timeline of executing the message, media, and creative decisions.

- The *control* aspect of marketing communications involves evaluating the success (effectiveness and cost-efficiency) of the communication campaign with respect to achieving its goals.

The key aspects of developing an advertising campaign are discussed in more detail in the following sections.

Setting a Communication Goal

Setting a goal typically involves two decisions: (1) identifying the focus of the communication campaign and (2) identifying the specific performance benchmarks to be reached.

- Identifying the *focus* of the communication campaign involves setting the ultimate criterion for success. There are three core goals, any of which can be the focus of a given communication campaign:

    - Create and/or raise *awareness* of the company's offering.

    - Create and/or strengthen buyer *preferences* for the company's offering.

    - Incite an *action* (e.g., purchasing the offering or contacting the company for information). In certain cases (e.g., when the offering is not readily available), communications may aim to create a behavioral intent (e.g., purchasing the offering) rather than incite an immediate action. For example, movie releases are often preceded by preannouncements designed to form a predisposition in target customers to view the movie when it is released.

    These goals are interdependent, such that some can be viewed as prerequisites for others. Thus, enhancing an offering's attractiveness implies that target customers are aware of its existence. Similarly, a call for action implies that customers are already aware of the offering and find it attractive.

- The *benchmark* aspect of the goal provides measurable *criteria* for success (e.g., creating awareness among 40% of a given market), as well as an identifiable *time frame* for achieving these criteria (e.g., two weeks prior to launching the new product).

Developing the Message

The message can concern any of the five value-design marketing mix variables (product, service, brand, price, and incentives), as well as the availability of the offering. For each of these marketing mix factors, the message articulates the specifics of the company's offering as follows:

- The *product- and service-related message* informs target customers of the characteristics of the company's products and services.

- *The brand-related message* focuses on the identity and the meaning of the company's or offering's brand.

- The *price-related message* communicates the offering's price.

- The *incentives-related message* depicts the incentives associated with the offering, such as temporary price reductions, volume discounts, rebates, coupons, and premiums.

- The *distribution-related message* highlights the offering's availability in distribution channels.

With respect to the strategy used to communicate the offering's value proposition, two types of messages can be distinguished: comparative and noncomparative. *Comparative messages* define the value of the offering by comparing it to a competitive offering. In contrast, *noncomparative messages* define the value of the offering in terms of its inherent ability to meet a particular customer need without necessarily comparing it to competitive offerings. In this context, the focus of comparative messages is on differentiating the company's offering and emphasizing the uniqueness, whereas the focus of noncomparative messages is on emphasizing the offering's fit with customers' needs. Furthermore, the frame of reference (i.e., how the customer should think about the offering) for the comparative message is the other offerings in the product category (e.g., product X is better than product Y), whereas in the case of noncomparative messages, the frame of reference is customer needs (e.g., product X fulfills need Z).

Selecting the Media

The media decision involves three aspects: media budget, media type, and media scheduling. These three aspects are discussed in more detail in the following sections.

Media Budget

Deciding on the magnitude of communications expenditures is one of the key decisions in planning a promotional campaign. There are several approaches to determine the total communication budget:

- The *goal-driven* approach is based on an estimate of the resources required to achieve the company's strategic goal. To illustrate, if the communication goal is to increase awareness of a company's new offering by 10% within three months, then the budget will reflect the estimated costs of achieving this goal, taking into account factors such as media costs, number of customers reached through a single exposure to the company's message per media dollar spent, and the average number of exposures necessary to create awareness.

- The *percentage-of-sales* approach implies setting the budget as a fraction of the company's sales revenues.

- The *competitive-parity* approach implies setting the budget at par with a key competitor (or a set of competitors). The approach in which the budget is set proportionally to the desired share of total media expenditures in a given category is also referred to as share-of-voice budgeting.

- The *legacy* approach implies setting the budget based on prior-year expenditures.

- The *affordability* approach implies setting the budget based on resources available for promotional activities.

While all of the above budgeting strategies have merit (some more than others), the goal-driven approach dominates the others in its ability to estimate most effectively the resources required to achieve the company's communication goals. Competitive-parity and percentage-of-sales approaches can also provide useful insights into the budgeting decision. Because they are detached from market realities, the legacy and affordability approaches are the least likely to provide an accurate budget estimate.

Media Type

Media type involves the means used by the company to convey its message. The most popular types of media include advertising, public relations, direct marketing, personal selling, event sponsorship, product-based communications, and product samples. These media types are discussed in more detail below.

- *Advertising* involves nonpersonal marketing communications in which the company/sponsor develops the message and absorbs most or all of the media costs (e.g., air time and print space). The most popular forms of advertising involve audio–visual (e.g., television, video, and film), radio, print (e.g., promotional brochures, advertisements in newspapers and magazines, and newspaper and magazine inserts), online (e.g., website advertisement), outdoor (e.g., posters and billboards), point-of-sale (e.g., front-of-the-store, end-of-aisle, and shelf-talkers— signs displayed in close proximity to the promoted item). In the United States, advertising is the most popular media type, with most of the advertising dollars spent on television commercials.

- *Public relations* involve communications by third parties that are not controlled by the company. Unlike advertising, with public relations the company does not pay for the media and does not control the content of the message; all it can do is encourage a third party (e.g., opinion leaders and press) to promote the offering (e.g., in newspaper, television, and radio coverage). Because the message comes from a third party that typically has no vested interest in the company's offering, public relations communications are often viewed as more credible than communications directly initiated by the company.

- *Direct marketing* involves individually targeted communications (e.g., catalogs, direct mail, telemarketing, and online), typically designed to elicit a direct response.

- *Personal selling* involves direct (typically face-to-face) interaction with a company representative (e.g., a salesperson).

- *Event sponsorship* involves sponsoring events and activities of interest to the offering's target customers. A form of event sponsorship is product placement, where the sponsor secures the rights to embed (place) its offering within a particular form of entertainment, such as a sports event, television show, or a movie.

- *Product-based communications* are those embedded in the product itself, such as product labels, signs, and packaging.

- *Product samples* and *free trials* enable customers to experience product benefits directly.[1] Samples and free trials are often used in new product introductions to encourage customers to try the offering. They are typically distributed via direct mail (e.g., in the case of consumer packaged goods); online (e.g., in the case of digital content products such as electronic newspapers, music samples, and movie trailers); or at the point of sale (e.g., in the case of items that can be readily consumed, such as food samples).

The allocation of resources across different media types is a function of the effectiveness and cost-efficiency of each media format with respect to its ability to communicate the desired message. For certain types of products (e.g., alcohol and tobacco), legal restrictions exist that also determine the choice of advertising medium.

In addition to deciding on the allocation of resources across different types of media, the media decision involves determining the specific media channels within each of the media types. For example, within the domain of television advertising, the media channel decision involves selecting particular shows and time slots in which the company's message will be best positioned to reach and influence its target customers. Thus, beer companies often choose to advertise during popular sport events with predominantly male audiences, whereas beauty products are typically advertised during shows with predominantly female audiences.

Media Scheduling

Deciding on media scheduling involves identifying factors such as time horizon, pattern, reach, and frequency.

- Based on the *time horizon*, media scheduling typically involves two types of planning: macro-scheduling and micro-scheduling. Macro-scheduling involves deciding on the allocation of media impact within a longer-term time frame, such as on an annual basis (e.g., in the case of seasonal products like flowers, chocolates, and champagne) or as a function of the offering's business cycle (e.g., when launching a new offering, the media impact is typically greater at the time of introduction, slowing down as the offering reaches the desired level of market penetration). In contrast, micro-scheduling involves media allocation decisions within a shorter time frame, such as a month, a week, or a day.

- Based on the *pattern*, three common scheduling formats can be distinguished: continuous, concentrated, and intermittent. Continuous scheduling (also referred to as flighting) involves allocating exposures evenly throughout the individual periods within a given time frame. Concentrated scheduling involves allocating the majority of exposures in a single period. Intermittent scheduling (also referred to as pulsing) involves alternating periods with high and low (or zero) levels of advertising (e.g., every other week). The decision on a particular timing format is a function of the characteristics of the company's offering and target customers' pattern of product adoption and usage.

- The *frequency* decision reflects the number of times target customers are exposed to a particular message over a given period. The number of exposures necessary is a function of a variety of factors, such as communication goals (e.g., creating awareness, strengthening preferences, or inciting action), the novelty of the offering's benefits, the relevance of these benefits to customers' goals, the nature of the media carrying the message (e.g., television commercial, print advertisement, or direct mail), the creative solution used to generate awareness, and the level of involvement of the target customers viewing the advertisement. In certain cases, a single exposure could be sufficient, although in most cases, multiple exposures are required to achieve communication goals.

- The *reach* decision reflects the number of target customers that are exposed to a particular message at least once in a given period. The communication reach is typically a function of the size of the target market.

Creative Solution

The creative solution involves translating the company's message into the language of the selected media format (e.g., television, print, or radio advertising). The creative solution has two main aspects: appeal type and execution style.

- *Appeal type* refers to the approach used to communicate the company's message. Most creative solutions involve at least one of two types of appeals: information-based (also referred to as cognitive) and emotion-based (also referred to as affective). Information-based appeals typically rely on methods such as factual presentations (straightforward presentation of the relevant information), demonstrations (illustration of the offering's key benefits in a staged environment), slice-of-life stories (illustration of the offering's key benefits in everyday use), and testimonials (praise by an individual based on his or her experience with the offering and endorsements by ordinary users or celebrities). In contrast, emotion-based appeals typically play on emotions such as love, romance, humor, and fear. Communication campaigns often combine informational and emotional appeals—an approach consistent with the "Think-Feel-Do" paradigm, according to which consumer actions are preceded by learning and affective evaluation of the offering.

- *Execution style* refers to the method used to translate a particular appeal into the language of the selected media format. Style decisions are media-specific. Thus, print advertising involves decisions concerning the copy text (e.g., wording of the headline and the body text), visual elements (e.g., pictures, photos, graphics, and logos), format (e.g., size and color scheme), and layout (i.e., the arrangement of different parts of the advertisement). Radio/audio advertising involves decisions concerning the text (e.g., wording of the dialogue and narration), audio (e.g., music, dialogue, and sound effects), and format (e.g., length). Television/video advertising involves decisions concerning the visual/video elements (e.g., imagery), text (e.g., wording of the dialogue, voice-over narration, and printed text), audio (e.g., music, dialogue, and sound effects), and format (e.g., length).

Implementing the Communication Campaign

The implementation of a communication campaign involves three decisions: (1) designing the infrastructure necessary for implementing the communication campaign; (2) defining the processes that enable the company to implement the message, media, and creative solutions; and (3) setting the implementation schedule.

- The *infrastructure* aspect of implementing the communication campaign involves deciding on the organizational structure of the team managing the campaign, identifying the relevant collaborators (e.g., advertising and public relations agencies), and formalizing the relationship between the company and the collaborators.

- The *processes* aspect of implementation typically involves identifying the specific actions to be taken during the following four steps: preproduction (e.g., identifying the technical aspects of the message, media, and creative solution), production (e.g., the actual filming, videotaping, recording, or printing of the advertisement), postproduction (e.g., editing, duplicating, legal compliance, and client approval), and distribution (e.g., airing, printing, and shipping).

- The *scheduling* aspect of implementation involves deciding on the timing and the optimal sequence in which individual tasks should be performed to ensure effective and cost-efficient execution of the communication campaign.

Evaluating Communication Effectiveness

John Wanamaker's famous quote, uttered nearly a century ago, "I know that half of my advertising money is wasted. I just don't know which half," succinctly reflects the current state of evaluating communication effectiveness. There is no general agreement on the part of marketers, advertising agencies, and research companies as to the best way to measure advertising effectiveness. As a result, companies use diverse criteria to measure the effectiveness of an advertising campaign. The most commonly used criteria involve measuring the following six factors: exposure, comprehension, recall, persuasion, intent, and behavior. These factors are discussed in more detail below.

- *Exposure* reflects the number of times a given advertisement has been seen by the target audience.

- *Comprehension* reflects the degree to which the target audience understands the message embedded in the advertisement.

- *Recall* reflects the degree to which the target audience remembers an advertisement. Two types of recall measures are commonly utilized: aided and unaided. In the case of aided recall, respondents are given a list of brand names following the presentation of a series of advertisements and are asked to recall whether they have seen any of these brands. In contrast, in the case of unaided recall, respondents are simply asked to recall all brands they have seen during the presentation. Overall, retention is a very popular (although not always very useful) benchmark among advertising agencies.

- *Persuasion* reflects the degree to which the advertisement is able to change the attitudes of the target audience and enhance their preference for the advertised product. Because preferences for established brands (which often are among the largest advertisers) are difficult to change with a single advertisement, many advertising agencies measure the attitude toward the advertisement (rather than the attitude toward the brand) on the premise that if the target audience likes the advertisement, then this attitude will translate into liking the brand.

- *Intent* reflects a mental disposition in the consumer to act favorably toward the offering (e.g., buy the product, visit the store, or contact the company). Intent is typically measured by asking respondents to indicate the likelihood of purchasing the product within a given time frame.

- *Behavior* reflects the impact of an advertisement on respondents' actual behavior, such as purchasing the product, inquiring about product features, and researching the product on the Internet. Behavior is typically measured by the number of sales, sales inquiries, and website visits.

A great deal of disagreement exists about which of the above measures is the most reliable indicator of the effectiveness of a given advertisement. Intuitively, it may seem that sales volume is the best measure of communication effectiveness. Unfortunately, this is not the case. The key problem with relying on customers' behavior as a measure of communication effectiveness is that, in most cases, the impact of communications is not immediate (especially in cases of brand-building communications); as a result, the impact of communications is confounded with a variety of nonrelated factors such as changes in price, incentives, competitive actions, and purchase cycle.

The decision which metric to use depends on three main factors: (1) the goal of the campaign, (2) the selected media format, and (3) the message being communicated.

- *Communication goal.* Measuring the success of a communication campaign is a function of the nature of the communication goal. Thus, if the communication goal is to create awareness (e.g., in the case of a new product introduction), then exposure, comprehension, and/or recall should be measured. If the communication goal is to strengthen preferences, then the persuasiveness of the advertisement should be measured. Finally, if the communication goal is to incite action, then behavior should be measured.

- *Media format.* Measuring the effectiveness of a communication campaign is also a function of the particular media format. Thus, in cases where the media are not directly linked to a particular performance measure, such as public relations and event sponsorship, performance tends to be gauged through indirect measures of awareness and preference. In contrast, in cases where the media are directly linked to performance measures (e.g., direct marketing, personal selling, and click-through advertising), the effectiveness of the communication campaign can be directly estimated using behavior-based measures.

- *Communication message.* Evaluating the effectiveness of a communication campaign is also a function of the nature of the message type. Unlike communicating incentives that tend to have an immediate impact on sales, building a brand has a delayed impact on sales. As a result, using sales as a benchmark of effectiveness is likely to lead to an underestimation of the impact of brand-building communications, while at the same time overestimating the role of incentive-focused communications.

Summary

Managing communications involves two types of decisions: (1) strategic decisions, which are a function of the offering's target market defined by the 5-C framework (customers, company, collaborators, competition, and context), and (2) tactical decisions, which are a function of the other marketing mix variables (product, service, brand, price, incentives, and distribution).

Managing the communication aspect of an offering involves six key decisions: setting the goal, developing the message, selecting the media, developing the creative solution, implementing the communication campaign, and evaluating the campaign results.

The *goal* identifies a set of criteria (e.g., create awareness, strengthen preferences, and incite action) to be achieved by the communication campaign within a given time frame.

The *message* identifies the information to be communicated to target customers. The message can focus on one or several of the five value-design marketing mix variables: product, service, brand, price, and incentives.

The *media* describes the means used by the company to convey its message. The media decision involves three aspects: media budget (goal-based, percentage of sales, competitive parity, legacy, and affordability), media type (advertising, public relations, personal selling, product samples, event sponsorship, and product placement), and media scheduling (time horizon, pattern, reach, and frequency).

The *creative solution* involves the execution of the company's message in a given media. Among the key aspects of the creative solution are appeal type (e.g., information-based or emotion-based) and execution style (e.g., text, format, and layout).

The *implementation* aspect of marketing communications identifies the timeline and the logistics of executing the message, media, and creative decisions.

The *control* aspect of marketing communications involves evaluating the success (effectiveness and cost-efficiency) of the communication campaign with respect to achieving its goals. The most commonly used criteria involve measuring the following five factors: exposure, comprehension, recall, persuasion, intent, and behavior.

Relevant Concepts

Above-the-Line (ATL) Communications: Company communications are often divided into two categories: Above-The-Line (ATL) communications, which encompass mass media advertising such as television commercials, radio, and print advertisements; and Below-The-Line (BTL) communications, which include public relations, event sponsorship, personal selling, and direct mail. Historically, the term ATL was used in reference to communications for which an advertising agency charged a commission to place in mass media, whereas the term BTL was used in reference to communications that involved a standard charge rather than a commission. Currently, the terms ATL and BTL are loosely used to indicate an emphasis on mass media (ATL) versus one-to-one communications (BTL). The current use of BTL often includes customer and trade incentives as well.

Advertising Allowance: A form of trade promotion in which retailers are given a discount in exchange for promoting a product in their own advertisements.

Advertising Awareness: The number of potential customers who are aware of the offering. Awareness is a function of the total volume of advertising delivery to the target audience and the number of exposures necessary to create awareness. In cases where a single exposure is sufficient to create awareness, the awareness level equals the advertising reach.

$$\text{Awareness} = \frac{\text{Advertising reach} \cdot \text{Frequency of exposure}}{\text{Number of exposures necessary to create awareness}}$$

Advertising Reach: The size of the audience that has been exposed to a particular advertisement at least once in a given period (multiple viewings by the same audience do not increase reach). Reach may be stated either as an absolute number or as a fraction of a population. For example, if 40,000 of 100,000 different households are exposed to a given commercial at least once, the reach is 40%.

Advertising Frequency: The number of times the target audience is exposed to an advertisement in a given period. Also used in reference to the number of times an advertisement is repeated through a specific medium during a specific period.

Affiliate Marketing: A communications strategy that involves revenue sharing between advertisers and online content providers. An affiliate is rewarded based on specific performance measures, such as sales, click-throughs, and registrations, or a combination of these factors.

Awareness Rate: The number of potential customers aware of the offering relative to the total number of potential customers. Depending on the manner in which it is measured, two types of awareness are commonly distinguished: aided awareness, in which respondents are provided with the name of the target offering (e.g., "Have you seen any advertisements for Coca-Cola in the past month?"), and unaided awareness, in which respondents are not provided with any offering-specific information (e.g., "Which soft drinks have you seen advertised during the past month?").

Below-the-Line (BTL) Communications: See *above-the-line communications.*

Carryover Effect in Advertising: Impact of an advertising campaign that extends beyond the time frame of the campaign. To illustrate, an advertising effort made in a given period may generate sales in subsequent periods.

Comparative Advertising: Advertising strategy whereby a given offering is directly compared with another offering.

Competitive Parity Budgeting: Budget allocation strategy based on (1) matching the competitors' absolute level of spending or (2) the proportion per point of market share.

Cooperative Advertising: Advertising strategy in which a manufacturer and a retailer jointly advertise their offering to consumers. In this case, the manufacturer pays a portion of a retailer's advertising costs in return for featuring its products, services, and brands.

Cost Per Point (CPP): Measure used to represent the cost of a communications campaign. CPP is the media cost of reaching one percent (one rating point) of a particular demographic.

$$CPP = \frac{\text{Advertising cost}}{\text{GRP}}$$

Cost Per Thousand (CPM): Measure used to represent the cost of a communications campaign. CPM is the cost of reaching 1,000 individuals or households with an advertising message in a given medium (M is the Roman numeral for 1,000). For example, a TV commercial that costs $200,000 to air and reaches 10M viewers has a CPM of $20. The popularity of CPM derives in part from its being a good comparative measure of advertising efficiency across different media (e.g., TV, print, and Internet).

$$CPM = \frac{\text{Advertising cost}}{\text{Total impressions}} \cdot 1,000$$

Gross Rating Point (GRP): A measure of the total volume of advertising delivery to the target audience. It is equal to the percent of the population reached times the frequency of exposure. To illustrate, if a given advertisement reaches 60% of the households with an average frequency of three times, then the GRP of the media is equal to 180. GRP can also be calculated by dividing the gross impressions by the size of the total audience. A single GRP represents 1% of the total audience in a given region.

$$GRP = Reach \cdot Frequency$$

Impression: A single exposure of an advertisement to one person.

Infomercial: A long-format television commercial, typically five minutes or longer.

Institutional Advertising: Advertising strategy designed to build goodwill or an image for an organization (rather than to promote specific offerings).

Integrated Marketing Communications (IMC): An approach to designing marketing communications programs that emphasizes the importance of consistency of all communication activities. In particular, this approach calls for consistency on at least three levels: strategic, tactical, and internal. *Strategic consistency* implies coordination between the different aspects of the communication campaign and the elements of the offering's overall marketing strategy. *Tactical consistency* implies coordination between communications and the other elements of the marketing mix. Thus, an offering's message should be consistent with the perceived product and service benefits, brand image, price, incentives, and distribution channel. *Internal consistency* implies that the message, media, creative solution, implementation, and control metrics evaluating the success of the campaign need to be consistent with the communication goal as well as in and of themselves. The concept of internal consistency can also be applied with respect to the different media types (e.g., advertising, public relations, and direct marketing) to ensure that they work in a coordinated fashion rather than independently of one another.

Net Promoter Score: A popular metric designed to measure customers' word of mouth about a company and/or its products.[2] The basic idea is fairly simple: A company's current and potential customers are asked to indicate the likelihood that they will recommend the company and/or its products to another person (e.g., "How likely is it that you would recommend this company to a friend or colleague?"). Responses are typically scored on a 0–10 scale, with 0 meaning extremely unlikely and 10 meaning extremely likely. Based on their responses, customers are categorized into one of three categories: promoters (those with ratings of 9 or 10), passives (those with ratings of 7 or 8), and detractors (those with ratings of 6 or lower). The net promoter score is then calculated as the difference between the percentage of a company's promoters and detractors. For example, if 40% of a company's customers are classified as promoters and 25% are classified as detractors, the company's net promoter score is 15%.

Point-of-Purchase Advertising: Promotional materials displayed at the point of purchase (e.g., in a retail store).

Public Service Announcement (PSA): Nonprofit advertising that uses free space or time donated by the media.

Reminder Advertising: Advertising strategy designed to maintain awareness and stimulate repurchase of an already established offering.

Share of Voice: A company's communications expenditures relative to those of the entire product category.

$$Share\ of\ voice = \frac{An\ offering's\ communications\ expenditures}{Product\ category's\ communications\ expenditures}$$

Target Rating Point (TRP): A measure of the total volume of advertising delivery to the target audience. TRP is similar to GRP, but its calculation involves using only the target audience (rather than the total audience watching the program) as the base. Thus, a single TRP represents 1% of the targeted viewers in any particular region.

Teaser Advertising: Communication strategy designed to create interest in an offering while providing little or no information about it.

Top-of-Mind Awareness: The first brand identified by respondents when asked to list brands in a given product category.

Wearout: A decrease in the effectiveness of a communication campaign from decreased consumer interest in the message, often resulting from repetition.

Additional Readings

Belch, George E. and Michael A. Belch (2007), *Advertising and Promotion: An Integrated Marketing Communications Perspective* (7th ed.). Boston, MA: McGraw-Hill Irwin.

Ogilvy, David (1983), *Ogilvy on Advertising* (1st American ed.). New York, NY: Crown.

Sutherland, Max and Alice K. Sylvester (2000), *Advertising and the Mind of the Consumer: What Works, What Doesn't, and Why* (2nd ed.). St. Leonards, NSW: Allen & Unwin.

Wells, William D., John Burnett, and Sandra E. Moriarty (2006), *Advertising: Principles & Practice* (7th ed.). Upper Saddle River, NJ: Pearson/Prentice Hall.

Notes

[1] Product samples are often misclassified as a form of incentive. Because product samples aim to inform customers about the benefits of the offering without influencing its value proposition, they should be viewed as a form of communication rather than as an incentive.

[2] Reichheld, Fred (2003), "The One Number You Need to Grow," *Harvard Business Review*, (December), 1-11.

Chapter Twenty

Managing Distribution

*If you make a product good enough, even though you live in the depths of the forest,
the public will make a path to your door . . . But if you want the public
in sufficient numbers, you better construct a highway.*
William Randolph Hearst, American newspaper publisher

The distribution aspect of the marketing mix involves the process of delivering a company's offering to its target customers and collaborators. The key aspects of managing distribution channels are the focus of this chapter.

A Framework for Managing Distribution

Managing distribution involves two types of decisions: (1) strategic decisions that aim to optimize distribution as a function of the offering's target market, and (2) tactical decisions that aim to optimize distribution as a function of the other marketing mix variables. These two types of decisions are outlined in more detail below.

Managing Distribution: Strategy

From a strategic standpoint, channel decisions involve analyzing five key factors: customers, company, collaborators, competition, and context. These five factors are illustrated in Figure 1 and outlined in more detail below.

Figure 1. Distribution Management as a Function of the Target Market

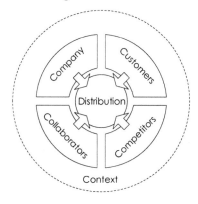

- *Customers.* An offering's distribution strategy is influenced by its target customers. Offerings pursuing a mass-marketing strategy are more likely to in-

177

volve extensive distribution through different channels and across different geographic markets, whereas offerings targeting a smaller customer base, such as niche offerings, are more likely to involve a more selective distribution strategy.

- *Company.* A company's goals, strategic assets, and core competencies have a great influence on the distribution of its offerings. To illustrate, a company seeking market share dominance is likely to utilize diverse channels for its offerings to achieve extensive distribution coverage. In the same vein, an offering's distribution strategy is influenced by the company's existing strategic assets and core competencies, such as an established distribution network and retailing expertise.

- *Collaborators.* An offering's distribution strategy reflects the company's relations with its collaborators and, in particular, its channel partners. Because indirect distribution implies collaboration with intermediaries, it is influenced by their goals, strategic assets, and core competencies. An offering's distribution strategy can be also influenced by the dynamics of the relationship between the company and its collaborators and, in particular, by the balance of power between channel partners. For example, a company may choose to shift from a single to multiple distributors to minimize the percentage of sales through an individual intermediary, thus reducing the power of any particular channel. Similarly, a company may adopt a direct distribution strategy (e.g., by opening its own retail stores) to decrease its reliance on its collaborators.

- *Competitors.* An offering's distribution strategy is also influenced by its competitors' distribution strategy. For instance, increasing competition in the traditional distribution channels has forced many companies to seek alternative distribution formats. Similarly, in the case of new offerings, the likelihood that competitors also will enter the market is a key factor in determining the coverage and speed of the distribution strategy.

- *Context.* Distribution is also a function of various economic, technological, socio-cultural, regulatory, and physical factors describing the environment in which the offering is delivered to its customers. To illustrate, the consolidation of retail outlets and the emergence of superstores and specialized retail chains in many industries have resulted in increased power of retailers with respect to the other channel members (e.g., manufacturers and wholesalers).

Managing Distribution: Tactics

From a tactical standpoint, distribution needs to be coordinated with the other marketing mix variables (i.e., product, service, brand, price, incentives, and communication). The key aspects of these decisions are illustrated in Figure 2 and outlined in more detail below.

Figure 2. Distribution Management as a Function of the Marketing Mix

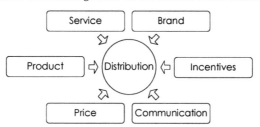

- *Product and service.* An offering's distribution strategy is a function of the characteristics of its product and service characteristics. For example, offerings predominantly defined by experience and credence attributes (characteristics that are unobservable at the time of purchase, such as reliability, durability, and consumption experience) are more likely to benefit from the endorsement of an established distribution channel than offerings predominantly characterized by search attributes (characteristics that are readily observable, such as color, size, and shape). In the same vein, novel, complex, and/or nondifferentiated products tend to benefit from being distributed through channels offering higher levels of sales support.

- *Brand.* To ensure the success of an offering, its distribution strategy needs to be consistent with its branding strategy. To illustrate, brands associated with a distinct lifestyle (e.g., Ralph Lauren, Lacoste, Apple, and Cartier) tend to benefit from employing a direct distribution model that enables the company to achieve better control over the environment in which its brand is delivered to customers.

- *Price.* An offering's distribution channel is a function of its pricing strategy. For instance, penetration pricing is typically associated with extensive distribution through multiple channels and in different geographic areas, whereas skim pricing is typically associated with limited distribution through selected channels and/or geographic areas. Similarly, the price tier of the distribution channel is typically selected based on the price tier of the offering.

- *Incentives.* The selection of a distribution channel is contingent on the offering's incentive strategy. For example, a promotional strategy that implies frequent use of incentives typically calls for channels that also frequently utilize monetary incentives (sometimes referred to as "High–Low" retailers), whereas a promotional strategy that implies limited use of monetary incentives is more consistent with an everyday low pricing (EDLP) retail strategy.

- *Communication.* An offering's distribution channel is also an important vehicle for implementing its communication strategy. The selection and design of a distribution channel is often a function of its ability to effectively communicate the offering's benefits. To illustrate, offerings relying on a "push" strategy, in which the channel is a key factor in promoting the offering to target customers, are likely to use channels that can facilitate this function (e.g., retailers with an extensive and experienced sales force).

Distribution Channel Design

The process of designing and managing distribution channels involves several pivotal decisions: channel structure, channel coordination, channel type, channel coverage, and channel exclusivity. The main aspects of these decisions are outlined in the following sections.

Channel Structure

Based on their structure, three basic types of value-delivery models can be identified: direct, indirect, and hybrid (Figure 3). These three types of distribution channels and their pros and cons are discussed in more detail below.

Figure 3. Distribution Channel Structure

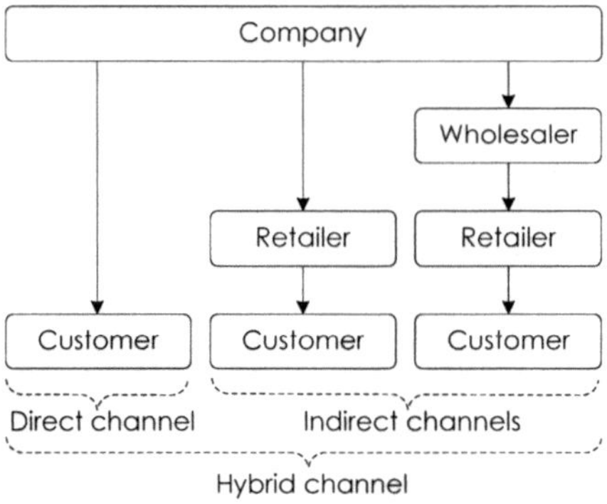

- *Direct distribution* is a business model in which the manufacturer and the end customer interact directly with each other without intermediaries.

  The direct distribution model affords multiple advantages, such as (1) a more effective distribution system resulting from better coordination of the different aspects of the value-delivery process; (2) greater cost-efficiency resulting from eliminating intermediaries; (3) greater control over the environment in which the offering is delivered to customers (level of service, product display, and availability of complementary offerings); and (4) closer contact with end users, allowing the manufacturer to have firsthand information about their needs and their reactions to its offerings.

  Despite its numerous advantages, the direct-distribution model also has a number of disadvantages: (1) establishing a direct-distribution channel, especially a brick-and-mortar one, takes time; (2) in most cases, it is difficult to achieve the same breadth of distribution outlets with direct distribution as with multiple intermediaries; (3) launching and managing a distribution channel requires a different set of strategic assets and core competencies that many manufacturers do not readily have; and (4) in most cases, direct-distribution channels require a large upfront fixed-cost investment.

- *Indirect distribution* is a business model in which the manufacturer and the end customer interact with each other through intermediaries, such as wholesalers and retailers.

The indirect distribution model has a number of advantages, such as: (1) rapid distribution that can be implemented instantly; (2) broad coverage that enables the company to reach all or the majority of its target customers; (3) greater effectiveness of the value-delivery process since manufacturers can benefit from the assets and core competencies of intermediaries; (4) potential economies of scale because intermediaries perform similar activities for a variety of manufacturers; and (5) no large upfront investment necessary because a manufacturer using intermediaries is "renting" rather than buying shelf space for its products.

Despite its advantages, the use of intermediaries in the indirect distribution model is associated with a number of disadvantages, such as: (1) a more complex channel structure could have a negative impact on the efficiency of the distribution system; (2) the possibility that intermediaries can add an extra layer of profit margins, thus increasing the total costs of the indirect distribution system; (3) loss of control over the selling environment; (4) greatly diminished ability to communicate with and collect information directly from customers; and (5) potential for vertical channel conflicts resulting from different strategic goals and profit-optimization strategies for the manufacturer and its intermediaries.

- *Hybrid distribution* is a business model in which the manufacturer and the end customer interact with each other through multiple channels, both directly and through intermediaries (e.g., wholesalers and/or retailers).

The hybrid channel has numerous advantages that stem from combining the benefits of direct and indirect distribution. At the same time, hybrid channels are also subject to many of the disadvantages of both direct and indirect channels. An additional problem with using hybrid channels is the potential for a channel conflict in cases where the both the company and its intermediaries target the same customers and aim to perform the same value-delivery function (e.g., selling an offering that will satisfy the same need of the same target customers).

Channel Coordination

Conventional marketing channels comprise independent companies (e.g., manufacturers, wholesalers, and retailers), each maximizing their own profitability. Because the profitability of the channel as a whole can be increased by coordinating the activities of each individual member, there is an increasing trend toward channel coordination. The coordination could be (1) ownership-based, in which different channel members are parts of the same company; (2) contractual, in which coordination is achieved through binding contractual agreements between channel members (e.g., between manufacturers and distributors); and (3) implicit, in which channel coordination is achieved without explicit contractual agreements. The pros and cons of these channel coordination strategies are outlined below.

- Channel coordination based on *common ownership* of channel members offers numerous potential advantages, such as: (1) better optimization of channel functions, resulting in greater effectiveness and cost-efficiency (e.g., through joint profit optimization and system integration); (2) greater degree of information sharing; and (3) better control and performance monitoring. Despite its multiple advantages, single-ownership distribution channels have a number of potential disadvantages: (1) high initial investment; (2) potential internal inefficiencies because of lack of competition; (3) lower cost-efficiency resulting from a smaller scale; and (4) the need to develop distribution channel expertise when moving from one business function (e.g., manufacturing) to another (e.g., distribution). In addition, in the case of hybrid distribution, in which some but not all channels are company owned, ownership often results in channel conflicts with independent distributors.

- Channel coordination based on *contractual relationships*—such as long-term contractual agreements, joint ventures, and franchise agreements—has several key advantages: (1) lower initial investment, (2) fast implementation, and (3) lower cost-efficiency resulting from partners' scale and/or specialization. Despite its advantages, contractual channel coordination has a number of drawbacks: (1) potential inefficiencies stemming from less coordination, (2) strategic risk of creating a potential competitor (e.g., in the case of backward integration) by sharing know-how and strategic information (e.g., pricing policies, profit margins, and cost structure), and (3) monitoring performance.

- *Implicit channel coordination* is similar to contractual coordination with the advantage of being much more flexible. This flexibility, however, comes at the cost of the inability to predict the behavior of various channel members. Another shortcoming of implicit coordination is a lower level of commitment, resulting in unwillingness to invest resources to customize the channel for a particular manufacturer. Implicit coordination is also likely to lead to lower cost-efficiency resulting from a lower degree of channel coordination.

Channel Type

Channels vary in terms of the breadth and depth of their assortments. Based on the breadth of assortment of items carried by a distributor, channels can be classified into one of two categories: specialized or broad. Specialized distributors, such as Foot Locker, Office Depot, CarMax, and Toys"R"Us, tend to carry a relatively narrow assortment. In contrast, nonspecialized distributors, such as Wal-Mart, Costco, and Carrefour, tend to carry much more extensive assortments.

Based on the depth of the item assortment carried by a distributor, channels can be classified into one of two categories: limited and extensive. Limited-assortment distributors (e.g., 7-Eleven and Circle K), carry relatively small assortments, whereas extensive-assortment distributors, such as Home Depot and Wal-Mart, carry fairly large assortments. Specialized retailers carrying an extensive assortment of items (e.g., Best Buy, Office Depot, and SportMart) are often referred to as category killers.

Channel Coverage

Channel strategies vary in the degree to which they can make an offering available to customers in a given market (e.g., the number of outlets at which offerings are made available to target customers). Extensive distribution implies that an offering is readily accessible by a fairly large proportion of customers in a given market, whereas limited distribution implies that the accessibility of the offering is fairly limited (e.g., the offering is available only through specialized retailers). The key trade-off here is between achieving high offering availability, which typically comes at a high cost and often leads to channel conflicts, and limited availability, which aims to achieve more targeted distribution at the risk of missing some potential customers.

Channel Exclusivity

Channel exclusivity refers to the degree to which an offering is made available through different distribution channels. Channel exclusivity is commonly used to reduce the potential for horizontal channel conflicts, which occur when distributors with different cost structures and profit margins sell identical offerings to the same customers. To mitigate the negative impact of a direct price comparison of the same offering across retailers, manufacturers often release channel-specific product variants in which individual offerings vary in functionality and, therefore, cannot be directly compared.

Distribution Channel Functions

Channels facilitate the value exchange between the company and its customers. Their primary function is delivering the company's offering to its target customers. In addition to its value-delivery functions, channels often take part in the process of enhancing the value of the company's offering and communicating the offering's benefits to target customers. The value-delivery, value-design, and value-communication functions of distribution channels are discussed in more detail in the following sections.

Value-Delivery Functions of a Distribution Channel

Channel functions are not limited to delivering the company's products and services to customers; they can involve all five value creation marketing mix variables: product, service, brand, price, and incentives.

- *Delivering products.* The product-delivery function involves transfer of the physical possession and ownership rights (title) of the product from the manufacturer to intermediaries (e.g., wholesales and retailers) and to end users. It can involve value-added functions such as storage, inventory management, sorting, and repackaging.

- *Delivering services.* The service-delivery function involves performing services (e.g., customization, repair, technical assistance, and warranty support) that are part of the company's offering.

- *Delivering brands.* The brand-delivery function involves enabling customers to experience the brand. To illustrate, Disney, Sony, and Harley-Davidson retail stores function as channels delivering these brands to their customers.

- *Delivering prices.* The price-delivery function involves collecting and processing payments from customers. Unlike other marketing mix variables, in the case of pricing the flow is reversed: The price is collected from customers and delivered to the company.

- *Delivering incentives.* The incentive-delivery function involves the mechanisms for distributing incentives to customers (e.g., delivering coupons, rebates, and premiums to customers), as well as the processes established to implement these incentives (e.g., implementing price reductions, processing coupons, and rebates).

In addition to delivering the offering to target customers, the functions of distribution channels also involve managing reverse flow, often referred to as reverse logistics (Figure 4). Reverse logistics can involve product-delivery (processing returns), price-delivery (processing refunds and partial credits), and incentives-delivery (collecting and processing coupons and rebates).

Figure 4. Forward and Reverse Value-Delivery Flows

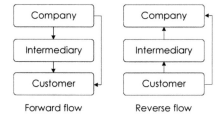

Forward flow   Reverse flow

Value-Design and Value-Communication Functions of a Distribution Channel

In addition to their value-delivery function, channels typically participate in the process of designing and communicating the value of the offering. The value-design function of distribution channels can involve products (e.g., product assembly), services (e.g., financing and extended warranty), brand (e.g., using the retail environment to enhance the meaning of the brand), price (e.g., negotiating the price to the end user), and incentives (e.g., managing channel-specific incentives). The value-communication function of distribution channels can involve products and services (e.g., explaining product and/or service benefits), brands (e.g., communicating the brand essence), price (e.g., informing customers about the offering's price), and incentives (e.g., making customers aware of the availability of an incentive). The value-communication function of channels also involves managing the reverse flow—customer feedback, suggestions, and complaints.

Summary

Managing distribution involves two types of decisions: (1) strategic decisions, which are a function of the offering's target market defined by the 5-C framework (customers, company, collaborators, competition, and context), and (2) tactical decisions, which are a function of the other marketing mix variables (product, service, brand, price, incentives, and communication).

The process of designing and managing distribution channels involves several pivotal decisions: channel structure (direct, indirect, and hybrid), channel coordination (ownership-based, contractual, and implicit), channel type (specialized vs. broad and limited vs. extensive), channel coverage (limited vs. extensive), and channel exclusivity.

Channels facilitate the value exchange between the company and its customers. Their primary function is delivering the company's offering (product, service, brand, price, and incentives) to its target customers. In addition to its value-delivery functions, channels often take part in the process of enhancing the value of the company's offering and communicating the offering benefits to target customers.

Relevant Concepts

All-Commodity Volume (ACV): A measure of an offering's availability, typically calculated as the total annual volume of the company's offering in a given geographic area relative to the total sales volume of the retailers in that geographic area across all product categories (hence, the term "all-commodity volume"). Also refers to the gross sales in a specific geographic area (i.e., total sales of all stores).

$$ACV = \frac{\text{Total sales of stores carrying the company's offering}}{\text{Total sales of all stores}}$$

Category Killers: Specialty retailers that focus on one product category, such as electronics or business supplies at very competitive prices (e.g., Best Buy, Office Depot, and PetSmart).

Contractual Vertical Marketing System: Channel structure in which the relationships between the manufacturer and the distributor are set on a contractual basis (rather than common ownership).

Corporate Vertical Marketing System: Channel structure in which the manufacturer and the distributor have common ownership rather than a contractual relationship.

Detailers: Indirect sales force promoting pharmaceuticals to doctors and pharmacists so that they, in turn, recommend the brand to the consumer.

Direct Channel: Distribution strategy in which the manufacturer and the end customer interact directly with each other without intermediaries.

Forward Buying: Increasing the channel inventory (also referred to as "channel stuffing"), usually to take advantage of a manufacturer's promotion and/or in anticipation of price increases.

Gray Market: A market in which products are sold through unauthorized channels.

Hybrid Channel: Distribution strategy in which the manufacturer and the end customer interact with each other through multiple channels (e.g., directly and through intermediaries).

Indirect Channel: Distribution strategy in which the manufacturer and the end customer interact with each other through intermediaries.

Inventory Turnover: The number of times that inventory is replenished, typically calculated as the ratio of annual revenues generated by a given offering to average inventory.

Merchandisers: Indirect sales force that offers support to retailers for in-store activities, such as shelf location, pricing, and compliance with special programs.

Parallel Importing: The practice of importing products from a country in which the price is lower into a country in which the same product is priced higher. A hypothetical example of this practice is importing drugs from Canada to the United States. In most cases, parallel importing is illegal in the United States.

Reverse Logistics: The process of reclaiming recyclable and reusable materials and returns for repair, remanufacturing, or disposal.

Same-Store Sales: A metric used in the retail industry to compare sales of stores that have been open for a year or more and have historical data to compare the current year's sales to the same time frame last year. Same-store sales is a popular metric because it takes store closings and chain expansions out of the mix, indicating the portion of new sales that resulted from sales growth and the portion that resulted from the opening or closing of new stores.

Share of Shelf Space: Shelf space allocated to a given offering relative to the total shelf space in a given geographic area.

Shrinkage: A term used by retailers to describe theft of goods by customers and employees.

Vertical Marketing Systems: Centrally coordinated distribution channel.

Additional Readings

Anderson, Erin, Anne T. Coughlan, Louis W. Stern, and Adel I. El-Ansary (2006), *Marketing Channels* (7th ed.). Upper Saddle River, NJ: Prentice Hall.

Rolnicki, Kenneth (1998), *Managing Channels of Distribution: The Marketing Executive's Complete Guide.* New York, NY: AMACOM.

Zoltners, Andris A., Prabhakant Sinha, and Sally Lorimer (2004), *Sales Force Design for Strategic Advantage.* Basingstoke, NH: Palgrave Macmillan.

Part Five

Managing Growth

Introduction

Managing growth is of primary concern to most organizations. Compared to cost-cutting—the alternative route to profitability—ensuring top-line growth is the preferred strategy to sustainable profitability. Cost-cutting measures are only a temporary means to increase profits and at some point all cost-cutting programs reach diminishing returns. In contrast, top-line growth has the potential of providing the company with a viable solution for achieving sustainable profit growth. In addition to enhancing profits, focus on growth adds vitality to organizations by providing challenges and fostering creativity.

- Ensuring sustainable growth calls for managing a company's *market position* vis-à-vis its competitors. A company's market position is determined by two main activities: gaining market share and defending its present market position. Strategies for managing these two activities are discussed in Chapter 21.

- *Managing top-line growth* involves increasing sales volume and is typically achieved through acquiring new customers and/or by increasing sales to existing customers. These two strategies for increasing sales volume—product adoptions by new customers and product usage by existing customers—are examined in Chapter 22.

- *New product development* is a universal route to ensure sustainable growth. The key issues in developing new offerings—understanding new product adoption, forecasting market demand, and designing new offerings—are the focus of Chapter 23.

- Most companies aim to grow by developing and managing a series of related offerings—or product lines—tailored to the diverse needs of their target customers. *Product line management* adds an extra level of complexity to managing individual offerings by introducing the need for coordinating their goals, strategies, tactics, implementation, and controls. The key aspects of product line management are discussed in Chapter 24.

The selection of a growth strategy is ultimately determined by the company's strategic goals, core competencies, and strategic assets, as well as by its target customers, collaborators, competitors, and the overall economic, technological, socio-cultural, regulatory, and physical context. An integrative approach to analyzing these factors is essential for the development of a successful growth strategy.

Chapter Twenty-One

Gaining and Defending Market Position

The first man gets the oyster, the second man gets the shell.
Andrew Carnegie, American industrialist and philanthropist

The constantly evolving nature of the competitive landscape calls for developing dynamic strategies to manage a company's market position. Managing market position presents companies with two perennial questions: (1) how to gain market share and (2) how to defend their current market position. These two issues and strategies to address them are the focus of this chapter.

Gaining Market Position

There are three basic strategies for a company to gain market position: (1) by stealing share from competitors already serving this market, (2) by growing the market by attracting new customers to the category, and (3) by creating new markets. These three strategies are discussed in more detail in the following sections.

Steal-Share Strategy

The steal-share strategy refers to a company's activities aimed at attracting its competitors' customers (Figure 1). A company's steal-share strategy can vary in terms of its breadth: It can either be narrowly focused on a specific subsegment of competitors' customers with well-defined needs (e.g., Pepsi targeting the younger Coke drinkers with its "new generation" campaign), or it can be broadly focused on the competitor's market as a whole (e.g., RC Cola trying to steal share from all competitors, including Coke and Pepsi). Because of its focus on attracting only those customers who are already using competitors' products, the steal-share strategy is also referred to as selective demand stimulation.

Figure 1. Steal-Share Strategy

Current users

To succeed in attracting competitors' customers, a company needs to present these customers with a compelling value proposition. In this context, there are two basic value proposition strategies: a differentiation-based strategy and a similarity-based strategy.

- *Differentiation strategy* aims to establish a single or multiple point(s) of differentiation and steal share from the competition by demonstrating the superiority of the company's offering. The differentiation may involve superior benefits (e.g., better performance) and/or lower costs (e.g., lower price).

- *Similarity strategy*, also referred to as a "me-too" strategy, aims to establish multiple points of parity and steal share from a competitor, typically the market leader, by showing that a company's and a competitor's offerings are, in fact, identical. One particular form of the "me-too" strategy is cloning, which involves emulating the incumbent's offering, usually with slight variations to avoid patent and trademark infringement liability.

Market-Growth Strategy

Unlike the steal-share strategy, which competes for customers who are currently using competitors' offerings, the market-growth strategy aims to attract customers who are new to the category (Figure 2). For example, an advertising campaign promoting the consumption of milk (e.g., the "Got milk?" campaign) builds the entire category, whereby switching occurs between substitute products (milk vs. non-milk) rather than between different brands within the same category (Brand A milk vs. Brand B milk). Because of its focus on increasing the overall category demand, the market-growth strategy is sometimes referred to as primary demand stimulation.

Figure 2. Market-Growth Strategy

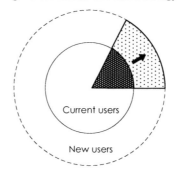

Because the market-growth strategy is aimed at growing the entire category represented by the offering, it typically benefits all companies serving that category. Because offerings often gain share proportionately to their current market position, this strategy is usually adopted in the early stages of an offering's life cycle when the overall market growth is high and competition is not a primary issue, and/or by the market leader.

A notable exception to the scenario illustrated in Figure 2 involves a case in which a company's offering has a superior value proposition relative to the competition (e.g., due to a technological breakthrough, the addition of unique product benefits, and/or price-based advantage), such that it is likely to gain a disproportionally large share (relatively to its current share) of new customers. In this case, the offering's current market share tends to be less relevant to its ability to benefit from growing the overall market, whereby a small-share offering can be as successful as the market leader. In addition to ensuring a larger share of the expanded market, the offering's competitive advantage is also likely to attract some of its competitors' current customers. Thus, even when targeting new users, offerings with a superior value proposition are likely to end up stealing share from competitors (Figure 3).

Figure 3. Market-Growth Strategy for an Offering with a Superior Value Proposition

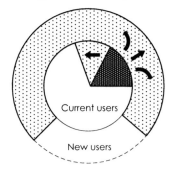

Market-Innovation Strategy

The market-innovation strategy is similar to the market-growth strategy in that that a company gains market position by attracting customers who have not used any products and services within the same category (Figure 4). The key difference is that instead of converting new customers to the existing category in which the company faces its current rivals, it defines an entirely new category in which competition is limited or absent. Because of its focus on uncontested markets, the market-innovation strategy is sometimes referred to as the Blue Ocean Strategy (described in more detail at the end of this chapter).

Figure 4. Market-Innovation Strategy

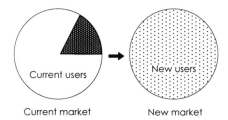

Because it targets customers that are new to the particular product category, the market-innovation strategy typically involves pioneering new markets. The main issues in market pioneering are discussed in more detail in the following section.

Pioneering New Markets

The term *pioneer* or *first-mover* is used in different contexts. A company that is first to introduce a new technology is referred to as the *technology pioneer*. A company that is first to commercially introduce a conceptually new ("new-to-the-world") product aimed at satisfying a particular customer need is referred to as a *product pioneer*. A company that is first to introduce a particular business process (e.g., supply-chain management) is referred to as a *process pioneer*. Finally, a company that is first to introduce a given offering to a particular target market is referred to as a *market pioneer*.

For the purposes of marketing analysis, the terms *pioneer* and *pioneering advantage* are used in reference to the first company to introduce its offering to a given market defined by a particular customer need. Thus, a pioneer in a market is the company that first reached a given segment with its offering. Even though, from a chronological standpoint, another company may have pioneered a product by introducing it to a different customer segment, the company that first introduced it to target customers is considered the pioneer for these customers. For example, Apple's iPod, which was introduced in United States in 2001, is typically thought of as the pioneer of portable hard drive MP3 players, even though MPMan, which used the same technology, was introduced in Asia in 1998 by the Korean company Saehan.

When pioneering new markets, a company's goal is not only to gain share but also to create a business model that cannot be copied by its current and future competitors. Thus, creating a sustainable competitive advantage is the underlying mechanism of any successful pioneering strategy. Being the pioneer in a given market offers a company several potential benefits that may be the source of a sustainable competitive advantage. The key benefits of being a market pioneer are as follows:

- By being a pioneer, a company has the unique opportunity to *shape customer preferences* and at the same time create a close association between its brand and the underlying customer need. For example, products such as Coke, Xerox, Jeep, Walkman, and TiVo not only helped shape customer preferences (e.g., in terms of flavor, functionality, and design) but also became synonymous with the entire category.

- By being a pioneer, a company has the opportunity to build loyalty by creating *switching costs* for its customers. These switching costs could be functional (e.g., loss of the unique benefits of the pioneer's offering), monetary (e.g., the cost of replacing proprietary equipment or a penalty for breaking a contract), or psychological (e.g., the cost of learning the functionality of a competitor's offering).

- The pioneer can benefit from *preempting scarce resources* such as raw materials, human resources, geographical locations, and collaborator networks. Thus, the pioneer may be able to lock out the competition by securing exclusive access to strategically important mineral resources. Similarly, the pioneer may preempt competitors' access to a particular human resource in short supply, such as engineers, designers, and managers. The pioneer may also preempt strategically important geographic locations in both real space (e.g., Starbucks and Wal-Mart) and cyberspace (e.g., flowers.com, drugstore.com, and buy.com). Finally, the pioneer can preempt the competition by forging collaborator alliances with strategically important partners, such as distributors or advertisers. For example, sporting goods manufacturers offer exclusive long-term contracts to promising athletes early in their careers when they believe that these athletes are likely to become strategic assets, differentiating these companies from the competition.

- The pioneer can create *technological barriers to entry* to prevent competitors from entering the market. For example, the pioneer may secure the exclusive rights to use a particular invention or design that is essential for developing offerings that will successfully address a specific customer need. Being the pioneer also enables a company to establish a proprietary technological standard (e.g., operating system, communication protocol, and video compression) that ensures the sustainability of the incumbent's technological advantage in the marketplace.

- The pioneer often benefits from *learning curve advantages,* whereby its production effectiveness and efficiency increase as its cumulative output increases over time. Simply put, being in business longer than its competitors often gives the pioneer a competitive edge in technological know-how, level of workforce experience, and production efficiency.

Being a pioneer, however, does not always lead to a sustainable competitive advantage. In fact, pioneers face a distinct set of disadvantages that may actually impede rather than facilitate their strategy.

- *Free riding* is one of the key problems facing the pioneer. A later entrant may be able to free ride on the pioneer's resources, including its investments in technology, product design, customer education, regulatory approval, infrastructure development, and human resource development. To illustrate, after spending millions of dollars to develop the technology and educate the American audience about the advantages of a personal digital recorder, TiVo found itself in competition with cable and satellite operators selling similar services to its already educated target customers. Alternatively, a follower could reverse-engineer the pioneer's product and improve upon it, while investing only a fraction of the resources required to develop the original product. Federal Express built on DHL's idea to start overnight deliveries in the United States. IBM launched its PC, building on the earlier product introductions from Apple and Atari. Best Buy launched a rapid expansion of superstores based on the success of the Circuit City model.

- *Incumbent inertia* is another very important, yet often overlooked, source of competitive disadvantage. Being a market leader often leads to a feeling of complacency, thus leaving technological and market opportunities open to competitors. To illustrate, IBM's reliance on mainframes, even when mainframes were being replaced by networked computers, enabled competitors such as Dell and Hewlett-Packard to gain a foothold in IBM's markets and steal some of its most valuable clients. Incumbent inertia may also be driven by a reluctance to cannibalize existing product lines by adapting a new technology or a new business model. For example, brick-and-mortar booksellers, such as Barnes & Noble and Borders, failed to recognize the importance of e-commerce, allowing Amazon.com to establish a dominant presence in online book retailing. Incumbent inertia may also be a result of a "sunk-cost mentality," whereby managers feel compelled to utilize their large investments in extant technology or markets, even when technological advancements and/or market forces make these investments unfeasible. For example, one of the reasons Ford lost its leading market position to General Motors in the 1930s was its reluctance to make the necessary investments to modify existing manufacturing facilities to diversify its product line.

- Another potential disadvantage in being a pioneer is the *uncertainty* associated with the offering. Indeed, whereas the pioneer has to deal with the uncertainty surrounding the technology and market demand, a follower can learn from the pioneer's successes and failures and design a superior offering. Because of the uncertainty associated with the introduction of a new offering, companies with strong brands and distribution capabilities often choose to be late market entrants, which enables them to learn from the pioneer's experience and develop an effective and cost-efficient market entry strategy. These companies use their brand and channel power to manage the risk associated with new product development and new market entry, allowing them to be successful late entrants into a given market. To illustrate, the first sugar-free soft drink was introduced in the United States by Cott in 1947, and the first sugar-free cola was introduced by Royal Crown in 1962, only to be overtaken by Coke and Pepsi, which used their branding and distribution power to dominate the consumer soft drink market.

Defending Market Position

Because business success inevitably attracts competition, a company needs to develop strategies to defend its market position. There are three basic ways in which a company can react to a competitor's actions: (1) by doing nothing, (2) by repositioning its existing offering (e.g., by increasing benefits and/or decreasing costs), and (3) by adding a new offering(s). These strategies are illustrated in Figure 5 and discussed in more detail in the following sections.

Figure 5. Defensive Marketing Strategies[1]

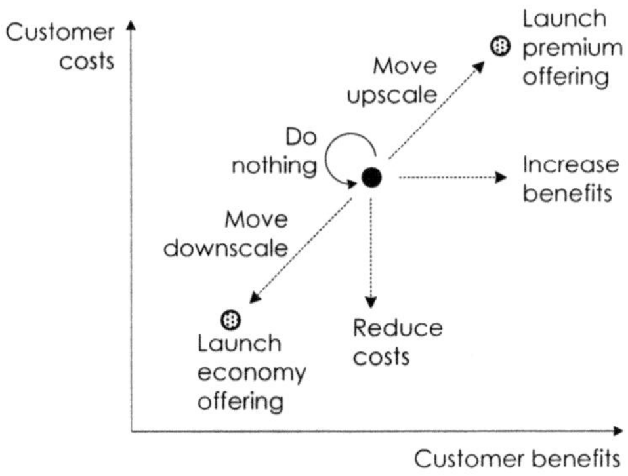

Doing Nothing

The decision to ignore a competitor's action(s) reflects a company's belief either that these actions will have no material impact on the company's market position or that the competitive threat is not sustainable and will dissipate by itself. For example, a company may decide that its upscale offering will not be affected by the entry of a low-price, low-quality competitor and therefore not consider this action a direct threat. In the same vein, a company may not react to a competitor's price reduction if it believes that this low-price position is not sustainable in the longer term.

Repositioning the Existing Offering

A company may choose to reposition its offering in one of two ways. It may change the offering's value proposition to become more attractive to the company's current customers or, alternatively, it may reposition the offering to make it appealing to a different customer segment.

- *Enhancing the offering's value to current customers.* Because value is a function of benefits and costs, enhancing the value of an offering may be achieved by two basic strategies: increasing benefits and decreasing costs. These two strategies are outlined in more detail below.

  - *Increasing an offering's benefits.* To enhance the customer benefits of its offering, a company may choose to adopt one of the following three strategies: (1) enhance the functional benefits of its offering (e.g., by improving the offering's performance), (2) increase its monetary benefits (e.g., by adding monetary rewards), and/or (3) increase its psychological benefits (e.g., by enhancing the offering's image). For each of these strategies to succeed, the increase in benefits must actually be perceived as such by customers. Improving the offering's performance on attributes that do not create readily observable customer value will most likely not enhance its customer value.

  - *Decreasing an offering's costs.* As in the case of increasing benefits, decreasing an offering's costs can be achieved by decreasing its functional, monetary, and psychological costs. Because the price of an offering is typically the most important component of customers' costs, price reduction is the most common form of cost decrease. Based on the endurance of price reductions (i.e., whether they are permanent or temporary) and their reach (i.e., whether they are available to all customers or target a particular subset of customers), four types of price reductions can be identified: (1) widespread price cuts in which the price of an offering is permanently reduced; (2) targeted price cuts in which the price of an offering is permanently reduced only to a select group of customers (e.g., senior citizens, repeat customers, or high-volume buyers); (3) widespread price incentives (e.g., temporary price reductions); and (4) targeted price incentives (e.g., selective discounts, coupons, and rebates). These four price-reduction strategies can be summarized in a 2×2 matrix, as shown in Figure 6.

Figure 6. Strategies for Lowering an Offering's Monetary Costs

- *Repositioning the offering to attract new customers.* In addition to increasing an offering's value to existing customers, a company may decide to reposition its offering to better address the needs of target customers. Repositioning implies

a change in the value proposition of a given offering and typically involves one of two distinct strategies: vertical or horizontal.

-   *Vertical repositioning* refers to a scenario in which a company modifies the value proposition of an offering by moving it into a different price tier (and typically modifying its benefits). There are two general vertical repositioning strategies: upscale and downscale. In the case of an upscale repositioning, the company increases the price of an offering while at the same time enhancing its benefits. In contrast, in the case of a downscale repositioning, the company decreases an offering's price while at the same time decreasing its benefits.

-   *Horizontal repositioning* refers to a scenario in which a company modifies the value proposition of an offering by altering its benefits without necessarily moving it to a different price tier. To illustrate, in an attempt to break away from the traditional association of prunes as a means to regularity for the elderly and make them appealing to younger customers, California prune manufacturers began marketing prunes as "dried plums," highlighting their high level of antioxidants.

Extending the Product Line

In addition to repositioning its existing offering(s), a company can respond to competitive actions by extending its product line. Conceptually, product line extension is similar to repositioning, with the key distinction that instead of modifying the value proposition of an existing offering, the company launches a new offering with a different value proposition. In this context, there are two common product line extension strategies used to fight low-price rivals: vertical and horizontal.

*   *Vertical extensions* are new offerings differentiated by both benefits and price (e.g., an economy car vs. a luxury car). A company can use both upscale and downscale extensions to defend its market position. One popular strategy to fight low-price rivals involves launching a *fighting brand*—a downscale offering introduced to shield the core offering from low-priced competitors. A slightly more complex approach to dealing with low-priced competitors is the sandwich strategy, which involves both the introduction of a downscale offering and upscale repositioning of the core brand. A third commonly used approach to deal with low-priced rivals is the good-better-best strategy, which involves introducing both an upscale and a downscale offering, resulting in a three-tier product line. The fighting brand strategy, the sandwich strategy, and the good-better-best strategy are discussed in more detail at the end of this chapter.

*   *Horizontal extensions* are new offerings that are differentiated primarily by performance/functionality and not necessarily by price (e.g., a sedan vs. a minivan). As product categories mature, their user base becomes more diverse, calling for specialized offerings customized to the needs of different customer segments. In this context, a market leader might preempt the competition by extending its product line with offerings tailored to each strategically important customer segment.

A more detailed discussion on managing product lines and product line extensions is offered in Chapter 24.

Summary

The constantly evolving nature of the competitive landscape calls for developing dynamic strategies to manage a company's market position. Managing market position presents companies with two perennial questions: (1) how to gain market share and (2) how to defend their current market position.

There are three basic strategies for a company to gain market position: (1) by stealing share from competitors serving this market (steal-share strategy), (2) by growing the market by attracting new customers to the category (market-growth strategy), and (3) by creating new markets (market-innovation strategy).

Gaining market position often involves pioneering new markets. The key benefits of market pioneering involve the opportunity to shape customer preferences, creating switching costs, preempting scarce resources, creating technological barriers to entry, and reaping learning curve benefits. The key drawbacks of being a pioneer involve free riding, incumbent inertia, and the uncertainty associated with the offering's technology and with customer demand.

Because business success inevitably attracts competition, a company needs to develop strategies to defend its market position. There are three basic ways in which a company can react to a competitor's actions: (1) by doing nothing, (2) by repositioning its existing offering (e.g., by increasing benefits, decreasing costs, and moving upscale or downscale), and (3) by adding a new offering(s) to its product line.

Relevant Concepts: The Blue Ocean Strategy

The Blue Ocean Strategy[2] posits that instead of competing in overcrowded existing markets (red oceans) and trying to steal share from direct competitors, a company should focus its efforts on uncovering new, uncontested markets (blue oceans). Examples used to illustrate this strategy include the Ford Model T (affordable mass-produced car), Apple (all-in-one, user-friendly personal computer), Dell (built-to-order value-priced computers), and Cirque du Soleil (a new form of entertainment combining elements from circus and theater).

The Blue Ocean Strategy can be related to the concept of product life cycle, according to which maturing markets are more competitive and, hence, less profitable (see Chapter 23 for mode detail). In the same vein, the Blue Ocean Strategy argues that mature markets are "red oceans" that should be avoided and priority given to the search for the "blue oceans"—new markets that a company can shape and in which it can be the dominant player.

According to this strategy, technology innovation is most often not the key driver in discovering uncontested markets; instead it is the company's ability to find an innovative way of creating value for target customers that determines its success in discovering "blue oceans." Thus, the Blue Ocean Strategy implies business model innovation rather than imitation.

The Blue Ocean Strategy further asserts that the competition should never be used as a benchmark in strategic planning. Instead of focusing on the competition, the company should focus on creating value for its target customers in a way that benefits the company itself. With its focus on optimizing value for target customers and the company, the Blue Ocean Strategy is consistent with the 3-V framework advanced in this book.

The Blue Ocean Strategy is a fairly general concept that provides the company with overall guidance in its strategic planning activities. The notion of creating new markets and making the competition irrelevant intuitively appeals to most managers—a factor contributing to the popularity of the Blue Ocean Strategy.

Relevant Concepts: The Fighting Brand Strategy

A popular strategy to compete with low-priced rivals involves launching a fighting brand—an offering that matches or even undercuts the competitor's price (Figure 7). For example, to compete with low-price rivals while preserving the market position of its flagship Marlboro brand, Philip Morris aggressively priced its Basic cigarette label, effectively making it a fighting brand. Similarly, Procter & Gamble launched the low-priced Oxydol laundry detergent to complement its flagship brand Tide.

Figure 7. The Fighting-Brand Strategy

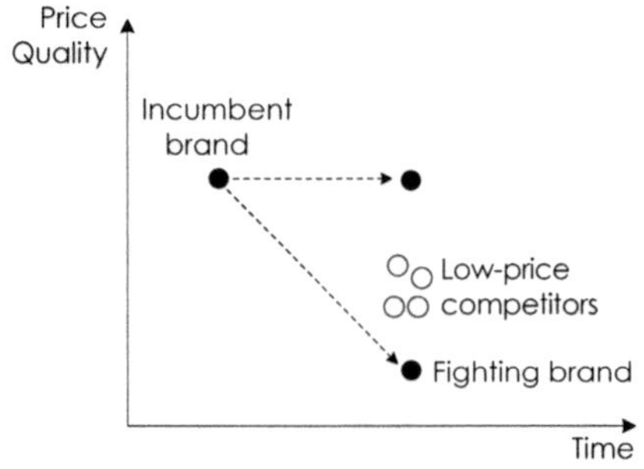

Essential to the fighting brand strategy is the notion that the offering's buyers have diverse (heterogeneous) preferences that cannot be successfully addressed by simply repositioning the existing offering (e.g., by lowering price). This strategy further assumes a two-tiered market comprised of buyers who are quality-focused and buyers who are more price sensitive.

Relevant Concepts: The Sandwich Strategy

The simplest form of the sandwich strategy involves introducing a two-tier product line comprising a high-quality and a low-price offering, effectively sandwiching low-price competitors.[3] This strategy is typically achieved by introducing a downscale extension while simultaneously moving the existing offering upscale (Figure 8). For example, in the anticipation of an inflow of cut-price competitors following the patent expiration of its blockbuster prescription drug Prilosec, AstraZeneca launched a low-priced, over-the-counter version (Prilosec OTC), and at the same time replaced Prilosec with Nexium—a premium-priced and slightly more effective version of the drug.

Figure 8. The Sandwich Strategy

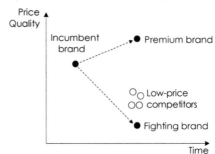

The sandwich strategy in many respects resembles a *fighting-brand* strategy in which the market leader introduces its own low-priced (fighting) brand. Despite their similarities, the sandwich strategy differs from the fighting-brand strategy in that in addition to the introduction of a downscale offering it also involves repositioning the core offering by moving it upscale.

The upscale repositioning of the core brand in the sandwich strategy has important strategic implications. Thus, prior to the entry of cut-price competitors, the incumbent brand is optimized to appeal to its target segment, which comprises both quality-oriented and price-sensitive customers. Following the entry of cut-price competitors, the incumbent brand loses some of its more price-sensitive customers. This defection of price-sensitive consumers redefines the target market of the incumbent brand, such that the customers left in its target segment are more quality-oriented. As a result, the core brand, which was originally optimized to appeal to both quality-focused and price-sensitive customers, ends up underpriced and, hence, no longer optimally positioned for this market. In this context, the upscale repositioning of the core offering can create value for the company by providing increasing profit margins—a counterintuitive result given the increasingly competitive environment. Thus, because it maximizes a company's profitability by taking into account the dynamic changes in its target market, the sandwich strategy yields results that are superior to the fighting-brand strategy.

Relevant Concepts: The Good-Better-Best Strategy

The good-better-best strategy involves introducing a downscale offering (fighting brand) as well as an upscale offering (premium brand) while preserving the core brand. Thus, the good-better-best strategy is similar to the sandwich strategy in that it involves the introduction of a low-priced offering. However, instead of a two-tier product line (e.g., by moving its core brand upscale), the good-better-best strategy calls for a three-tier product line (e.g., by launching a new premium offering) in which brands vary in terms of both performance and price (Figure 9).

Figure 9. The Good-Better-Best Strategy

Consider Apple's response to low-price competitors of its iPod music player. Instead of directly competing with lower priced offerings, Apple extended its product line downscale by first introducing iPod Nano and then iPod Shuffle. iPod's good-better-best product line reflects Apple's view of the market as comprising three key segments: a segment seeking a fully functional player (iPod), a segment seeking basic functionality (iPod Nano), and a segment seeking a low-priced offering with limited functionality (iPod

Shuffle). The good-better-best strategy has been successfully employed by a number of companies such as Microsoft (Works, Office Home Edition, and Office Professional), Dell (Mini, Inspiron,, and Studio laptops), and Gap (Old Navy, Gap, and Banana Republic).

The good-better-best strategy works well in tiered markets comprising three key segments: a quality-focused segment, a price-focused segment, and a segment seeking a compromise between high quality and low price. In such three-tiered markets the two-prong sandwich strategy would not work because moving the core offering upscale without having a mid-tier option leaves the company vulnerable to competitive offerings of average quality and price.

In addition to being an effective tool to fence off cut-price competitors in three-tiered markets, the good-better-best strategy can be used in markets in which buyers have uncertain preferences. In such cases, buyers tend to prefer options that offer a compromise among the extreme alternatives. To illustrate, when choosing from a set composed of a high-priced/high-quality brand, a low-priced/low-quality brand, and an average-priced/average-quality brand, buyers often select the middle option because it allows them to avoid trading off price and quality. Buyers' tendency to choose the middle option in the absence of articulated preferences has important implications for choosing a strategy to compete with low-priced rivals. In this case, trying to "sandwich" the low-priced brand by simply launching a fighting brand and moving the core brand upscale without offering a mid-priced/mid-quality option might backfire because the low-priced competitor might benefit from becoming the compromise option.

Additional Readings

Day, George S., David J. Reibstein, and Robert E. Gunther (2004), *Wharton on Dynamic Competitive Strategy*. New York, NY: John Wiley & Sons.

Kotler, Philip, Dipak C. Jain, and Suvit Maesincee (2002), *Marketing Moves: A New Approach to Profits, Growth, and Renewal*. Boston, MA: Harvard Business School Press.

Treacy, Michael and Fred Wiersema (2006), *The Discipline of Market Leaders: Choose Your Customers, Narrow Your Focus, Dominate Your Market* (2nd ed.). London: Profile.

Notes

[1] Adapted from Hoch, Stephen J. (1996), "How Should National Brands Think about Private Labels?" *Sloan Management Review*, 37 (2), 89–102.

[2] Kim, W. Chan and Renée Mauborgne (2005), *Blue Ocean Strategy: How to Create Uncontested Market Space and Make the Competition Irrelevant*. Boston, MA: Harvard Business School Press.

[3] Jain, Dipak C. (2006), *Market Pricing and the Sandwich Strategy*. Kellogg Schol of Management, Northwestern University, Evanston, IL.

Chapter Twenty-Two

Managing Sales Growth

He who moves not forward, goes backward.
Johann Wolfgang von Goethe, German writer and philosopher

Sales growth is an essential component of a company's efforts to achieve sustainable profitability. Understanding the main factors influencing sales volume and identifying strategies for effectively managing sales growth are the focus of this chapter.

Overview

There are two basic strategies for growing sales volume: increasing the rate of adoption of a company's offerings by new customers and increasing the offerings' sales to existing customers. Increasing the rate of adoption can result from attracting two types of customers: (1) customers who are new to the particular product category and are currently not buying this type of offering and (2) customers who are already category users and are buying competitors' offerings. In this context, three basic strategies for growing sales volume can be identified: (1) increasing product adoptions by new-to-the-category customers (market-growth strategy), (2) increasing product adoptions by encouraging competitors' customers to switch (steal-share strategy), and (3) increasing purchase quantity by existing customers (market-penetration strategy).

A particularly useful approach for developing an effective sales-growth strategy involves identifying the key impediments to increasing sales for each of the three types of customers identified above and developing specific solutions to remove these impediments. This approach calls for identifying the gaps between customers' current and desired behavior and developing an action plan to close these gaps (Figure 1).

Figure 1. Managing Sales Growth

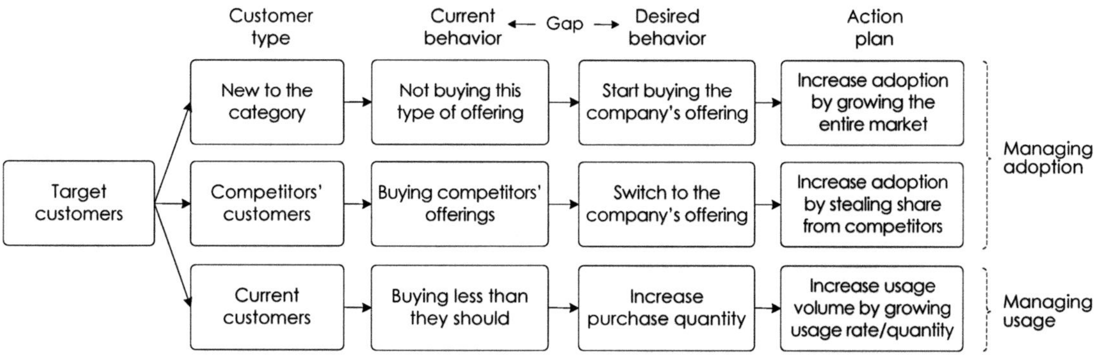

The gap approach to developing an effective, cost-efficient strategy and the two core strategies for increasing the sales volume of a company's offerings—managing product adoptions by new customers and managing product usage by current customers—are examined in more detail in the following sections.

Managing Adoption

To identify the optimal strategy for increasing sales volume, a company first needs to understand the process by which its target customers adopt new products, then to identify the impediments to new product adoption in different stages of the process, and, finally, to develop an action plan to remove these impediments. These various aspects of managing product adoption are discussed in more detail below.

Understanding the Adoption Process

From a customer's perspective, offering adoption can be viewed as a multistage process comprising a sequence of six key steps: awareness, understanding, attractiveness, affordability, availability, and purchase intent. This view of adoption implies that for customers to adopt an offering, they should (1) be aware of its availability, (2) understand its value proposition, (3) perceive the offering to be attractive, (4) perceive it to be affordable, (5) have access to the offering, and (6) intend to purchase it within a particular time frame (Figure 2).[1]

Figure 2: Managing Adoption

The key steps of offering adoption can be summarized as follows:

- *Awareness* reflects customers' knowledge of the availability of the offering. Awareness can be generated by the company's direct communications to its target customers, by communications initiated by the company's collaborators (distribution partners, supplier partners, co-developers, and co-promoters), as well as by third-party communications, such as word of mouth, media coverage, and noncompensated endorsements.

- *Understanding* reflects customers' comprehension of the benefits and costs of the offering. Understanding the value of the offering goes beyond simply being aware of the existence of the offering; it must include comprehension of its benefits and costs. As in the case of creating awareness, understanding the value of the offering can be facilitated by the company's direct communications to its target customers, by communications initiated by the company's collaborators, and by third-party communications.

- *Attractiveness* reflects the utility customers expect to receive from the offering. This implies that consumers should not only be aware of the offering's existence and understand its benefits and costs, but should also find this offering's value proposition attractive. An offering's attractiveness is a function of two factors: its intrinsic value, which reflects the offering's innate ability to deliver value to its target customers in the absence of competitive offerings, and its competitive advantage, which reflects the offering's ability to deliver value superior to that of competitors' offerings. Thus, attractiveness reflects an offering's ability to satisfy a particular need of target customers better than competitors' offerings can.

- *Affordability* reflects customers' perceptions of the monetary cost of the offering with respect to their ability to pay for it. Thus, affordability implies that consumers not only find the offering attractive, but can also come up with the money to acquire it. Because affordability is a function of customers' financial resources, it often is the key impediment to product adoption in developing countries and in financially strained demographic areas.

- *Availability* reflects the degree to which the offering is accessible by target customers. An offering's availability is a function of factors such as the density of the distribution channels catering to its target customers, as well as the availability of the offering in these channels on a day-to-day basis (e.g., absence of stock-outs).

- *Purchase intent* reflects customers' intention to purchase the offering within a particular time frame. Thus, even though customers may find the company's offering attractive, affordable, and accessible, they may not necessarily have the intention to purchase it within the time frame outlined by the company's sales goals.

- *Purchase* involves customers' actual acquisition of the offering. Purchase intent does not necessarily translate into an actual purchase. Numerous factors can either delay the intended action (e.g., anticipation of future price cuts) or void the purchase intent altogether (e.g., the introduction of a superior competitive offering).

Identifying and Closing Adoption Gaps

Managing product adoption calls for identifying and eliminating impediments at different stages of the adoption process. These impediments, often referred to as adoption gaps, can be illustrated by mapping the dispersion of customers across different stages of the adoption process. The goal of this analysis is to provide a better understanding of the dynamics of the adoption process and identify problematic areas that require specific actions.

The dispersion of customers across different stages of the adoption process can be represented by a series of bars—a format that visualizes the potential hurdles in the adoption process (Figure 3). Here, the blank part of each bar corresponds to the share of potential customers who have not transitioned to the next stage of the adoption process, whereas the ratio of the blank part to the shaded part reflects the effectiveness of the company's actions at each step in acquiring new customers.

Figure 3: Identifying Adoption Gaps

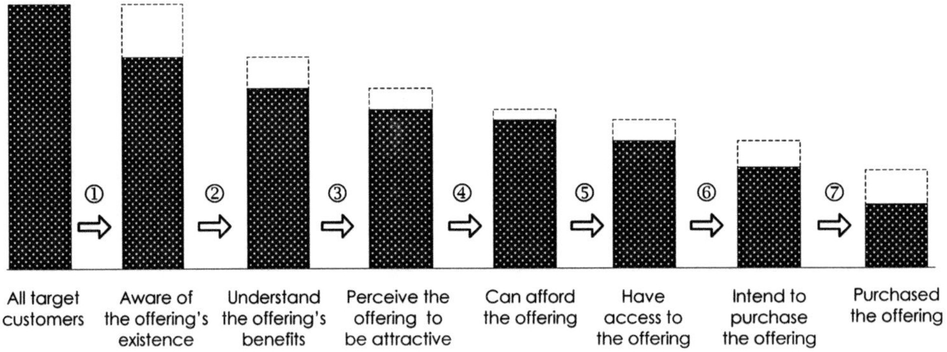

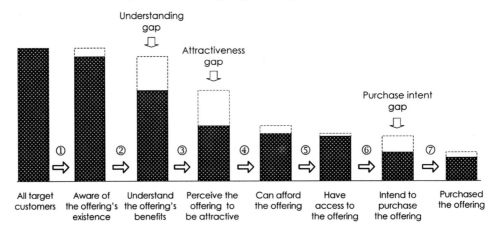

Comparing the loss of potential customers at each step of the process offers a simple way to identify steps with a disproportionate drop in product adoption. These disproportionate drops in the product adoption process are also referred to as *adoption gaps*. To illustrate, consider the adoption chart in Figure 4. It indicates that the largest drops occur in step 2 (communicating the benefits of the offering) and step 3 (perceived attractiveness of the offering). The next largest drop in adoptions occurs at the point of forming intent to purchase the offering within the given time frame (step 6).

Figure 4: Identifying Adoption Gaps: An Illustration

The gap analysis can be used both to pinpoint the problem spots in product adoption and to identify specific *solutions* to close adoption gaps. Some of the most common solutions for closing performance gaps at the different stages of the adoption process are outlined below.

- A gap at *step 1* calls for increasing target customers' awareness of the offering. This type of gap calls for optimizing company, collaborator, and third-party communications. Optimizing company communications can be achieved by increasing the magnitude of communication expenditures and increasing the effectiveness and cost-efficiency of these resources (e.g., by streamlining the message, developing a better creative solution, and using more effective media in a more cost-efficient manner). In addition to directly communicating the availability of the offering to target customers, the company can also involve some of its current collaborators to create awareness among target customers, as well as to identify new collaborators explicitly for the purpose of promoting the offering. Finally, the company may stimulate third-party communications that promote the offering (e.g., by encouraging product adoption by opinion leaders and facilitating the creation and functioning of early-adopter forums and user groups).

- A gap at *step 2* calls for increasing target customers' understanding of the true benefits and costs of the offering. As in the case of closing awareness gaps, a gap in customers' understanding of the offering's value can be closed by optimizing company, collaborator, and third-party communications. The key difference is that the focus of communications here is on improving the understanding of the value of the offering rather than simply creating awareness of its existence. In addition to using advertising, public relations, and personal communications, communicating the benefits of an offering can be effectively achieved by providing target customers with an option to experience the offering (e.g., using product samples and demos).

- A gap at *step 3* calls for improving the expected value of the offering. This typically can be achieved by reformulating/redesigning the offering to increase its perceived benefits and/or decrease its expected costs. This reformulation can involve permanent changes in the product, service, branding, and pricing aspects of the offering, as well as the use of incentives to improve the overall value proposition of the current offering.

- A gap at *step 4* indicates that target customers do not consider the offering to be affordable. For example, a customer may be aware of the existence of the Porsche GT, understand its benefits and costs, and find its value proposition attractive, yet not be able to afford its hefty price tag. One solution to increase sales volume in this case is to improve affordability of the offering. The intuitive solution is to lower the price or introduce price incentives targeting the desired customer segment. Lowering the price and introducing price incentives, however, while potentially increasing the sales volume, may eventually lead to a decline in sales revenues as well—a scenario that can occur when the marginal increase in the sales volume generated by the price cut cannot offset the decline in revenues associated with the drop in price. An alternative approach to circumvent the affordability barrier involves changing the perceived importance of the benefits provided by the offering so that customers reallocate additional resources to this offering in their budget planning.

- A gap at *step 5* indicates that the offering is not available to all target customers. To illustrate, an offering may be in short supply because a company underestimated its appeal to target customers or because of inadequate distribution coverage. The logical solution to increase sales volume in this case is to improve the offering's availability. This can be achieved by (1) ramping up production to meet demand, (2) improving the geographical coverage of the offering's distribution channels to offer its target customers better accessibility to the offering, and (3) improving channel operations to minimize logistical stock-outs.

- A gap at *step 6* indicates that target customers have no intention to purchase the offering within the time frame set by the company. For example, a customer may have a general intention to buy a new car without having a specific time frame in mind. The logical solution to increase sales volume in this case is to facilitate the formulation of purchase intent within the desired time frame. Strategies to achieve this involve introducing time-sensitive incentives as well as making salient the immediate gratification from purchasing the offering.

- A gap at *step 7* indicates that target customers fail to act upon purchase intention. To illustrate, a consumer may fail to act upon the intent to purchase the offering because of unexpected budgetary constraints. To increase sales volume in this case, a company needs to improve the conversion of the purchase intent into purchase behavior. As in the case of facilitating the formation of purchase intent, the conversion of this intent into actual behavior can be facilitated by introducing time-sensitive incentives, as well as making salient the immediate gratification from purchasing the offering.

Managing Usage

The discussion so far has focused on growing sales volume by increasing product adoption by new customers. In addition to increasing adoption by new customers, in many cases an offering's sales volume can also be increased by growing its usage by current customers. To identify the optimal product usage strategy for increasing sales volume, it is important to first understand factors that determine the process by which customers repurchase the offering, identify impediments to achieving the desired product usage, and develop an action plan to remove these impediments. These aspects of managing product usage are discussed in more detail in the following sections.

Understanding the Repurchase Process

From a customer's perspective, product repurchase can be viewed as a multistep process in which each step identifies a factor essential for repurchase. In particular, four key factors in product repurchase can be distinguished: satisfaction, usage frequency, usage quantity, and repurchase intent (Figure 5).

Figure 5: Managing Usage

The key steps of offering repurchase can be summarized as follows.

- *Satisfaction* reflects the degree to which customers find the offering attractive after having experienced it. Unlike the attractiveness stage in product adoption, which is based on customers' expectations of an offering's attractiveness, satisfaction reflects customers' postconsumption evaluation of the offering and is a function of customers' experience of the benefits and costs of the offering.

- *Frequency* reflects the rate at which customers use the offering. For example, in the case of toothpaste, frequency refers to the number of times people use toothpaste to brush their teeth. The frequency of usage is a function of factors such as customers' satisfaction with the offering, their awareness of the offering and its optimal usage frequency, their understanding of the optimal usage rate, the affordability of the offering and its availability for repurchase, as well as customers' existing usage habits.

- *Quantity* reflects the amount of the offering customers consume on each usage occasion. This step is relevant for offerings where the quantity consumed on a given usage occasion is determined by customers. For example, in the case of toothpaste, quantity refers to the amount of toothpaste people use to brush their teeth.

Based on the nature of the offering, two types of usage can be distinguished: volume-based usage and time-based usage. Volume-based usage reflects a scenario in which the usage quantity is determined by the actual amount of the item consumed on a given usage occasion (e.g., soft drinks, laundry detergent, toothpaste, and mobile phone service). In contrast, time-based usage reflects a scenario in which the product is offered in units, and each unit is used across multiple usage occasions (e.g., printer cartridges, water filters, and shaving blades). Here the usage quantity is determined by the number of occasions on which the item is used.

Similar to the case of usage frequency, usage quantity is a function of factors such as customers' satisfaction with the offering, their awareness of the optimal usage rate, their understanding of the optimal usage rate, the affordability of the offering, its availability for repurchase, and customers' existing usage habits. In addition, usage quantity is also a function of the physical characteristics of the offering, such as packaging size and usage management features (e.g., measuring cup in laundry detergent).

- *Repurchase intent* reflects customers' intent to repurchase the offering within a particular time frame. Thus, customers' satisfaction with the offering does not guarantee that they will necessarily form an intent to repurchase the company's offering; they may instead decide to purchase a competitor's offering. Even if customers remain loyal to the company, this does not necessarily imply that they will form an intention to repurchase the offering within the time frame determined by the company's sales goals.

- *Repurchase* involves customers' actual reacquisition of the offering. Formulating intent to repurchase the offering in a given time frame does not guarantee that customers will actually do so. A number of factors may either delay customers' acting on their intent (e.g., anticipation of future price cuts) or lead to customers deciding not to repurchase the product (e.g., introduction of a superior offering).

Identifying and Closing Usage Gaps

A practical approach to managing usage calls for identifying and eliminating impediments at the different stages of the repurchase process. This can be achieved by identifying the dispersion of customers across different stages of the usage process (Figure 6).

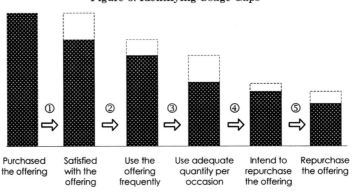

Figure 6: Identifying Usage Gaps

Comparing the loss of potential customers at each stage of the repurchase process offers a simple way to identify stages in which there are disproportionate drops in product usage. These disproportionate drops are commonly referred to as *usage gaps*. In addition to pinpointing the hurdles in product repurchase, usage gap analysis also identifies specific *solutions* for closing these gaps. The most common solutions for closing usage gaps at the different stages of the repurchase process are outlined below.

- A gap at *step 1* calls for improving customer *satisfaction* with the offering. This can be achieved by improving actual product performance, for example, by optimizing its design, functionality, and user friendliness.

- A gap at *step 2* calls for increasing customers' usage rate of the offering. This can be achieved by improving customers' satisfaction with the offering, their awareness of the optimal usage rate, and their understanding of its benefits by increasing the affordability of the offering and its availability for repurchase, as well as by changing customers' usage-rate habits. To illustrate, to increase sales volume from its current customers, Campbell Soup Company launched an advertising campaign to promote the use of its soup during summer. In the same vein, Arm & Hammer promotes baking soda not only for baking, but also as a household cleaner and deodorizer.

- A gap at *step 3* calls for increasing the *usage quantity* of the offering. This can be achieved by improving customers' satisfaction with the offering, their awareness of the optimal usage quantity and their understanding of its benefits; by increasing the affordability of the offering and its availability for repurchase; and by changing customers' existing usage-quantity habits. For example, to change consumers' usage habits, many shampoo companies have included the word "repeat" in usage instructions.

Usage quantity can also be managed by reformulating and/or redesigning the product in ways that lead to greater consumption. One approach to achieve this goal involves increasing the size of the packaging in categories where increased package size typically leads to a greater usage quantity (e.g., laundry detergents as well as many food and beverage products). For example, PepsiCo's introduction of the larger, two-liter bottle in 1970 resulted in increased consumption of Pepsi products.

An alternative strategy to increasing usage quantity involves designing the product in a way that ensures dispensing the optimal quantity per usage occasion. To illustrate, to increase the quantity of ketchup consumed at each usage occasion, Heinz introduced a plastic squeeze bottle, increased the size of the opening in the bottle neck, and designed the "upside-down bottle" in which ketchup is ready to be poured without having to wait for the contents to slide down to the opening of the bottle. Similarly, liquid laundry detergents often have caps that can be used to measure the optimal usage quantity, and solid detergents typically include measuring cups inside the box.

Using product design can also be effective in cases of time-based usage, where usage quantity is determined by the number of occasions on which the same item is used. For example, to encourage customers to replace their toothbrush, Gillette added blue indicator bristles on its Oral-B Indicator toothbrush, which at a certain point fade halfway to alert users of the need to replace their brush. The new design was prominently featured in its advertising: "When the blue is gone, it's time to move on."

- A gap at *step 4* calls for facilitating the formulation of an *intent to repurchase the offering* within the desired time frame. This can be achieved by creating awareness of the product's scarcity as well as by offering time-sensitive incentives encouraging customers to repurchase the offering within a specific time frame. For example, printer manufacturers include toner-level indicators to alert users that the cartridge will soon need replacement. Similarly, to ensure that customers have milk in ready supply, the California Milk Processor Board launched the famous "Got Milk?" campaign in 1993, featuring scenarios in which customers consuming complementary products (e.g., chocolate-chip cookies and cereal) are deprived of milk.

- A gap at *step 5* calls for improving the conversion of repurchase intent into repurchase behavior. As in the case of facilitating the formation of repurchase intent, the conversion of this intent into actual behavior can be facilitated by creating awareness of the product's scarcity, as well as by offering time-sensitive incentives that encourage customers to repurchase the offering within a specific time frame. Ensuring an offering's availability at the time of purchase is also an important factor in encouraging the desired repurchase behavior. Another important and often overlooked aspect of managing the conversion of repurchase intent into behavior involves ensuring continuity in the product's appearance, functionality, and availability. Indeed, a dramatic change in an offering's marketing mix (e.g., packaging, branding, pricing, and distribution) can result in customers reevaluating their purchase intent, postponing their purchase decision, or even switching to a competitor's offering.

Summary

Sales growth is a key factor for achieving sustainable profitability. The two core strategies for increasing the sales volume of a company's offerings include (1) increasing product adoptions by new customers and (2) increasing product usage by current customers.

Product adoption can be viewed as a multistage process comprising the following six key factors: awareness (knowledge of the existence of the offering), understanding (comprehension of the benefits and costs of the offering), attractiveness (utility that customers expect to receive from the offering), affordability (customer perceptions of their ability to pay for the offering), availability (degree to which the offering is accessible by target customers), and purchase intent (intention to purchase the offering within a particular time frame). A useful approach to managing product adoption involves identifying and eliminating impediments (adoption gaps) at the different stages of the adoption process.

In addition to increasing adoption by new customers, in many cases an offering's sales volume can also be increased by influencing its usage (and, hence, repurchase frequency) by current customers. Product repurchase can be viewed as a multistage process comprising the following four factors: satisfaction (the degree to which customers find the offering attractive after having experienced it), usage frequency (rate at which customers use the offering), usage quantity (amount of the offering that customers consume on each usage occasion), and repurchase intent (intent to repurchase the offering within a particular time frame). A practical approach to managing product usage involves identifying and eliminating impediments (usage gaps) at the different stages of the repurchase process.

Relevant Concepts

Conversion Rate: The number of potential customers who have tried the product/service relative to the total number of customers aware of the product/service.

$$\text{Conversion rate} = \frac{\text{Current and former customers}}{\text{Potential customers aware of the offering}}$$

Customer Attrition Rate (Churn Rate): The number of customers who discontinue using a company's product or service during a specified period relative to the average total number of customers over that same period.

$$\text{Customer attrition rate} = \frac{\text{Number of customers who disadopt an offering during a specific period}}{\text{Total number of customers during that period}}$$

Market Size: Monetary value of an existing or potential market, typically measured on an annual basis. Market size is also used in reference to the number of customers comprising a particular market.

Pareto Principle: The 80/20 relationship discovered in the late 1800s by the economist Vilfredo Pareto.[2] Pareto established that 80% of the land in Italy was owned by 20% of the population. He later observed that 20% of the peapods in his garden yielded 80% of the peas that were harvested. The Pareto Principle, or the 80/20 Rule, has proven its validity in a number of other areas. In marketing, the most common illustration of the 80/20 rule is that 80% of revenues are often generated by 20% of customers (or products).

Penetration Rate: The number of customers who have tried the offering at least once relative to the total number of potential customers.

$$\text{Penetration rate} = \frac{\text{Current and former customers}}{\text{Potential customers}}$$

Purchase Intent: The intent to purchase a particular offering within a given time frame. A popular approach to estimating the purchase likelihood involves using a five-point scale with the following anchors: "definitely would buy," "probably would buy," "might or might not buy," "probably would not buy," and "definitely would not buy." To account for an overestimation bias, whereby respondents tend to overestimate the probability of actually purchasing the surveyed product, the stated purchase probabilities are typically corrected. A common methodology for correcting this overestimation bias involves using generalized industry estimates. To illustrate, with consumer packaged goods, these responses are sometimes corrected as follows: "Definitely would buy" responses are reduced by 20% (which implies that only 80% of those stating that they will definitely buy the product actually end up buying it); "probably would buy" responses are reduced by 70% (which implies that only 30% of those stating that they will probably buy the product actually end up buying it); and responses falling into the three remaining categories are considered to be no-purchase responses.

Retention Rate: The number of customers who have repurchased the offering during the current buying cycle (e.g., month, quarter, or year) relative to the number of customers who have purchased the offering during the last cycle. Also used in reference to the number of customers who have repurchased the offering relative to the total number of customers who have tried the product at least once.

$$\text{Retention rate} = \frac{\text{Active customers during the current period}}{\text{Active customers during the last period}}$$

Additional Readings

Aaker, David A. (2007), *Strategic Market Management* (8th ed.). New York, NY: John Wiley & Sons.

Best, Roger J. (2008), *Market-Based Management: Strategies for Growing Customer Value and Profitability* (5th ed.). Upper Saddle River, NJ: Prentice Hall.

Kumar, Nirmalya (2004), *Marketing as Strategy: Understanding the CEO's Agenda for Driving Growth and Innovation*. Boston, MA: Harvard Business School Press.

Notes

[1] The sequence of these steps in the adoption process may vary across products and customers. The model presented in Figure 2 reflects the most common sequence.

[2] Koch, Richard (1998), *The 80/20 Principle: The Secret to Success by Achieving More with Less.* New York, NY: Doubleday.

Chapter Twenty-Three

Managing New Products

I don't design clothes. I design dreams.
Ralph Lauren, founder of Polo Ralph Lauren

New product offerings are a key tool used by companies to ensure sustainable growth. The main aspects of designing and managing new product offerings are the focus of this chapter.

Overview

The term "new products" has dual meaning: It is used in reference to offerings that are new to the company but not new to target customers (often referred to as "new-to-the-company" products), as well as to offerings that are new both to the company and its target customers (often referred to as "new-to-the-world" products). New-to-the-company offerings usually involve using new processes to create the product, devising new ways to communicate its benefits, and finding new distribution channels to deliver the product to target customers. The key in this case is that while these innovations are novel to the company, they have already been adopted by competitors and, hence, are already familiar to target customers. In contrast, new-to-the-world innovations are novel not only to the company, but to target customers as well.

Depending on their novelty to target customers, new-to-the-world products can be either extensions of an existing category (also referred to as "slightly new" products) or can create their own category (also referred to as "really new" products). Slightly new products typically operate within the boundaries of an existing product category, target customers who are familiar with the offering's core value proposition, and compete with offerings from the same product category. To illustrate, slightly new products are different variants of an existing offering (e.g., different colors, flavors, tastes, sizes, designs, or packaging variations of an existing core product). In contrast, really new offerings typically create a new product category. Examples of really new products include Amazon.com (online retailing), eBay (consumer-to-consumer online auctions), Priceline.com (reverse-price auctions), TiVo (personal digital recorders), and Slingbox (TV-to-computer video streaming). Because the boundaries between the slightly new and really new products are not well-defined, the newness of the offering to target customers can be thought of as a continuum, where minor variations to existing offerings are at one extreme and truly novel offerings that create their own category are at the other extreme.

Understanding New Product Adoption

The process of new product adoption describes the diffusion of new ideas, products, services, and technologies. This diffusion process can be represented by an S-shaped curve, which depicts the total number of adoptions at any given point in time (Figure 1). The pattern of the diffusion process can be defined by two key characteristics: (1) the size of the potential market, indicating the total number of users that will ultimately adopt the innovation, and (2) the speed of diffusion, which can be defined by the time frame for reaching the inflection point—the point at which the rate of growth slows down and starts declining (the place where the shape of the diffusion curve turns from convex to concave).

Figure 1. The Typical S-Shaped Pattern of New Product Adoption

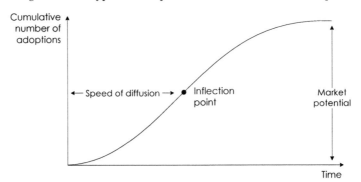

The diffusion process can also be represented in terms of the number of new (rather than cumulative) adoptions of the innovation at any given point in time. In this context, new product adoption can be represented by a bell-shaped curve, whereby, after a relatively slow start, an increasing number of people adopt the innovation until it reaches a peak, then starts declining as the number of potential adopters decreases. The noncumulative pattern of adoption illustrated in Figure 2 directly corresponds to the cumulative pattern given in Figure 1, with the key difference that Figure 2 illustrates the pattern of dispersion of new adoptions over time instead of the total number of current users.

Figure 2. The Typical Bell-Shaped Pattern of New Product Adoption

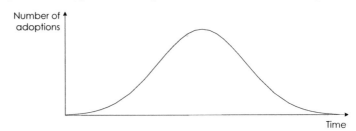

The bell-shaped diffusion pattern is based on the assumption that the adoption of an innovation can be represented by a normal distribution. This assumption, however, is not always realistic. Indeed, some innovations are adopted very rapidly, whereas others take a substantial amount of time to achieve their peak adoption period (e.g., in the case where benefits are not readily apparent or the innovation is not heavily promoted by the company). Thus, a new offering may be adopted almost instantly by a large segment of the population and then diffused at a much slower rate until it is adopted by all target customers or, alternatively, it might start at much slower rate and reach the point at which it is adopted by the majority of target customers relatively late in the adoption process (Figure 3).

Figure 3. New Product Adoption: Fast and Slow Diffusion Scenarios

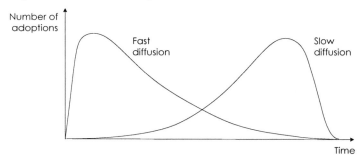

A popular interpretation of the bell-shaped curve of noncumulative product adoptions involves classifying customers into distinct categories based on their adoption pattern. The two most influential frameworks offering such classifications are the ones advanced by Everett Rogers and Geoffrey Moore, discussed at the end of this chapter.

Forecasting Market Demand

Demand forecasting is important for new product launch decisions, for resource allocation decisions (e.g., to determine the level of support for a given offering), for setting goals and performance benchmarks, and for developing the strategy of a particular offering.

There are two common types of market estimates: market potential forecast and sales forecast. *Market potential forecast* is an estimate of the total sales volume that ultimately can be achieved by all companies in a given market. Forecasting market potential is typically used to make market entry and exit decisions, resource allocation decisions, and to set goals and evaluate performance. Unlike market potential forecasts, which indicate the sales volume that ultimately could be achieved in a particular market, *sales forecasts* impose a specific time frame for achieving the sales volume. Thus, sales forecast is an estimate of the total sales volume attainable within a given time frame. Similar to the estimates of market potential, sales forecasts typically are used to make entry and exit decisions, allocate resources, plan production capacity, and evaluate the impact of various marketing mix variables on sales.

In general, two types of demand-forecasting methods can be identified: methods that involve collecting and analyzing primary data (data collected especially for the purpose of demand forecasting) and methods that involve analyzing secondary data (existing data). These two types of methods are discussed in more detail in the following sections.

Forecasting Demand Using Primary Data

Primary-data forecasting methods can be divided into two types: *expert-judgment forecasts* and *customer-research forecasts*. These two forecasting methods are discussed in more detail below.

- *Expert-judgment forecasting* relies on experts' opinions to estimate market demand. Depending on the nature of the expert's background, there are three main categories of forecasts: executive forecasts, sales force forecasts, and industry forecasts.

  - *Executive forecast* is a top-down approach in which the forecast is based on the aggregated opinion of a company's top executives and senior managers.

  - *Sales force forecast* is a bottom-up approach in which the forecast is based on the aggregated opinion of a company's sales force and sales managers.

  - *Industry forecast* is based on the aggregated opinion of industry experts, such as industry analysts, executives, managers, and sales forces from competitive companies.

  Because most expert-judgment forecasts are based on aggregating the opinions of multiple experts, an important issue concerns the process of aggregating individual judgments to arrive at the final estimate. A popular method for eliciting group expert judgments is the Delphi method, described in more detail at the end of this chapter.

- *Customer-research forecasting* examines customers' reaction to the offering at different stages of the product development process. The two most popular forms of customer-based forecasting are concept testing and market testing.

  - *Concept testing* is the process of evaluating consumer response to a particular offering prior to its introduction to the market. Concept testing can be based on a description of the offering or, alternatively, can also involve a fully functional prototype. One approach to concept testing involves using a representative sample of the target segment (e.g., a focus group) with the purpose of revealing insights, ideas, and observations related to the key aspects of the offering. Another methodology involves estimating the probability of the offering's purchase by target customers based on a description of its main benefits and costs. Because it is based on customers' estimates of their future behavior, concept testing provides only rough estimates of sales volume.

  - *Market testing* relies on test markets to estimate market potential and/or future sales volume. It is often used as the litmus test for a go or no-go decision to launch a new product, as well as for testing specific aspects of the offering's marketing mix. Test markets aim to replicate all relevant aspects of the environment in which the company's offering will be launched (e.g., offering-related advertising and incentives, competitive offerings, and point-of-purchase environment) so that the test market outcome can be extrapolated to more general (e.g., national) sales forecasts. To ensure greater validity for the results, multiple test markets, typically located in different geographic areas, are often used. Because of its relatively high costs, market testing is normally used only for products that successfully pass the concept testing stage.

Forecasting Demand Using Secondary Data

Forecast methods involving already existing (secondary) data can be divided into three categories based on whether the available data pertain to (1) the offering that is the object of the forecast, (2) a related offering, or (3) an entire product category. These three forecasting methods are discussed in more detail below.

- *Offering-specific forecasting* involves using past data from the sales of the same offering for which the demand is being forecast. A popular approach relies on past sales data to identify trends, then extrapolates these trends to a sales forecast. A variety of time-series statistical approaches may be employed for this type of analysis, such as linear trend analysis, moving-average analysis, and exponential smoothing. Another popular approach involves identifying the relationships among the offering's sales and a variety of internal factors (e.g., the offering's price, incentives, and communications) and external factors (e.g., competitors' price, incentives, and communications).

- *Forecasting by analogy* involves forecasting an offering's performance by comparing its adoption cycle to a functionally similar product for which sales data are available. This approach is useful for new-to-the-world products (e.g., Amazon's Kindle, Slingbox, and Segway Personal Transporter) for which adoption data are not available, or for nontraditional marketing activities involving existing products (e.g., drastic price change, novel incentives, nontraditional communications campaign) for which the market reaction is unknown. The key assumption of analogy-based forecasts is that the pattern of adoption of the new product (e.g., speed and depth of market penetration) follows a similar pattern to that of the analogous product.

- *Category-based forecasting* involves utilizing available product-category data to estimate a particular product's performance. One category-based forecasting approach to quantifying the sales potential of a given category involves estimating the degree to which sales in a given category have captured the total market potential in a particular geographical area based on the population of that area and average consumption per user nationally (also referred to as Category Development Index, or CDI). An alternative approach to category-based demand forecasting involves estimating the degree to which sales of a specific offering (rather than the entire category) have captured the total market potential in a particular market (also referred to as Brand Development Index, or BDI). Comparing these two indexes reveals a an offering's performance relative to the category. Thus, a combination of high BDI and low CDI indicates that the brand is doing better than competitive offerings in a given market, whereas a combination of low BDI and high CDI indicates that the brand is doing worse than competitive offerings.

Developing the Marketing Mix

The process of managing a new offering involves deciding on its product, service, brand, price, incentives, communication, and distribution characteristics. The key aspects of these decisions are outlined below.

Product Management

Product strategies vary as a function of the product's stage in its life cycle. At the introduction stage, companies typically offer a single product variant, targeted at the most likely adopters. As the product enters the growth stage, the number of customers adopting the product increases and so does the heterogeneity of these customers. To address the different needs of their current and potential customers, companies add product extensions designed to better meet the needs of various customer subsegments. The variety of product variants peaks at maturity and starts decreasing as the product enters its decline stage; profit margins shrink, and companies focus on best-selling products, phasing out products with insufficient volume to meet their profitability benchmarks.

The successful introduction of a new offering is a function of the following factors.

- *Relative advantage.* The greater the relative advantage of an offering over the product it replaces, the more likely it is to be adopted.

- *Transparency.* An offering is more likely to be adopted when its relative advantage is readily observable and can be experienced by customers.

- *Compatibility.* An offering compatible with customers' existing systems and processes is more likely to be adopted than an incompatible one.

- *Perceived risk.* An offering is more likely to be adopted when the uncertainty associated with its performance is low. This uncertainty might involve customer uncertainty about their own preferences, uncertainty about the product's future performance, and uncertainty about the magnitude of the risks associated with the new product.

An important aspect of new product decisions involves managing the evolution of the company's products over time. As products become obsolete, they are often replaced by a new generation of products that take advantage of changes in target markets, such as changes in customer preferences, alterations in the competitive landscape, advances in technology, and changes in the regulatory environment. Thus, through innovation, companies can extend the life cycle of their individual products (Figure 4). To illustrate, consider Gillette's product development strategy leading to the introduction of Fusion, its eighth-generation wet-shaving razor. Gillette's original razor introduced in 1903 was replaced by the second-generation razor Trac II (1971), followed by Sensor (1990), Sensor Excel (1995), MACH3 (1998), MACH3 Turbo (2002), M3Power (2004), and Fusion (2006).

When developing a new generation of products, companies often develop strategies to make the earlier generation obsolete, a process often referred to as planned obsolescence. Planned obsolescence involves designing new products in a way that makes prior generations inferior (and, therefore, obsolete) on key dimensions such as functionality, compatibility, and style. To illustrate, to facilitate user migration to later versions of their software, companies systematically terminate support (e.g., software upgrades) for earlier versions. In addition, the added functionality of the new generations of its software often limits this software's backward compatibility; as a result, once the new software has been adopted by a critical mass of users, the earlier versions become obsolete because of their incompatibility.

Figure 4. Extending Product Life Cycle through Innovation

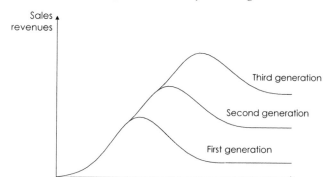

One important implication of planned obsolescence for new product design involves managing a new product's costs by optimizing its performance during its expected lifetime, a process often referred to as value engineering. For example, a company expecting its product to be obsolete within a given time frame may optimize costs by designing the durability of a product's components according to the expected product lifetime.

Brand Management

An important question in developing new offerings is that of branding. There are several options that a company can choose: extend an existing brand to a new category (e.g., Heinz mustard), launch a new sub-brand under an existing umbrella brand (e.g., Honda Accord), or create a new, free-standing brand (e.g., Nexium).

The primary reason to use an existing brand for a new offering is to leverage its customer equity. Indeed, using an existing brand is likely to facilitate the adoption of the offering by customers for whom the brand has positive equity in a cost-efficient and timely fashion. Using an established brand can also facilitate the company's ability to convince channel members to carry the new product. An important drawback of this strategy is that using an existing brand may limit the company's ability to attach a specific meaning to this brand in the context of the new product category (e.g., Heinz All-Natural Cleaning Vinegar, Harley-Davidson Cake Decorating Kit, and Kellogg Special K2O Protein Water). Brand extensions may also dilute the meaning associated with the original brand. Furthermore, poor performance of the new product can easily spill over and hurt the reputation of the entire brand.

Developing a strong new brand, on the other hand, typically requires significant resources and time. Launching a new brand is generally a better strategy in cases where the meaning associated with the existing brands in the company's portfolio is inconsistent with the image that the company needs to create for its new offering in order to optimize its value to target customers. Creating its own brand when pioneering a new category creates a unique opportunity for the company to associate its name with the entire category. To illustrate, brands like Google (information search), Amazon.com (e-commerce), eBay (online auctions), and Xerox (copying) have become virtual synonyms for the entire category. Creating strong brand-category associations enables the company to recapture some of its marketing expenses in the form of brand equity.

Price Management

When launching a new offering, two core pricing strategies can be distinguished: skim pricing and penetration pricing.

- *Skim pricing* involves setting a high initial price to "skim the cream" off the top of the market, represented by customers who value the offering's benefits and are not price sensitive. By setting high initial prices, skim pricing maximizes profit margins, usually at the expense of market share. Skimming is more appropriate in cases where: (1) demand is relatively inelastic and lowering the price is not likely to substantially increase sales volume, (2) there is little or no competition for the target segment, (3) cost is not a direct function of volume—significant cost savings are not achieved as cumulative volume increases, (4) being the market pioneer is unlikely to result in a sustainable competitive advantage, and (5) the company lacks the capital expenditures required for volume production.

- *Penetration pricing* involves setting relatively low prices in an attempt to gain higher sales volume, albeit at relatively low margins. Penetration pricing is more appropriate in cases where: (1) demand is relatively elastic—that is, lowering the price is likely to substantially increase sales volume, (2) the target segment becomes increasingly competitive, (3) cost is a function of volume and, as a result, significant cost savings are expected as cumulative volume increases, and (4) being the market pioneer is likely to result in a sustainable competitive advantage.

Incentives Management

Most new-product incentives fall into one of three categories: incentives given to customers, incentives given to collaborators (e.g., channel members), and incentives given to company personnel.

- *Customer incentives* (e.g., coupons, rebates, volume discounts, price reductions, premiums, rewards, and sweepstakes) are used by companies to achieve three primary goals: (1) to tailor the value of a new offering to the needs of different customer segments, (2) in response to a competitor's promotion, and (3) to better manage the rate at which customers adopt the new product. Thus, a company may offer different incentives to different customer segments based on the needs and resources of these customers and the strategic importance of these customers to the company (e.g., by giving substantial discounts to opinion leaders who can influence other potential buyers). Similarly, when introducing a new offering, companies often face competitive reaction, usually in the form of incentives given to potential buyers, and have to counter these incentives to make their offering appealing to target customers. Incentives are also used to manage the speed of adoption of the new offering by target customers. Thus, customers may form an intention to purchase a product without acting upon it (e.g., because of monetary and/or time constraints). In this case, by offering time-sensitive incentives, a company can encourage these customers to act upon their intent within a given time frame. Incentives are often used to stimulate off-season sales (e.g., convertible cars introduced in the fall can use incentives to encourage forward buying).

- *Channel incentives* are typically used for several reasons: (1) to gain shelf space for new products (e.g., through slotting allowances), (2) to encourage channel members to carry higher levels of inventory to avoid stock-outs (e.g., through stocking allowances, inventory financing, and volume discounts), (3) to encourage channel members to promote new products (e.g., through advertising and display allowances), and (4) to offset the impact of competitive promotions (e.g., through competitive price-matching incentives).

- *Company incentives* involve various rewards aimed at the company's personnel, which can include the functional areas involved in developing and managing the new offering, such as management, engineers, and the sales force. Company incentives can involve monetary bonuses, recognition awards, contests, free goods and services, prizes, sweepstakes, and games.

Communication Management

The communications associated with a new offering typically pursue one or more of the following three goals: (1) create awareness of the new offering, (2) create a preference for the offering, and (3) incite an action (e.g., purchase the offering). The selection of a communication goal is typically a function of the offering's stage in its life cycle. Thus, at the early stages of new product introduction, the communication campaign aims primarily at creating awareness among early adopters, as well as among channel partners. As the product enters the growth stage, a company's communication goals shift to creating awareness of the product among the mass market while at the same time differentiating its offerings from those of competitors in response to increasing competition. As the product enters its maturity stage and the majority of customers are aware of the category benefits, the communication focus shifts from creating awareness of the category benefits to differentiating the company's offering by highlighting its benefits vis-à-vis the competition. This emphasis on product differentiation continues as the product enters its decline stage; however, at this point overall communication expenditures tend to decline.

Communications associated with a new offering can be initiated by the company, its collaborators, and/or by a third party. Company and collaborator communications include activities such as advertising, press releases, event sponsoring, product placement, trade shows, free samples, free trials, sales force communications, and various other promotional incentives. In contrast, third-party communications include word of mouth, third-party media coverage (e.g., reviews, blogs, and endorsements), and noncompensated endorsements. From a chronological perspective, a company's own communications typically precede third-party communications, whereby the release of a new product is accompanied by (and often preceded by) a targeted promotional campaign. Third-party communications are then generated by early adopters of the offering, who either deliberately or unintentionally make other potential buyers aware of the existence and the benefits of the offering (Figure 5). On many occasions, however, third-party communications precede the company's promotions. For example, Google, eBay, and Netscape relied primarily on third-party effects to build their initial customer base and started promoting their offerings on a large scale only after achieving a certain level of growth.

Figure 5. Product Adoptions as a Function of Company, Collaborator, and Third-Party Communications

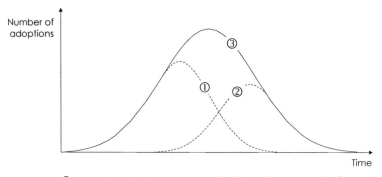

① Adoptions due to company and collaborator communications
② Adoptions due to third-party communications
③ Total adoptions

In general, while third-party communications can facilitate the new product adoption process, they also can have a detrimental impact on product adoptions. Indeed, in cases where a new offering is perceived as unattractive, it can generate unfavorable third-party communications that may slow down the rate of the adoption process and decrease the overall market potential of the offering. To illustrate, helped by a massive advertising campaign, the movie *Hulk*, released by Universal Pictures in 2003, became number one at the box office, with one of the highest grossing opening weekends of all time, only to be followed by a record 70% drop in ticket sales the second week. The drop stemmed from mixed reviews and negative word of mouth. In contrast, *My Big Fat Greek Wedding*, released by IFC Films in 2002 with a relatively small advertising budget, was ranked twentieth at the box office its first week, steadily gained share from positive word of mouth and twenty weeks later became the second highest-grossing movie.

Managing promotional efforts in an effective and cost-efficient manner requires optimizing the impact of company, collaborator, and third-party communications. When the anticipated effects of third-party communications are likely to be strong (e.g., because of the shared consumption experience as in the case of movies and computer games), then an effective and cost-efficient communications strategy may involve an emphasis on third-party communications. In contrast, in cases where third-party communications are unlikely (e.g., because of the private nature of consumption or competitive issues in business-to-business markets), reliance on company and collaborator communications is crucial to ensure adoption.

Distribution Management

When designing the distribution aspect of its new offerings, a company needs to decide on several key factors: channel structure (e.g., direct, indirect, or hybrid), channel ownership (e.g., ownership-based or contractual), channel type (e.g., specialized or broad), channel coverage (e.g., selective or intensive), and channel exclusivity (e.g., exclusive or not exclusive).

As a general rule, the distribution strategy is a function of the offering's overall strategy as well as the other marketing mix elements. Thus, in the case of offerings following a skimming strategy, distribution at the introduction stage tends to be more selective (e.g., specialty distributors), aiming to make the product available to early adopters. As the number of likely adopters increases, distribution becomes more intensive to include a broad range of distribution channels (e.g., mass merchandisers and volume resellers). In contrast, an offering following a market-penetration strategy is likely to pursue an intensive distribution strategy even at the early stages of its life cycle. As the popularity of the offering starts decreasing and it enters its decline stage, companies begin phasing out less profitable channels, focusing on those channels that are either likely to remain profitable or have strategic importance to the company (e.g., resulting from synergies with other offerings).

Summary

The term "new product" is used in reference to offerings that are new to the company but not new to target customers (often referred to as "new-to-the-company" products), as well as to products and services that are new to the company and its target customers (often referred to as "new-to-the-world" products).

The process of new product adoption can be represented using an S-shaped curve, which depicts the total number of adoptions at any given point in time. The diffusion process can also be represented in terms of the number of new (rather than cumulative) adoptions of the innovation at any given point in time. In this context, the process of adoption of innovation can be represented by a bell-shaped curve, whereby after a relatively slow start, an increasing number of people adopt the innovation until it reaches a peak, then starts declining as the number of potential adopters decreases.

Understanding market demand is essential for managing new products. There are two basic types of demand forecasting methods: methods that involve collecting primary data (data collected especially for the purposes of demand forecasting) and methods that involve analyzing secondary data (existing data). Primary-data forecasting comprises two types of methods: expert-judgment forecasts and customer-research forecasts. Forecast methods involving already existing (secondary) data include offering-specific forecasting, forecasting by analogy, and category-based forecasting. Because most forecasting methods use a variety of assumptions, a more accurate forecast can be achieved by using multiple methods.

The process of managing a new offering typically involves deciding on its product, service, brand, price, incentives, communication, and distribution aspects. All of the marketing mix decisions need to be optimized to facilitate an offering's adoption by new customers.

Relevant Concepts

Brand Development Index (BDI): A measure of the degree to which sales of a given offering (or a product line associated with a particular brand) have captured the total market potential in a particular geographical area based on the population of that area and average consumption per user nationally. BDI quantifies the sales potential of a given brand in a particular market.

$$BDI = \frac{\text{Percent of an offering's total U.S. sales in market X}}{\text{Percent of the total U.S. population in market X}} \cdot 100$$

Category Development Index (CDI): A measure of the degree to which sales in a given category have captured the total market potential in a particular geographical area based on the population of that area and average consumption per user nationally. In other words, CDI quantifies the sales potential of a given category in a particular market.

$$CDI = \frac{\text{Percent of a category's total U.S. sales in market X}}{\text{Percent of the total U.S. population in market X}} \cdot 100$$

Delphi Method: A popular method for eliciting group expert judgments, named after the site of the most revered oracle in ancient Greece, the Temple of Apollo in Delphi. The Delphi method involves multiple rounds of anonymous collection of expert opinions. The primary goal of the Delphi method is to ensure an accurate forecast from a group of experts by controlling for many of the potential decision biases, such as social conformity (e.g., agreeing with the majority), status (e.g., seniority within the organization), confirmation bias (e.g., ignoring new information that is inconsistent with the original forecast), and other related effects (e.g., experts' ability to eloquently articulate their forecast). To achieve this degree of control, individual forecasts are collected by a moderator who ensures anonymity of the expert opinions. Each forecast typically consists of two parts: the forecast and its rationale. In the Delphi method, after each round of forecast elicitation, the moderator provides the experts with the anonymous forecasts and their rationale, and gives them the option to revise their opinion. This process is repeated until a consensus is reached. In cases where consensus is unlikely after several rounds, the individual forecasts are typically aggregated into an overall estimate (e.g., by averaging the individual numeric forecasts).

Relevant Frameworks: The Product Life Cycle Framework

Managing new products and services can be better understood when considered in the context of their entire life cycle. The product life cycle describes the general trend of products and services as they progress through different stages in the marketplace.[1] It can be defined in terms of a product category (e.g., flat screen TVs), a product class (e.g., LCD TVs), or a particular product form (e.g., 42" LCD TVs). The concept of a product life cycle is based on four key assumptions: (1) products have a limited life, (2) they pass through distinct stages, (3) their profitability depends on the stage, and, as a result, (4) different stages require different marketing strategies. In this context, four key product life cycle stages are identified: introduction, growth, maturity, and decline.

During the introduction stage, product awareness is low and there are very few competitors; hence, the company's primary goal tends to be creating awareness and educating customers about the benefits of the product. As the product takes off during the growth stage, the number of competitors entering the market increases. At maturity, the number of competitors tends to peak, the market becomes saturated, and industry profitability starts to decline because of intensifying competition. Finally, the decline stage is characterized by declining demand for the product, relatively low profitability, and a decreasing number of competitors stemming from consolidation and exit from the market.

The four stages of product life cycle and the corresponding market conditions at each stage are illustrated in Figure 6.

Figure 6. Product Life Cycle[2]

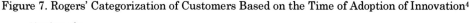

	Introduction	Growth	Maturity	Decline
Market size	Small	Moderate	Large	Moderate/Small
Market growth	Low	High	Low	Negative
Competition	Low	Moderate	High	Moderate/Low

The bell-shaped curve shown in Figure 7 is merely a stylized example of the product life cycle. In reality, many products and services follow different patterns that, for example, may include multiple peaks at different stages of the life cycle. In this context, the product-life-cycle curve is primarily a descriptive tool used to illustrate the general trend of products as they go through different stages in the market. It is not designed to predict the future market success of a particular product or exactly when the product will reach the growth, maturity, and decline stages.

Relevant Frameworks: Rogers' Model of Adoption of Innovations

The key premise underlying the Rogers model is that some consumers are inevitably more open to adaptation than others.[3] Based on the relative time of adoption of innovations, the Rogers model distinguishes five categories of customers (Figure 7): innovators (the first 2.5% of the adopters), early adopters (the 13.5% of the adopters following the innovators), early majority (the next 34% of adopters), late majority (the next 34%), and laggards (the remaining 16%).

Figure 7. Rogers' Categorization of Customers Based on the Time of Adoption of Innovation[4]

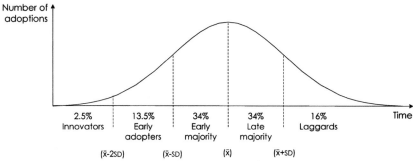

The respective percentage values associated with each category are based on the assumption that the process of adoption of innovations can be represented by a normal distribution, which is defined by two key parameters: its mean ($\overline{x}$) and its standard deviation (SD), a measure of the variation from the mean. In this context, the early and late majorities are defined as being one standard deviation from the mean (34%), whereas early adopters are defined as being two standard deviations from the mean. This classification is not symmetric: There are three categories on the left of the mean and only two on the right. The reason is that the segment on the far left end is further divided into two categories: innovators and early adopters, which cumulatively add up to the size of the laggards segment on the right. The rationale for this division is that these two categories display distinct patterns of adoption behavior and, therefore, from a theoretical standpoint, need to be considered separately.

Despite its popularity, the Rogers model has a number of limitations. One of its key limitations is that it is essentially a classification model; although it identifies the five different categories of adopters of innovation, it does not explain the factors that determine this classification. For example, this model does not offer a decision rule to determine whether a particular individual will become an early adopter or a laggard. Another limitation is that individuals' classification into one of the five categories is linked to relatively stable personality traits, even though in reality, individuals who are innovators in one domain often may be laggards in another. Additional limitations can be traced back to some of its assumptions, such as the normally shaped distribution of adoption of innovation across the population and the preset percentage allocation of individuals into each of the five categories. As a result, the application of the Rogers model is limited to a general description of the adoption of the innovation process and to classifying adopters into one of the five categories for descriptive purposes.

Relevant Frameworks: Moore's Model of Adoption of New Technologies

A popular application of Rogers' diffusion theory to technology products is Moore's[5] "chasm" model.[6] Moore argued that the adoption of technology-based innovations is discontinuous because different groups of adaptors have different adoption patterns and, therefore, require different marketing strategies. Moore's model identifies five distinct categories of customers based on their attitudes toward technology, which correspond to Rogers' five categories: technology enthusiasts (innovators), visionaries (early adopters), pragmatists (early majority), conservatives (late majority), and skeptics (laggards). These five categories of adopters can be described as follows:

- *Technology enthusiasts* (innovators) are fundamentally committed to new technology and derive utility from being the first to experience new technologies.

- *Visionaries* (early adopters) are among the first to apply new technologies to solve problems and exploit opportunities in the marketplace.

- *Pragmatists* (early majority) view technology innovation as a productivity tool. Unlike enthusiasts, they do not appreciate technology for its own sake. Unlike visionaries, they do not use technology innovations to change existing business models but rather to optimize the efficiency and effectiveness of existing business models.

- *Conservatives* (late majority) are generally pessimistic about their ability to significantly benefit from new technological innovations and are reluctant to adopt them.

- *Skeptics* (laggards) are critics of any innovative technology and are not likely to adopt such technologies even when they offer distinct benefits.

Unlike Rogers' model, which implies smooth and continuous progression across segments over the life of an offering, Moore's model assumes that the adoption of technology-based innovations follows a discontinuous pattern. This discontinuity in the adoption process is attributed to the fact that different groups of adaptors have different adoption patterns and, therefore, require different marketing strategies. Thus, once a technology has reached its market potential within a given segment, it may not naturally roll over to the next segment.

To illustrate, even though an innovation has been adopted by technology enthusiasts, it may never be widely accepted by the next segment, the visionaries. In this context, a company's biggest hurdle in promoting technology innovations is to bridge the gaps among different segments. According to Moore, the key gap among segments—typically referred to as a "chasm"—is the one between the early market (enthusiasts and visionaries) and the mainstream market (pragmatists, conservatives, and skeptics). In this context, the chasm describes the impediments to mainstream commercialization of technology innovations that prevent pioneers from gaining mainstream acceptance of their offerings (Figure 8). Thus, to be successful, an offering needs to "cross the chasm" between the early and the mainstream market.

Figure 8. Moore's Application of Rogers' Model to Technology Markets[7]

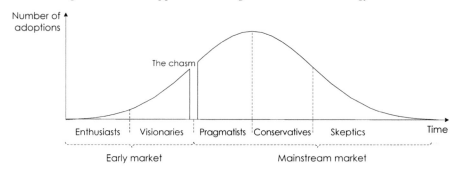

To avoid the perils of discontinuity of adoption of innovations, Moore's model suggests promoting innovations first to technology enthusiasts so that they help educate visionaries. Visionaries, in turn, are likely to serve as a reference for pragmatists, one of the two largest market segments. Leveraging its success with pragmatists, the company should be able to gain the know-how and achieve the economies of scale necessary to make the product reliable and inexpensive, allowing it to meet the needs of conservatives. With respect to skeptics, referred to as "gadflies of high tech," the prescription is to let them be and not promote the innovation to them.

Despite the intuitive appeal of the idea that customers vary in terms of the speed and likelihood of adapting new technologies, Moore's model of technology adoption is subject to several important assumptions that limit the validity of its predictions. Dividing adopters into five distinct categories, as well as predefining the size of each category (e.g., enthusiasts/innovators are the first 2.5% of adapters), often involves an unrealistic assumption that does not apply to all high-tech innovations. This assumption is not an issue for Rogers' model, which assumes continuous adoption across different segments. In contrast, because the presence of gaps among segments is the cornerstone assumption for Moore's model, the identification and size of each segment are crucial. To illustrate, the assumption that a pronounced discontinuity ("chasm") in the adoption process is likely to occur after 16% of customers (the "early market") have adopted the product is not likely to hold universally across different innovation types and industries. In the same vein, relative segment sizes are likely to be a function of the degree to which the technology appeals to the broader market. Indeed, certain types of innovations are likely to have much broader appeal than others and, as a result, the dynamics of their adoption patterns are likely to vary.

Additional Readings

Davidow, William H. (1986), *Marketing High Technology: An Insider's View*. New York, NY: Free Press.

Rogers, Everett M. (2003), *Diffusion of Innovations* (5th ed.). New York, NY: Free Press.

Grieves, Michael (2006), *Product Lifecycle Management: Driving the Next Generation of Lean Thinking*. New York, NY: McGraw-Hill.

Kahn, Kenneth B. (2005), *The PDMA Handbook of New Product Development* (2nd ed.). Hoboken, NJ: John Wiley & Sons.

Notes

[1] Levitt, Theodore (1965), "Exploit the Product Life Cycle," *Harvard Business Review*, 43, (November–December), 81–94.

[2] Adapted from ibid.

[3] Rogers, Everett M. (1962), *Diffusion of Innovations*. New York, NY: Free Press.

[4] Adapted from ibid.

[5] Not to be confused with Intel's cofounder, Gordon E. Moore, widely known for "Moore's Law."

[6] Moore, Geoffrey A. (1991), *Crossing the Chasm: Marketing and Selling High-Tech Products to Mainstream Customers*, New York, NY: HarperBusiness.

[7] Adapted from ibid.

---------------------- Chapter Twenty-Four ----------------------

Managing Product Lines

The essence of the beautiful is unity in variety.
William Somerset Maugham, English writer

The term *product line* is typically used in reference to a set of related offerings that function in a similar manner, are sold to the same target customers, and/or are distributed through the same channels. Product-line management aims to optimize the value delivered by the individual offerings comprising a company's product line. The essential aspects of the product-line-management process are the focus of this chapter.

Overview

From a conceptual standpoint, product-line management is similar to managing an individual offering and involves the same structural aspects: goal, strategy, tactics, implementation, and control. The main difference is that in the case of product-line management, the focus is on the coordination of each of these aspects across individual offerings. Setting product-line goals relates to the objectives of the individual offerings in a company's product line; developing a product-line strategy identifies the relationship among the offerings' strategies; designing product-line tactics relates to the relationship among the tactical aspects of these offerings; developing a product-line implementation plan identifies the infrastructure, processes, and schedules across these offerings; and identifying product-line controls focuses on measures used to evaluate a company's progress toward its product-line goals. The key aspects of product-line management are illustrated in Figure 1 and discussed in more detail in the following sections.

Figure 1. Product-line Management: The Big Picture

Offering A	Offering B	Offering C	
Goal	Goal	Goal	⇐ Product-line goal
Strategy	Strategy	Strategy	⇐ Product-line strategy
Tactics	Tactics	Tactics	⇐ Product-line tactics
Implementation	Implementation	Implementation	⇐ Product-line implementation
Control	Control	Control	⇐ Product-line control

Managing Product-Line Goals

Offerings comprising a company's product line often have different goals. Some have monetary goals, such as profitability, revenue growth, and sales-volume growth, whereas others have nonmonetary goals, such as strengthening a company's and/or an offering's brand, providing synergies with other offerings, preventing competitive entry, and/or establishing market share dominance. Offerings in a company's product line also can vary in terms of their time horizon: Some offerings aim at providing an immediate impact, whereas others may have long-term goals. Finally, offerings may vary in the magnitude of the anticipated impact; some offerings are likely to have greater profit, sales volume, or market share impact than others.

Product-line management strives to coordinate the goals of individual offerings to optimize their joint performance in terms of their focus (e.g., monetary vs. functional) and benchmarks (e.g., time horizon and the magnitude of their impact). Thus, even though a particular offering may have relatively low direct profit potential, it may play an important role in the company's product line by offering synergies with other, more profitable offerings.

Managing Product-Line Strategy

The development of a product-line strategy calls for coordinating the *target markets* of the individual offerings and synchronizing the *value proposition* of each offering to its target customers, the company, and its collaborators. These two aspects of strategy analysis—managing multiple target markets and managing product-line value—are discussed in more detail below.

Managing Multiple Target Markets

Depending on the selection of target customers, two distinct product-line strategies can be identified: (1) a multi-segment strategy, in which offerings target different customer segments and (2) a single-segment strategy, in which offerings target the same customer segment.

Offerings targeting different customer segments typically feature substantively different benefits (e.g., higher quality/higher price offerings vs. lower quality/lower price offerings). In contrast, offerings targeting the same customer segment typically feature similar benefits (e.g., offerings differentiated by minor factors such as color or flavor). The multi-segment and single-segment product lines, illustrated in the context of the company's segmentation and targeting strategy, are depicted in Figure 2.

The multi-segment and single-segment strategies may also be represented in a matrix format as shown in Figure 3, which illustrates two basic approaches to allocating a company's offerings (O1, O2, and O3) across different target segments (S1, S2, and S3). In this case, the underlying customer segmentation is already given, and the key decision involves allocating individual offerings across the identified segments.

Figure 2. Multi-Segment and Single-Segment Product Line Strategies:
Customer-Segmentation Perspective

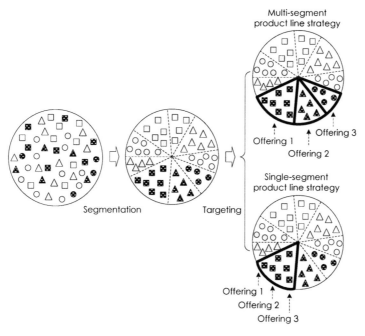

Figure 3. Multi-Segment and Single-Segment Product Line Strategies:
Product-Mix Perspective

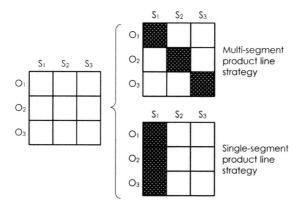

Deciding on whether the offerings in a company's product line target the same customers is important because it determines the degree of similarity across the company's target markets. Thus, offerings targeting the same customer needs are likely to have the same competitors and collaborators, be driven by the same core competencies and strategic assets of the company, and operate in the same business context. In contrast, offerings aimed at different segments are often characterized by different competitors and collaborators, require different competencies and assets from the company, and/or operate in a different business context. In general, the greater the similarity of offerings' market structures in a company's product line, the greater the overlap among the strategies of these offerings and the greater the potential for internal conflicts (e.g., sales cannibalization).

Product-Line Value Management

The key principle in managing product-line value is that individual offerings should be designed to optimize the value of the entire product line to target customers, the company, and its collaborators. Managing product-line value involves two key decisions: (1) deciding how many offerings to carry and (2) deciding how to differentiate these offerings. These two decisions and their impact on the value created to target customers, company, and its collaborators are discussed in more detail in the following sections.

Managing Product-Line Length

The key principle in deciding the length of a company's product line is that the product-line extensions should be designed in a way that optimizes their value to target customers, the company, and its collaborators.

- From a *customer's standpoint*, larger product lines offer the possibility of finding an option that best matches their inherent preferences. Thus, the greater the variety of available products and services, the greater the likelihood that a buyer will find an attractive product/service. Greater variety of offerings can also create value by creating a perception of freedom of choice. Larger product lines can also increase customers' confidence that the options in a company's product line adequately represent all potentially available options, thus reducing the likelihood that a potentially superior alternative is not represented in the product line.

  On the downside, larger product lines might hinder customer preferences because of the increased demand on their cognitive resources caused by the extra effort required to evaluate the additional product options. Extending an offering's product line also might confuse buyers, leading to weaker preferences and lower purchase likelihood.

- From a *company's standpoint*, extending the product line is likely to stimulate customer demand, leading to greater sales revenues. Product-line extensions can also help minimize channel conflicts that are likely to occur when distributors with different cost structures and profit margins have identical offerings (also referred to as horizontal channel conflicts; see Chapter 14 for more detail). By creating channel-specific product variants, a company can minimize the potential for such conflicts. A comprehensive product line is also likely to prevent competitors from taking advantage of an existing market opportunity.

  On the downside, increasing the number of offerings in a company's portfolio is usually associated with an increase in product development, production, distribution, and/or management costs. There is also the potential danger that the new offerings will ultimately cannibalize the sales of the company's existing offerings instead of stimulating new customer demand. Finally, while helping the company avoid horizontal channel conflicts, product-line extensions may lead to vertical channel conflicts (see Chapter 14 for more detail).

- The *collaborator's* perspective on managing product-line length can be illustrated in the context of channel-based collaboration. In this context, increasing the number of company offerings is likely to benefit retailers by making their assortments more attractive to customers searching for greater variety of offerings.

On the downside, expanding a company's product line typically leads to an increase in retailers' costs. Furthermore, when faced with stagnant customer demand, expanding a company's product line may lead to cannibalization of retailer sales, with the new offering stealing share from the retailer's other offerings. As a result, a retailer's total sales volume is likely to remain the same despite the larger inventory.

Designing a Product-Line Differentiation Strategy

An important issue in optimizing the product-line value proposition involves designing the differentiation strategy underlying the product line. Based on the type of differentiation, two common product-line strategies can be identified: vertically differentiated and horizontally differentiated. These two strategies are discussed in more detail below.

- Offerings in *vertically differentiated product lines* can be easily ordered in terms of the relative attractiveness of their benefits and costs, such that this preference ordering is the same for all target customers. To illustrate, most Marriott customers will rate Ritz-Carlton hotels as superior to Marriott hotels, which in turn are likely to be rated superior to Courtyard by Marriott hotels. Because better performance typically comes at a higher price, vertically differentiated products and services typically belong to different price tiers (hence, the name vertical differentiation). When designing its product line, a company may decide to extend its offerings upscale and/or downscale (Figure 4).

Figure 4. Vertically Differentiated Product Line

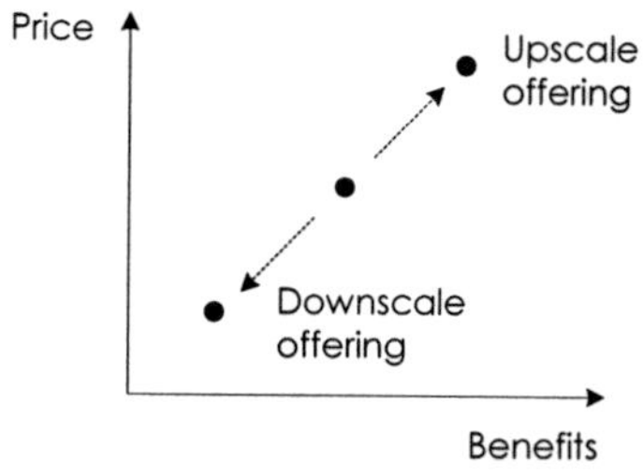

An *upscale extension* is characterized by a company's entry (either by developing its own offering or through acquisition) into a market to which it delivers a higher level of benefits at a higher price. Examples of upscale extensions include Volkswagen's entry into the sport/luxury sedan market with Jetta, Passat, and Phaeton; Fiat's entry into the racing car market with the acquisition of Ferrari; Gap's purchase of Banana Republic; Marriott's acquisition of Ritz-Carlton; and Black & Decker's launch of DeWalt. One of the main reasons for introducing an upscale extension is a company's desire to capture a more lucrative market.

Downscale extensions are characterized by a company's entry into a market to which it delivers a lower level of benefits at a lower price. Examples of downscale extensions include Intel's introduction of Celeron; United Airlines' launch of Ted, and Gap's introduction of Old Navy stores. Downscale extensions are typically driven by a desire to capture larger customer segments, even though a move downscale is typically associated with lower profit margins. Downscale extensions are especially beneficial to companies operating in industries requiring high fixed-cost investments and in which economies of scale may be achieved, such as the airline and automotive industries.

The simplest example of a vertically differentiated product line involves a set of two offerings, one of which delivers greater benefits at a higher price (e.g., economy vs. first-class airline service). Slightly more complex is three-tier positioning, often referred to as "Good–Better–Best," in which the "best" offering delivers the highest level of benefits at the highest price, whereas the "good" offering delivers the lowest level of benefits at the lowest price (e.g., airline service: first, business, and economy class; Figure 5). A more detailed discussion of the Good–Better–Best strategy is offered in Chapter 21.

Figure 5. "Good–Better–Best" Product-Line Strategy

- Offerings in a *horizontally differentiated product line* vary on benefits that do not imply a universal preference ordering. Thus, because taste preferences are idiosyncratic, offerings such as different types of soft drinks (regular, cherry, vanilla, diet, caffeine-free), different yogurt flavors, and different product colors comprise horizontally differentiated product lines. Although price may vary across horizontally differentiated offerings, it is not the key differentiating factor (Figure 6).

Figure 6. Horizontally Differentiated Product Line (Price–Benefit Perspective)

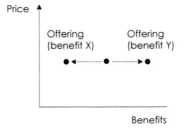

Because price is not the key distinguishing factor in the case of horizontally differentiated offerings, a more meaningful representation of the logic of the company's product line involves illustrating tradeoffs required from customers. This representation is shown in Figure 7, in which customers have to trade off an offering's performance on two of the key benefits (e.g., power and battery life of a laptop computer, effectiveness and mildness of a laundry detergent, or taste and nutrition of a meal).

Figure 7. Horizontally Differentiated Product Line (Benefit–Tradeoff Perspective)

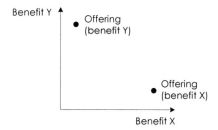

Product-Line Tactics

Managing product-line tactics involves optimizing the marketing mix—product, service, brand, price, incentives, communication, and distribution—of individual offerings in a way that maximizes the value created by the company's entire product line.

- *Product-line product and service management* aims to optimize the benefits delivered by the product and service aspects of an offering relative to those delivered by the other offerings comprising a company's product line. A key decision in product-line management involves deciding on the degree of differentiation of the products and services comprising a company's product line. Because product and service benefits are among the key determinants of an offering's value proposition, meaningful differentiation of these benefits is crucial for success. A common mistake involves insufficient differentiation among the offerings within the company's product line. In the case of vertical line extensions, this lack of differentiation is likely to lead to cannibalization of the share of upscale offerings since most customers will ultimately gravitate toward the lower-priced offerings. In the case of horizontal line extensions, the lack of differentiation can lead to customer confusion, choice deferral, and increased preference for competitors' offerings. Another common error involves "over-differentiating" the offerings in the company's product line. To illustrate, to avoid cannibalization, Intel overstretched its downscale extension Celeron, which resulted in inferior performance relative to its competitors AMD and Cyrix.

- *Product-line brand management* focuses on issues concerning the branding of the individual offerings comprising the product line. In this context, a key decision involves determining whether different offerings in a company's product line should share the same brand name (either using the same brand name or as a sub-brand) or be positioned as new brands.

The rationale for using the same brand for all offerings in a company's product line is straightforward: A single brand is not only cost-efficient but also can assure fast adoption of the new offering. Using a single brand when extending given product line can strengthen the existing brand by raising its image, as when adding a high-end offering carrying the same brand name. To illustrate, by introducing a line of premium, award-winning Gallo-branded wines, E. & J. Gallo Winery aimed in part to strengthen the image of the Gallo brand. Using a single brand can also strengthen the existing brand by increasing the brand's visibility to target customers. For example, extending the Starbucks brand to bottled coffee drinks was likely to strengthen the brand's image by demonstrating its coffee-related expertise.

The downside of a single-brand strategy is that applying the same brand to offerings delivering a variety of benefits to different customer segments could potentially weaken the brand by diluting its meaning to target customers. This brand dilution is likely to occur when a product line is extended by adding a low-end offering carrying the same brand name. For example, in 1986 General Motors introduced a Chevrolet-based compact car branded as Cadillac Cimarron and, by doing so, weakened the image of its upscale Cadillac brand. Brand dilution can also occur when a single brand is extended to diverse product categories that are inconsistent with the meaning of the brand. To illustrate, the introduction of Cayenne, Porsche's SUV, was likely to dilute its traditional image as a pure sports car manufacturer.

- *Product-line price management* aims to optimize the price of each individual offering to maximize the value delivered by the company's product line as a whole. Thus, product-line pricing can be used to influence the demand for a company's offerings by varying their prices. To illustrate, restaurants often price wine they are trying to dispose of as the second cheapest in its category because many customers who are not willing to spend much on wine are often embarrassed to select the least expensive one. The two common product-line pricing errors involve under-pricing (which is often a result of a company's desire to make its lower-end offerings superior to the low-priced competitor offerings) or overpricing (which is often a result of a company's desire to avoid the possibility for cannibalization of the higher end offerings by the lower-priced offerings) the lower-end offering. For example, Gap Warehouse, the forerunner to Old Navy, failed because, to avoid cannibalizing sales in Gap's core stores, it set relatively high prices, which in turn made it less attractive relative to its competitors.

- *Product-line incentives management* aims to optimize the impact of incentives applied to each individual offering with respect to the value delivered by the entire product line. Because incentives rarely affect the core functional benefits of the offering, they are often used to channel customer demand to a particular offering in a company's product line. For example, by offering incentives, airlines stimulate the demand on routes with excess capacity, hotels manage occupancy levels across different locations, and retailers manage demand for different items in their assortment.

- *Product-line communication management* aims to differentiate the offerings in the company's product line by highlighting their unique benefits and costs. To illustrate, in the case of vertically differentiated offerings with two or three price-tier levels, companies often use descriptions, such as "regular" vs. "premium" and "good" vs. "better" vs. "best" to indicate the relative place of each offering. In the case of vertically differentiated product lines, numbers are particularly useful because they inherently imply a certain ordering of the offerings (e.g., BMW 1-series, 3-series, 5-series, and 7-series). In the same vein, to communicate the differences among horizontally differentiated offerings, companies use letters, symbols, and numbers, as well as verbal descriptions (e.g., "diet" vs. "regular").

- *Product-line distribution management* aims to align the value-delivery strategies of individual offerings into a coordinated value-delivery strategy. This involves managing potential channel conflicts, which are driven by the difference in the profit optimization strategies among the various members of the distribution channel. In this context, product-line management aims to optimize different aspects of the value-delivery process in a way that maximizes the value of the entire product line to all participants in the marketing exchange.

Summary

The term *product line* refers to a set of related offerings that function in a similar manner, are sold to the same target customers, or are distributed through the same channels.

Product line management is conceptually similar to managing an individual offering and involves the same structural aspects: goal analysis, strategy analysis, tactical analysis, implementation, and control. The key difference is that in the case of product-line management, the focus is on the coordination of each of these aspects across individual offerings. Thus, setting product-line goals relates to the objectives of the individual offerings in a company's product line; developing a product-line strategy identifies the relationships among the offerings' strategies; designing product-line tactics relates to the relationship among the tactical aspects of these offerings; developing a product-line implementation plan identifies the infrastructure, processes, and schedules across these offerings; and identifying product-line controls focuses on measures used to evaluate a company's progress toward its product-line goals.

The development of a product-line strategy involves coordinating the target markets of the individual offerings and synchronizing the value proposition of each offering to its target customers, the company, and its collaborators.

Depending on whether the company offerings target the same customer segments, two distinct product line strategies can be identified: a multi-segment strategy, in which offerings target different customer segments, and a single-segment strategy, in which offerings target the same customer segment. Offerings targeting different customer segments typically feature substantively different benefits (e.g., higher quality/higher price offerings vs. lower quality/lower price offerings). In contrast, offerings targeting the same customer segment typically feature similar benefits (e.g., offerings differentiated by minor factors such as color or flavor).

The key principle in managing product-line (assortment) value is that individual offerings should be designed to optimize the value of the entire product line to target customers, the company, and its collaborators. Managing product-line value involves two key decisions: deciding how many offerings to carry and deciding how to differentiate these offerings.

Managing product-line tactics involves optimizing the marketing mix—product, service, brand, price, incentives, communication, and distribution—of individual offerings in a way that maximizes the value created by the company's entire product line.

Additional Readings

Cooper, Robert G., Scott J. Edgett, and Elko J. Kleinschmidt (2002), *Portfolio Management for New Products* (2nd ed.). Oxford: Perseus.

Kotler, Philip and Kevin Lane Keller (2008), *Marketing Management* (13th ed.). Upper Saddle River, NJ: Prentice Hall.

Lehmann, Donald R. and Russell S. Winer (2005), *Product Management* (4th ed.). Boston, MA: McGraw-Hill/Irwin.

Part Six

References

Chapter Twenty-Five

Writing a Strategic Marketing Plan

Plans are of little importance, but planning is essential.
Winston Churchill, British politician

The strategic marketing plan documents a proposed course of action pertaining to a particular offering, a product line, and/or an entire company. The basic aspects of developing a strategic marketing plan are the focus of this chapter.

Overview

Writing a marketing plan is often confused with strategic planning, partially because strategic planning is frequently driven by the need to generate a marketing plan. Strategic planning and writing a marketing plan, however, are two different activities. Strategic planning is the process of identifying a goal and developing a course of action to achieve this goal. Writing a marketing plan merely documents the identified goal and the decided-upon course of action.

Most marketing plans are organized in a similar fashion: they start with an executive summary, followed by an overview of the current situation; an outline of the company's goal(s), strategy, tactics, implementation, and controls; and conclude with a set of exhibits. This common approach to writing marketing plans is illustrated in Figure 1.

Figure 1. The Marketing Plan

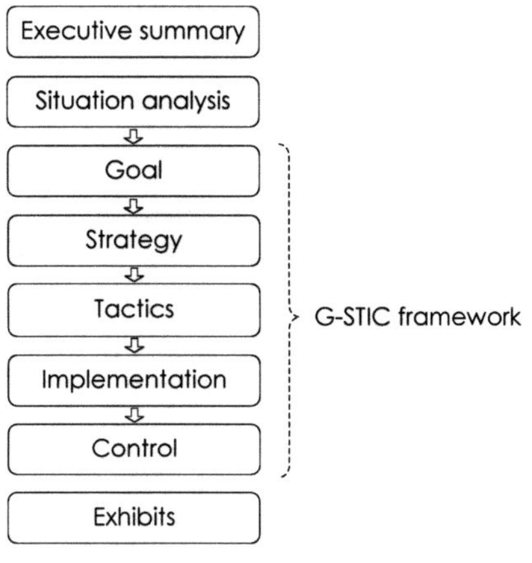

An example of a marketing plan following the value-centric approach advanced in this book is outlined in the following section. In addition, several alternative approaches to writing marketing plans are presented at the end of this chapter.

The Value-Centric Strategic Marketing Plan

Similar to most business documents, the marketing plan begins with an executive summary that highlights its most important aspects. The executive summary is followed by a situation analysis that evaluates market conditions in which the company operates, assesses its competitive position, and identifies target markets in which it will compete.

The core of the value-centric marketing plan is organized following the G-STIC framework. It begins with an outline of the *goals* identifying the *focus* and performance *benchmarks* to be achieved by the company. The goal analysis is followed by a description of the company's *strategy*, which identifies the *target market* and outlines the offering's *value proposition* to its customers, collaborators, and the company. The strategy analysis is followed by a description of marketing *tactics* reflected in the processes of *designing, communicating,* and *delivering value*. The tactical analysis is followed by an *implementation* plan that identifies the *infrastructure, processes,* and *schedules* involved in translating the planned strategy and tactics into reality. The *control* section of the marketing plan outlines a policy for *evaluating the company's performance* and *monitoring the environment* to ensure adequate progress toward the set goal. The G-STIC component of the marketing plan is summarized in the Action-Planning Pyramid illustrated in Figure 2.

Figure 2: The G-STIC Framework for Marketing Planning

The value-centric marketing approach to marketing planning illustrated in Figure 2 builds on three key principles: (1) from a structural standpoint, it follows the G-STIC framework (goal, strategy, tactics, implementation, and control); (2) its strategic aspect follows the 5-C (customers, collaborators, company, competitors, and context) and 3-V frameworks (customer value, company value, and collaborator value), and (3) its tactical aspect follows the D-C-D framework (designing, communicating, and delivering value).

The key steps of writing a value-centric marketing plan are outlined below.

The Strategic Marketing Plan

---

1. Executive Summary
Provide a brief overview of the situation, the company's goal, the proposed course of action, and its rationale.

2. Situation Analysis
Evaluate the environment in which the company operates and identify target market(s) in which it will compete.

3. Goal(s)
Identify the company's primary goal. Define its focus (e.g., net income) and key benchmarks (e.g., quantify the desired net income and identify the time frame for achieving it).

4. Strategy
Identify the target market (i.e., target customers, collaborators, the company, competitors, and context) and define the offering's value proposition to target customers, collaborators, and the company.

- *Target market*
    - *Customers.* Define the need(s) to be fulfilled by the offering and identify the distinguishing characteristics (profile) of customers with such needs.
    - *Collaborators.* Identify the key collaborators (e.g., suppliers, channel members, and communication partners) and their strategic goals.
    - *Company.* Define the strategic business unit responsible for the offering, the relevant personnel, and key stakeholders.
    - *Competitors.* Identify the competitive offerings that provide similar benefits to target customers and collaborators.
    - *Context.* Evaluate the relevant economic, technological, socio-cultural, regulatory, and physical context in which the company operates.
- *Value proposition*
    - *Customer value.* Define the offering's value proposition and positioning strategy to target customers.
    - *Collaborator value.* Define the offering's value proposition and positioning strategy to collaborators.
    - *Company value.* Outline the offering's value proposition and positioning strategy to company stakeholders and personnel.

5. Tactics

Outline the key aspects of the offering's marketing mix.

- *Product:* Define relevant product characteristics (attributes and benefits).
- *Service:* Identify relevant service characteristics (attributes and benefits).
- *Brand:* Determine the key elements (e.g., name, logo, and symbol) and the meaning of the offering's brand.
- *Price:* Identify the price(s) at which the offering is provided to customers and channel members.
- *Incentives:* Define the incentives offered to customers (e.g., price reductions), collaborators (e.g., trade allowances), and the company personnel (e.g., bonuses).
- *Communications:* Identify the manner in which the key aspects of the offering (product, service, brand, price, incentives) are communicated to target customers, collaborators, and the company personnel and stakeholders.
- *Distribution:* Describe the manner in which the key aspects of the offering (product, service, brand, price, incentives) are delivered to target customers, collaborators, and company personnel and stakeholders.

6. Implementation

Define the offering's implementation plan.

- *Infrastructure.* Outline the organizational structure of the business unit managing the offering and its relationship with collaborators.
- *Processes.* Outline the business processes involved in implementing the company's strategy and tactics.
- *Schedule.* Delineate the implementation schedule.

7. Control

Identify the metrics used to measure the company's performance and to monitor the environment in which the company operates.

- *Performance evaluation.* Define the criteria for evaluating the company's performance and progress toward its goals.
- *Environmental analysis.* Identify metrics for evaluating the environment in which the company operates and outline the processes for making adjustments to the plan to accommodate changes in the environment.

8. Exhibits

Provide additional information to support specific aspects of the marketing plan. This information may include target market data (e.g., industry overview, company overview, and customer trend analyses), financial calculations (e.g., breakeven analysis, best/worst case scenario analysis, and customer value analysis), details pertaining to the marketing mix (e.g., product specifications, communication plan, and distribution structure), the implementation (e.g., an overview of the infrastructure, processes, and schedules) and control (e.g., performance metrics and environmental analysis).

Summary

The strategic marketing plan delineates the key aspects of managing the value of a company's offering, its product lines, and/or the entire company. The marketing plan involves eight key components: an executive summary; situation analysis; an outline of the company's goal(s), strategy, tactics, implementation, and controls; and a set of relevant exhibits.

The value-centric marketing approach to marketing planning outlined in this chapter builds on three key principles: (1) from a structural standpoint, it follows the G-STIC framework (goal, strategy, tactics, implementation, and control); (2) its strategic aspect follows the 5-C (defining target customers, collaborators, company, competitors, and context) and 3-V frameworks (optimizing customer value, company value, and collaborator value), and (3) its tactical aspect follows the D-C-D framework (designing, communicating, and delivering value).

Alternative Marketing Plan Formats

Marketing Plan A[1]

1. Executive summary and table of contents
2. Current marketing situation
3. Opportunity and issue analysis
4. Objectives
5. Marketing strategy
6. Action programs
7. Financial projections
8. Controls

Marketing Plan B[2]

1. Executive summary
2. Situation analysis
   - Market summary (demographics, needs, trends, growth)
   - SWOT analysis
   - Competition
   - Product offering
   - Keys to success
   - Critical issues
3. Marketing strategy
   - Mission
   - Marketing objectives
   - Financial objectives
   - Target markets
   - Positioning
   - Strategies
   - Marketing mix
   - Marketing research
4. Financials
   - Break-even analysis
   - Sales forecast
   - Expense forecast

5. Controls
   - Implementation
   - Marketing organization
   - Contingency planning

Marketing Plan C[3]

1. Executive summary
2. Company description
3. Strategic focus and plan
   - Mission
   - Goals
   - Core competencies and sustainable competitive advantage
4. Situation analysis
   - SWOT
   - Industry analysis
   - Competition analysis
   - Company analysis
   - Customer analysis
5. Product-market focus
   - Marketing and product objectives
   - Target markets
   - Points of difference
   - Positioning
6. Marketing program
   - Product strategy
   - Price strategy
   - Promotion strategy
   - Distribution strategy
7. Financial data and projections
8. Implementation plan
9. Evaluation and control
10. Appendices

Marketing Plan D[4]

1. Executive summary
2. Introduction
3. Situational analysis
   - The situational environs
     - Demand
     - Social and cultural factors
     - Demographics
     - Economic conditions
     - Technology
     - Politics
     - Laws and regulations
   - The neutral environs
     - Financial environment
     - Government environment
     - Media environment
     - Special interest environment

- The competitor environs
- The company environs
4. The target market
5. Problems and opportunities
6. Marketing objectives
7. Marketing strategy
8. Marketing tactics
9. Implementation and control
10. Summary
11. Appendices

Marketing Plan E[5]

1. Executive summary
2. Situation analysis
   - Category/competitor definition
   - Category analysis
     - Aggregate market factors
       - Category size
       - Category growth
       - Stage in product life cycle
       - Seasonality
       - Profits
     - Category factors
       - Threat of new entrants/exits
       - Bargaining power of buyers
       - Bargaining power of suppliers
       - Pressure from substitutes
       - Category capacity
       - Current category rivalry
     - Environmental factors
       - Technological
       - Political
       - Economic
       - Regulatory
       - Social
   - Company and competitor analysis
     - Product features matrix
     - Objectives
     - Strategies
     - Marketing mix
     - Profits
     - Value chain
     - Differential advantage/resource analysis
       - Ability to conceive and design new products
       - Ability to produce/manufacture or deliver the service
       - Ability to market
       - Ability to finance
       - Ability to manage
       - Will to succeed in this category
     - Expected future strategies

- Customer analysis
  - Who are the customers?
  - What do they buy and how do they use it?
  - Where do they buy?
  - When do they buy?
  - How do they choose?
  - Why they prefer a product
  - How they respond to marketing programs
  - Will they buy it again?
  - Long-term value of customers
  - Segmentation
- Planning assumptions
  - Market potential
  - Category and product sales forecasts
  - Other assumptions

3. Objectives
   - Corporate objectives (if appropriate)
   - Divisional objectives (if appropriate)
   - Marketing objective(s)
     - Volume and profit
     - Time frame
     - Secondary objectives (e.g., brand equity, customer, and new product)
     - Program (marketing mix)

4. Product /brand strategy
   - Customer target(s)
   - Competitor target(s)
   - Product/service features
   - Core strategy
     - Value proposition
     - Product positioning

5. Supporting marketing programs
   - Integrated marketing communications plan
   - Advertising
   - Promotion
   - Sales
   - Price
   - Channels
   - Customer management activities
   - Website
   - Marketing research
   - Partnerships/joint ventures

6. Financial documents
   - Budgets
   - Pro forma statements

7. Monitors and controls
   - Marketing metrics
   - Secondary data
   - Primary data

8. Contingency plans

Marketing Plan F[6]

1. Executive summary
2. Agenda
3. State of the business
   - Vision and product positioning
   - Recent results
   - Business challenge
4. Objectives
5. Strategic initiatives
6. Tactics
7. Financial implications
8. Milestones
9. Executive summary

Notes

[1] Adapted from Philip Kotler (2003), *A Framework for Marketing Management* (2nd ed.). Upper Saddle River, NJ: Prentice Hall.

[2] Adapted from Philip Kotler and Kevin Lane Keller (2008), *Marketing Management* (13th ed.). Upper Saddle River, NJ: Prentice Hall.

[3] Adapted from Roger A. Kerin and Robert A. Peterson (2000), *Strategic Marketing Problems: Cases and Comments* (9th ed.). Upper Saddle River, NJ: Prentice Hall.

[4] Adapted from William A. Cohen (2001), *The Marketing Plan* (3rd ed.). Hoboken, NJ: John Wiley & Sons.

[5] Adapted from Donald R. Lehman and Russell S. Winer (2004), *Analysis for Marketing Planning* (6th ed.). New York, NY: McGraw-Hill.

[6] Adapted from Tim Calkins (2008), *Breakthrough Marketing Plans: How to Stop Wasting Time and Start Driving Growth*, New York, NY: Palgrave Macmillan.

Chapter Twenty-Six

Essential Financial Concepts in Marketing

Break-Even Analysis: Analysis aimed at identifying the break-even point at which the benefits and costs associated with a particular action are equal, and beyond which profit occurs. The four most common types of break-even analyses are: (1) break-even of a fixed-cost investment, (2) break-even of a price cut, (3) break-even of a variable cost increase, and (4) cannibalization break-even analysis.

Break-Even Analysis of a Fixed-Cost Investment: Analysis aimed at identifying the sales volume at which a company neither makes a profit nor incurs a loss after making a fixed cost investment (see Appendix 2 for more details).

Break-Even Analysis of a Price Cut: Analysis aimed at identifying the increase in the sales volume needed for the price cut to have no impact on profitability (see Appendix 3 for more details).

Break-Even Analysis of a Variable-Cost Increase: Analysis aimed at identifying the increase in the sales volume needed for the increase in variable costs to have no impact on profitability (see Appendix 4 for more details).

Break-Even Analysis of Cannibalization: Analysis aimed at identifying the ratio of the cannibalized sales volume of an existing offering to the sales volume generated by a new offering at which a company neither makes a profit nor incurs a loss (see Appendix 5 for more details).

Compound Annual Growth Rate (CAGR): The year-to-year growth rate of an investment over a specified period of time.

Contribution Margin ($): When expressed in monetary terms ($), contribution margin typically refers to the difference between total revenue and total variable costs. Contribution margin can also be calculated on a per-unit basis as the difference between the unit selling price and the unit variable cost. The per-unit margin, expressed in monetary terms ($), is also referred to as contribution (i.e., the dollar amount that each unit sold "contributes" to the payment of fixed costs).

$$\text{Margin}_{\text{Total}}(\$) = \text{Revenue}_{\text{Total}} - \text{Variable costs}_{\text{Total}}$$

$$\text{Margin}_{\text{Unit}}(\$) = \text{Price}_{\text{Unit}} - \text{Variable costs}_{\text{Unit}}$$

Contribution Margin (%): When expressed in percentages (%), contribution margin typically refers to the ratio of the difference between total revenue and total variable costs to total revenue. Contribution margin can also be expressed as the ratio of unit contribution to unit selling price.

$$\text{Margin (\%)} = \frac{\text{Revenue}_{\text{Total}} - \text{Variable cost}_{\text{Total}}}{\text{Revenue}_{\text{Total}}} = \frac{\text{Price}_{\text{Unit}} - \text{Variable cost}_{\text{Unit}}}{\text{Price}_{\text{Unit}}}$$

Cost of Goods Sold (COGS): Expenses directly related to creating the goods or services being sold. Cost of goods sold can have a variable (e.g., cost of raw materials, cost of turning raw materials into goods) and a fixed component (e.g., depreciation of equipment).

Economic Value Analysis: The process of translating the nonmonetary (i.e., functional and psychological) aspects of an offering's value proposition into financial terms (see Appendix 6 for more details).

Fixed Costs: Expenses that do not fluctuate with output volume within a relevant period (see Appendix 1 for more details).

Goodwill: Accounting term referring to a company's intangible assets. Goodwill is recorded on a company's books when it acquires another company and pays a premium over the listed book value of its assets. The excess paid is categorized as goodwill, added to the acquiring company's balance sheet as an asset, and then depreciated over time (usually fifteen years). The U.S. Internal Revenue Code defines goodwill as the value of a trade or business attributable to the expectancy of continued customer patronage. Such value results from several factors, including quality product lines and stable employees.

Gross (Profit) Margin: The ratio of gross (total) profit to gross (total) revenue (sometimes also used as a synonym for gross profit). Gross margin analysis is a useful tool because it implicitly includes unit selling prices of products or services, unit costs, and unit volume. Note, however, the difference between gross margin and contribution margin: Contribution margin includes all variable costs; in contrast, gross margin includes some, but often not all, variable costs, a number of which can be part of the operating margin.

$$\text{Gross margin} = \frac{\text{Gross profit}}{\text{Gross revenue}} = \frac{\text{Gross revenue} - \text{Cost of goods sold}}{\text{Gross revenue}}$$

Gross Profit: The difference between gross (total) revenue and total cost of goods sold. Gross profit can also be calculated on a per unit basis as the difference between unit selling price and unit cost of goods sold. For example, if a company sells 100 units, each priced at \$1 and each costing the company \$.30 to manufacture, then the unit gross profit is \$.70, the total gross profit is \$70, and the unit and total gross margins are 70%.

$$\text{Gross profit}_{\text{Total}} = \text{Revenue}_{\text{Total}} - \text{Cost of goods sold}_{\text{Total}}$$

$$\text{Gross profit}_{\text{Unit}} = \text{Price}_{\text{Unit}} - \text{Cost of goods sold}_{\text{Unit}}$$

Income Statement: Financial document showing a company's income and expenses over a given period (see Appendix 7 for more details).

Internal Rate of Return (IRR): The annualized effective compounded return rate that can be earned on the invested capital (i.e., the yield on the investment).

Margin: The difference between two factors, typically expressed either in monetary terms or percentages. There are two types of margins: (1) contribution margins, which reflect the relationship between variable and fixed costs and (2) income margins, which reflect the relationships between a company's gross (total) profit, income, and gross (total) revenue.

Marginal Cost: The cost of producing one extra unit.

Market Share: An offering's share of the total sales of all offerings within the product category in which the brand competes. Market share is determined by dividing an offering's sales volume by the total category sales volume. Sales can be defined in terms of revenues or on a unit basis (e.g., number of items sold or number of customers served).

$$\text{Market share} = \frac{\text{An offering's sales in market X}}{\text{Total sales in market X}}$$

Markup: See *trade margin*.

Net Earnings: See *net income*.

Net Income: Gross (total) revenue minus all costs and expenses (e.g., cost of goods sold, operating expenses, depreciation, interest, and taxes) during a given period of time.

$$\text{Net income} = \text{Gross revenue - Total costs}$$

Net Margin: The ratio of net income to gross (total) revenue.

$$\text{Net margin} = \frac{\text{Net income}}{\text{Gross revenue}}$$

Operating Expenses: The primary costs, other than cost of goods sold, incurred to generate revenues (e.g., sales, marketing, research and development, and general and administrative expenses).

Operating Income: Gross profit minus operating expenses. Operating income reflects the firm's profitability from current operations without regard to the interest charges accruing from the firm's capital structure.

$$\text{Operating income} = \text{Gross profit} - \text{Operating expenses}$$

Operating Margin: The ratio of operating income to gross (total) revenue.

$$\text{Operating margin} = \frac{\text{Operating income}}{\text{Gross revenue}}$$

Return on Investment (ROI): Net income as a percentage of the investment required to generate this income. Conceptually similar metrics are Return on Assets (ROA), Return on Net Assets (RONA), and Return on Capital (ROC).

$$\text{ROI} = \frac{\text{Gain from an investment} - \text{Cost of investment}}{\text{Cost of investment}}$$

Return on Marketing Investment (ROMI): A measure of the efficiency of a company's marketing expenditures. Most often calculated in terms of incremental net income, sales revenues, market share, or contribution margin. ROMI can also be calculated with respect to the overall marketing expenditures or to a specific marketing mix variable (e.g., branding, incentives, and communications).

$$\text{ROMI} = \frac{\text{Incremental net income generated by the marketing investment}}{\text{Cost of the marketing investment}}$$

Return on Sales (ROS): Net income as a percentage of sales revenues.

$$ROS = \frac{\text{Net income}}{\text{Sales revenue}}$$

Total Costs: The sum of the fixed and variable costs (see Appendix 1 for more details).

Trade Margin: The difference between unit selling price and unit cost at each level of a marketing channel (see Appendix 8 for more details). Trade margins can be expressed in monetary terms or as a percentage. Trade margins are typically determined on the basis of selling price, but practices vary among firms and industries.

Variable Costs: Expenses that fluctuate in direct proportion to the output volume of units produced (see Appendix 1 for more details).

Variable Profit: The difference between gross (total) revenue and variable costs.

Appendix 1: Fixed, Variable, and Total Costs

Cost accounting identifies three basic types of costs: fixed costs, variable costs, and total costs.

Fixed costs are expenses that do not fluctuate with output volume within a relevant period. Typical examples of fixed costs include research and development expenses, mass media advertising expenses, rent, interest on debt, insurance, plant and equipment expenses, and salary of permanent full-time workers. Even though their absolute size remains unchanged regardless of output volume, fixed costs become progressively smaller per unit of output as volume increases, a decrease that results from the larger number of output units over which fixed costs are allocated.

In contrast, *variable costs* are expenses that fluctuate in direct proportion to the output volume of units produced. For example, the cost of raw materials and expenses incurred by consumer incentives (e.g., coupons, price discounts, rebates, and premiums) are commonly viewed as variable costs. Other expenses, such as channel incentives (e.g., promotional allowances) and sales force compensation, can be classified as either fixed or variable costs depending on their structure (e.g., fixed salary vs. performance-based compensation).

Finally, the term *total costs* refers to the sum of the fixed and variable costs. The relationship between fixed, variable, and total costs is shown in Figure 1.

Figure 1: The Relationship between Fixed, Variable, and Total Costs

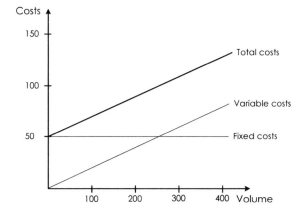

Deciding which costs are fixed and which costs are variable depends on the time horizon. For example, in the short run, the salaries of permanent full-time employees will be considered fixed costs because they do not depend on output volume. In the longer run, however, a company may adjust the number and/or salaries of permanent employees based on the demand for its products or services—a scenario in which these costs are considered variable rather than fixed. Thus, in the long run, all costs are considered variable.

Appendix 2: Break-Even Analysis of a Fixed-Cost Investment

Break-even analysis of a fixed-cost investment identifies the unit or dollar sales volume at which the company is able to recoup a particular investment, such as research and development expenses, product improvement costs, and/or the costs of an advertising campaign. The break-even volume of a fixed-cost investment (BEV$_{FC}$) is the ratio of the size of the fixed-cost investment to the unit margin.

$$BEV_{FC} = \frac{\text{Fixed cost investment}}{\text{Unit margin}}$$

Because the unit margin can be expressed as the difference between unit selling price and unit variable costs, break-even volume is also often given as:

$$BEV_{FC} = \frac{\text{Fixed-cost investment}}{\text{Unit selling price} - \text{Unit variable cost}}$$

The break-even analysis of a fixed-cost investment can be illustrated as shown in Figure 2.

Figure 2: Break-Even of a Fixed Cost Investment

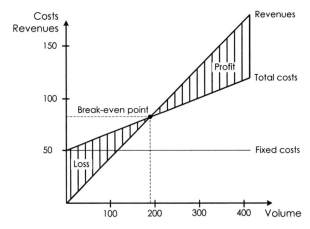

To illustrate, consider an offering priced at $100 with variable costs of $50 and fixed costs of $50M. In this case,

$$BEV_{FC} = \frac{\text{Fixed cost investment}}{\text{Unit margin}} = \frac{\$50M}{\$100-\$50} = 1,000,000$$

This implies that for a $50M fixed-cost investment to break even, sales volume should reach 1,000,000 items.

In addition to the break-even analysis of a fixed-cost investment associated with launching a new offering, a company may need to calculate the break-even volume of a change (most often an increase) in its current fixed-cost investment. Typical problems to which this type of analysis can be applied are estimating the incremental increase in sales necessary to cover the costs of an R&D project, the costs of an advertising campaign, and even the costs of increasing the compensation package of senior executives. The break-even analysis of such increase in the fixed-cost investment is shown in Figure 3.

Figure 3: Break-Even of an Increase in a Fixed-Cost Investment

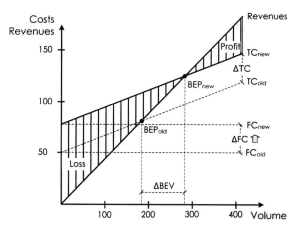

To illustrate, consider the impact of an increase in fixed costs from $50M to $60M for a product priced at $100 with variable costs of $50. In this case,

$$BEV_{\Delta FC} = \frac{\text{Increase in the fixed-cost investment}}{\text{Unit margin}} = \frac{\$60M - \$50M}{\$100 - \$50} = 200,000$$

This implies that for the $10M fixed-cost investment to break even, sales volume should increase by 200,000 items.

Appendix 3: Break-Even Analysis of a Price Cut

The impact of a price cut on profitability is twofold. On one hand, lowering price tends to increase the volume of units sold, thus increasing total revenues. On the other hand, lowering price decreases unit margin, thus lowering total revenues. In this context, break-even analysis estimates the increase in sales volume that needs to be achieved for a price cut to have a neutral impact on profitability. The break-even analysis of a price cut is shown in Figure 4.

Figure 4: Break-Even of a Decrease in Revenues (Resulting from a Price Cut)

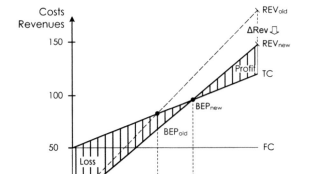

To break even, lost profits resulting from a lower margin after a price cut must be equal to the additional profits generated by the incremental volume from the lower price. Thus, to have a neutral or positive impact on the company's bottom line, the additional profits generated from the incremental volume resulting from a lower price must be equal to or greater than the lost profits that result from a lower margin.

$$\text{Profit}_{\text{NewPrice}} \geq \text{Profit}_{\text{OldPrice}}$$

Given that profit is a function of unit volume and unit margin, the above equation can be modified as follows:

$$\text{Volume}_{\text{NewPrice}} \cdot \text{Margin}_{\text{NewPrice}} \geq \text{Volume}_{\text{OldPrice}} \cdot \text{Margin}_{\text{OldPrice}}$$

Now, the above equation can be restructured as follows:

$$\text{Volume}_{\text{NewPrice}} \geq \frac{\text{Margin}_{\text{OldPrice}}}{\text{Margin}_{\text{NewPrice}}} \cdot \text{Volume}_{\text{OldPrice}}$$

Hence, the sales volume that needs to be achieved for a price cut to break even is:

$$\text{BEV}_{\text{PC}} = \frac{\text{Margin}_{\text{OldPrice}}}{\text{Margin}_{\text{NewPrice}}} \cdot \text{Volume}_{\text{OldPrice}}$$

In addition to calculating the break-even volume of a price cut, it may be useful to calculate the rate at which sales volume must increase for a price cut to be profitable. In this context, the break-even rate of a price cut (BER_{PC}) can be derived from the second equation as follows:

$$\frac{\text{Volume}_{\text{NewPrice}}}{\text{Volume}_{\text{OldPrice}}} \geq \frac{\text{Margin}_{\text{OldPrice}}}{\text{Margin}_{\text{NewPrice}}}$$

$$\frac{\text{Volume}_{\text{NewPrice}}}{\text{Volume}_{\text{OldPrice}}} - 1 \geq \frac{\text{Margin}_{\text{OldPrice}}}{\text{Margin}_{\text{NewPrice}}} - 1$$

$$\frac{\text{Volume}_{\text{NewPrice}} - \text{Volume}_{\text{OldPrice}}}{\text{Volume}_{\text{OldPrice}}} \geq \frac{\text{Margin}_{\text{OldPrice}}}{\text{Margin}_{\text{NewPrice}}} - 1$$

The left side of the equation reflects the increase in volume resulting from a price cut as a percentage of the initial volume before the price cut. Hence, the Break-Even Rate (BER$_{\text{PC}}$) at which sales should increase so that a price cut has a neutral impact on profitability is:

$$\text{BER}_{\text{PC}} = \frac{\text{Margin}_{\text{OldPrice}}}{\text{Margin}_{\text{NewPrice}}} - 1$$

To illustrate, consider the impact of a price cut from \$100 to \$75 for a product with a variable cost of \$50. In this case, Margin$_{\text{OldPrice}}$ = \$100 − \$50 = \$50 and Margin$_{\text{NewPrice}}$ = \$75 − \$50 = \$25. Therefore, the break-even volume can be calculated as follows:

$$\text{BEV}_{\text{PC}} = \frac{\text{Margin}_{\text{OldPrice}}}{\text{Margin}_{\text{NewPrice}}} \cdot \text{Volume}_{\text{OldPrice}} = \frac{\$50}{\$25} \cdot \text{Volume}_{\text{OldPrice}} = 2 \cdot \text{Volume}_{\text{OldPrice}}$$

This essentially means that for the price cut to break even, sales volume should double at the lower price. It is noteworthy that relatively small changes in sales price can require what may appear to be a disproportionately greater increase in sales volume. Indeed, in the example above, a 25% decrease in price requires a doubling of sales volume.

Alternatively, one may calculate the rate at which the current volume should increase so that the price cut has a neutral impact on profitability.

$$\text{BER}_{\text{PC}} = \frac{\text{Margin}_{\text{OldPrice}}}{\text{Margin}_{\text{NewPrice}}} - 1 = \frac{\$50}{\$25} - 1 = 1$$

The above calculation means that, for the price cut to break even, sales volume should increase by a factor of 1, or by 100%.

Appendix 4: Break-Even Analysis of a Variable-Cost Increase

Break-even analysis of a variable-cost increase identifies the sales volume at which a company neither makes a profit nor incurs a loss after increasing the variable costs associated with a particular offering. Typical problems to which this type of analysis can be applied are estimating the incremental increase in sales necessary to cover an increase in the cost of goods sold, estimating the costs associated with increasing an item-specific level of service, and estimating the costs associated with running item-specific incentives (e.g., premiums). The break-even analysis of a variable-cost increase is shown in Figure 5.

Figure 5: Break-Even of a Variable-Cost Increase

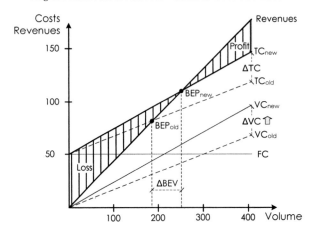

The basic principle of calculating the break-even point of an increase in an offering's variable costs is similar to that of estimating the break-even point of a price cut. The key difference in this case is that a decrease in the margin generated by the new offering is a result of an increase in the offering's costs rather than a decrease in revenues. Thus, the break-even volume of a variable-cost increase can be calculated as follows:

$$BEV_{VC} = \frac{Margin_{OldVC}}{Margin_{NewVC}} \cdot Volume_{OldVC}$$

Similarly, the break-even rate of an increase in variable costs can be calculated as follows:

$$BER_{VC} = \frac{Margin_{OldVC}}{Margin_{NewVC}} - 1$$

To illustrate, consider the impact of an increase in variable costs from \$50 to \$60 for a product priced at \$100. In this case, $Margin_{OldVC} = \$100 - \$50 = \$50$ and $Margin_{NewVC} = \$100 - \$60 = \$40$. Therefore, the break-even volume of a variable cost increase can be calculated as follows:

$$BEV_{VC} = \frac{Margin_{OldVC}}{Margin_{NewVC}} \cdot Volume_{OldVC} = \frac{\$50}{\$40} \cdot Volume_{OldVC} = 1.25 \cdot Volume_{OldVC}$$

Thus, for the variable-cost increase to break even, sales volume should increase by a factor of 1.25, or by 125%.

Alternatively, one could calculate the rate at which the current volume should increase so that the increase in variable costs has a neutral impact on profitability.

$$\text{BER}_{VC} = \frac{\text{Margin}_{OldVC}}{\text{Margin}_{NewVC}} - 1 = \frac{\$50}{\$40} - 1 = 0.25$$

The above calculation implies that, for the increase in variable costs to break even, sales volume should increase by a factor of .25, or by 25%.

Appendix 5: Break-Even Analysis of Cannibalization

The primary goal of extending a company's product line by launching a new offering is to increase the company's sales revenues by growing demand for the overall category and/or by stealing share from competitors. A typical side effect of such product line extensions is that, in addition to stealing share from competitors, the new offering also takes away share from a company's current offerings, a process commonly referred to as cannibalization (Figure 6).

Figure 6: Impact of Launching a New Offering on the Sales Volume of an Existing Offering

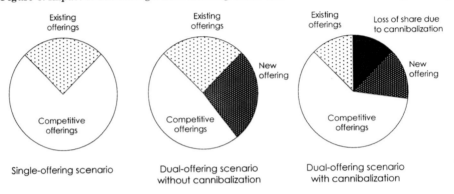

In this context, the break-even rate of a potential cannibalization of sales of an existing offering from a product line extension identifies the ratio of the cannibalized sales volume of the existing offering to the sales volume generated by the new offering at which a company neither makes a profit nor incurs a loss. Thus, the break-even rate of cannibalization indicates the maximum proportion of the sales volume of the new offering that could come from the company's existing offering(s) without incurring a loss. The break-even rate of cannibalization can be derived as follows:

To avoid loss of profit across all offerings, profit from the new product must be equal to or greater than the lost profits from cannibalization (the dark-shaded area in the above chart).

$$\text{Profit}_{\text{NewOffering}} \geq \text{LostProfit}_{\text{OldOffering}}$$

Given that profit is a function of unit volume and unit margin, the above equation can be modified as follows:

$$\text{Volume}_{\text{NewOffering}} \cdot \text{Margin}_{\text{NewOffering}} \geq \text{LostVolume}_{\text{OldOffering}} \cdot \text{Margin}_{\text{OldOffering}}$$

The above equation can be restructured as follows:

$$\frac{\text{LostVolume}_{\text{OldOffering}}}{\text{Volume}_{\text{NewOffering}}} = \frac{\text{Margin}_{\text{NewOffering}}}{\text{Margin}_{\text{OldOffering}}}$$

The left part of the equation is the ratio of sales volume of the old offering that was lost because of cannibalization of the sales volume of the new offering, which is exactly the definition of the break-even rate of cannibalization (BERc). Hence:

$$\text{BER}_C = \frac{\text{Margin}_{\text{NewOffering}}}{\text{Margin}_{\text{OldOffering}}}$$

For example, consider a company launching a new product priced at $70 with variable costs of $60, which may cannibalize the sales of an existing product priced at $100 that also has variable costs of $60. In this case, $\text{Margin}_{\text{NewOffering}} = \$70 - \$60 = \$10$ and $\text{Margin}_{\text{OldOffering}} = \$100 - \$60 = \$40$. Therefore, the break-even rate of cannibalization can be calculated as follows:

$$\text{BER}_{C} = \frac{\text{Margin}_{\text{NewOffering}}}{\text{Margin}_{\text{OldOffering}}} = \frac{\$10}{\$40} = 0.25$$

The break-even rate of cannibalization in this case is 0.25 or 25%, which means that to be profitable to the company, no more than 25% of the sales volume of the new offering should come from the current offering, which in turn implies that at least 75% of the sales volume should come from competitors' offerings and/or from increasing the overall size of the market.

Appendix 6: Economic Value Analysis

The concept of economic value analysis (EVA) is predicated on the idea that the monetary value of an offering should be estimated not only based on its purchase price but also on the overall value it delivers to target customers. In this context, EVA involves monetizing the nonmonetary aspects of an offering's value proposition. Building on the notion that an offering's value proposition has three distinct dimensions: functional, monetary, and psychological, EVA implies translating functional and psychological value into financial terms (Figure 7).

Figure 7. The Concept of Economic Value Analysis

Economic value analysis is typically used to evaluate the monetary value of an offering in two cases: (1) to identify the intrinsic value of an offering to its target customers (i.e., in the absence of competition) and (2) to identify an offering's monetary value relative to that of the competition. These two approaches are discussed in more detail below.

Identifying the intrinsic monetary value of an offering is particularly useful when developing a primary demand strategy that aims to gain share by attracting customers who are unfamiliar with this type of product. In this context, the monetary value of an offering is calculated as the difference between the monetary equivalent of its functional, monetary, and psychological benefits and its functional, monetary, and psychological costs (Figure 8).

Figure 8. Economic Value as a Function of an Offering's Benefits and Costs

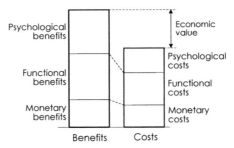

In addition to representing economic value as a function of the difference between benefits and costs, it can be represented as the relative advantage of an offering vis-à-vis its competitors. Defining the monetary value of an offering relative to the competition is particularly useful when developing a steal-share strategy that aims to gain share by attracting competitors' customers. In this context, an offering's economic advantage can be represented as the difference in the monetary value of the company's offering relative to its competitors (Figure 9).

Figure 9. Economic Value of the Relative Advantage of an Offering

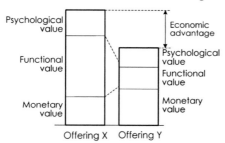

In business-to-business markets, the economic advantage of an offering is often calculated as the difference in the total costs of ownership of the offerings. This type of economic value analysis is especially useful to relate the price and nonprice aspects of the offering. To illustrate, consider the two offerings depicted in Figure 10. Although Offering Y is priced higher than Offering X, when all relevant costs (downtime, replacement, maintenance, usage, financing, inventory, and installation costs) are considered, the total cost of the higher priced Offering Y ends up being lower than that of the lower-priced Offering X.

Figure 10. Economic Value as a Function of the Differences in the Total Costs

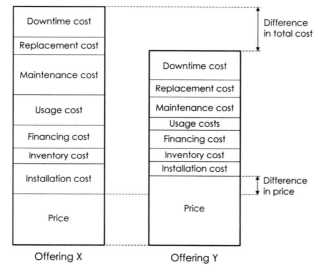

Calculating the economic value as a function of the difference in the total costs of an offering can be illustrated by the following example. Consider a farm equipment manufacturer selling a tractor priced at $180,000. Imagine that its price is $25,000 higher than functionally similar offerings from its competitors. Although this company's tractor is more durable, reliable, and has a longer warranty and faster response to service calls, justifying the $25,000 price difference is not a trivial task for its sales force. One approach to sales is to identify the monetary value of the functional differences between the company's tractor and its competitors, which involves estimating the incremental value of the benefits of the company's offering to the customer vis-à-vis its competitors. This approach is illustrated in Table 1, which indicates that the customer value of the functional benefits delivered by the company's offering is $41,000, significantly greater than the $25,000 price difference between the offerings. This analysis shows that the company's offering is *underpriced* by $16,000 relative to the competition.

Table 1. Economic Value Analysis: An Example

Value ($)	Benefit
$6,000	Greater durability (2 extra years of product usage)
$14,000	Greater reliability (2 fewer breakdowns per year × 10 years × downtime costs to the company)
$9,500	Longer warranty (2 years extra warranty × 3 service calls per year × value of replacement parts)
$11,500	Faster response to service calls (3 service calls per year × 10 years × 4-hour faster response × hourly downtime costs)
$41,000	Total monetary value of the competitive advantage

Appendix 7: Income Statement: An Overview

The income statement is a financial document showing a company's income and expenses over a given period. It typically identifies revenues, costs, operating expenses, operating income, and earnings (Figure 11).

Figure 11: An Example of Revenues, Costs, and Margins as Shown
in a Company's Income Statement

Gross Revenues	
Product sales	$ 12,000
Services	3,000
Total (Gross) Revenues	15,000
Cost of Goods Sold	
Product costs	4,000
Services costs	1,500
Depreciation	500
Total Cost of Goods Sold	6,000
Gross Profit	9,000
Gross Margin	60%
Operating Expenses	
Sales and Marketing	5,000
General and Administrative	1,000
Research and Development	1,500
Total Operating Expenses	7,500
Operating Income	1,500
Operating Margin	10%
Interest payments on loans	500
Earnings before taxes	1,000
Provision for taxes	250
Net Income (Earnings)	750
Net (Profit) Margin	5%

Appendix 8: Distribution Channel Margin Analysis

A useful approach to analyzing margins of the individual members of a distribution channel involves mapping the channel structure to identify margins for each channel member (Figure 12).

Figure 12: An Example of Distribution Channel Margins

Margins are almost universally calculated based on sales revenue (e.g., sales price) rather than based on cost (e.g., purchase price). To illustrate, the margin for an item purchased for $10 (cost) and sold for $15 (revenue) can be calculated as follows:

$$\text{Margin} = \frac{\text{Revenue - Cost}}{\text{Revenue}} = \frac{\text{Selling price - Purchase price}}{\text{Selling price}} = \frac{\$15 - \$10}{\$15} = 33\%$$

Chapter Twenty-Seven

Essential Marketing Metrics

Monitoring a company's progress toward its goals involves using performance benchmarks, commonly referred to as marketing metrics. Based on their focus, most marketing metrics can be divided into several categories: *company metrics,* which reflect a company's progress toward achieving its strategic goal(s), *customer metrics*, which capture customers' response to the company's actions, and *marketing mix metrics,* which depict an offering's performance on different marketing mix variables: *product, service, brand, price, incentives, communication,* and *distribution.* These different types of metrics are summarized in the following sections.

Company Metrics

Break-Even Analysis: An analysis aimed at identifying the break-even point at which the benefits and costs associated with a particular action are equal, and beyond which profit occurs (Chapter 26).

Compound Annual Growth Rate (CAGR): The year-to-year growth rate of an investment over a specified period of time (Chapter 26).

Contribution Margin ($): When expressed in monetary terms (e.g., in dollars), contribution margin typically refers to the difference between total revenues and total variable costs. Contribution margin can also be calculated on a per-unit basis as the difference between the unit selling price and the unit variable cost (Chapter 26).

Contribution Margin (%): When expressed in percentages, contribution margin refers to the ratio of the difference between total revenues and total variable costs to total revenues. Contribution margin also can be expressed as the ratio of unit contribution to unit selling price (Chapter 26).

Goodwill: An accounting term referring to a company's intangible assets (Chapter 26).

Gross Margin: The ratio of gross profit to gross revenues (Chapter 26).

Gross Profit: The difference between total sales revenue and total cost of goods sold (Chapter 26).

Internal Rate of Return (IRR): The annualized effective compounded return rate that can be earned on the invested capital (Chapter 26).

Market Share: An offering's share of the total sales of all offerings within the product category in which the brand competes. Market share is determined by dividing an offering's sales volume by the total category sales volume. Sales can be defined in terms of revenues or on a unit basis (Chapter 26).

Market Size: The monetary value of an existing or potential market, typically measured on an annual basis (Chapter 22).

Net Income: Gross revenues minus all costs and expenses (e.g., cost of goods sold, operating expenses, depreciation, interest, and taxes) in a given period of time (Chapter 26).

Net Margin: The ratio of net income to gross revenues (Chapter 26).

Operating Expenses: The primary costs, other than cost of goods sold, incurred to generate revenues (Chapter 26).

Operating Income: Gross profit minus operating expenses. Operating income reflects the firm's profitability from current operations without regard to the interest charges accruing from the firm's capital structure (Chapter 26).

Operating Margin: The ratio of operating income to gross revenues (Chapter 26).

Return on Investment (ROI): Net income as a percentage of the investment required to generate this income. Conceptually similar metrics are Return on Assets (ROA), Return on Net Assets (RONA), and Return on Capital (ROC; Chapter 26).

Return on Marketing Investment (ROMI): A measure of the efficiency of a company's marketing expenditures. Most often calculated in terms of incremental net income, sales revenues, market share, or contribution margin. ROMI can also be calculated with respect to the overall marketing expenditures or to a specific marketing mix variable (Chapter 26).

Return on Sales (ROS): Net income as a percentage of sales revenues (Chapter 26).

Customer Metrics

Brand Development Index (BDI): A measure of the degree to which sales of a given brand have captured the total market potential in a particular geographical area based on the population of that area and average consumption per user nationally (Chapter 23).

Category Development Index (CDI): A measure of the degree to which sales in a given category have captured the total market potential in a particular geographical area based on the population of that area and average consumption per user nationally (Chapter 23).

Conversion Rate: The number of potential customers who have tried the product/service relative to the total number of customers aware of the product/service (Chapter 22).

Customer Attrition Rate (Churn Rate): The number of customers who discontinue using a company's product or service during a specified time period relative to the average total number of customers over that same time period (Chapter 22).

Customer Equity: The lifetime value of a particular customer to the company. A common methodology for measuring customer equity involves estimating (1) the number of customer transactions per accounting period (e.g., quarter), (2) the average duration of the customer's lifetime with the company, measured in accounting periods, and

(3) the average transaction profitability, and then applying the appropriate discount rate for the future flow of profits generated from this customer.

Penetration Rate: The number of customers who have tried the offering at least once relative to the total number of potential customers (Chapter 22).

Retention Rate: The number of customers who have repurchased the offering during the current buying cycle (e.g., month, quarter, year) relative to the number of customers who have purchased the offering during the last cycle. Also used in reference to the number of customers who have repurchased the offering relative to the total number of customers who have tried the product at least once (Chapter 22).

Product and Service Metrics

Product/Service Preferences: A measure of the degree to which a product/service appeals to current and potential customers. Preferences can be measured in absolute terms (i.e., independent from the other products and services in the marketplace) or relative to other offerings (e.g., the degree to which the company's products and services are better than competitors' products and services). Preferences typically comprise two dimensions: the valence of preferences (e.g., positive vs. negative) and the strength of preferences (e.g., strong vs. weak). Product and service preferences can be measured using a variety of techniques such as questionnaires, conjoint analysis, and perceptual maps.

Product/Service Satisfaction: A measure of customers' experience with a product. Unlike product-preference metrics that can be measured prior to purchase as well as post-purchase, satisfaction requires consumers to have actual experience with the product or service. Satisfaction is typically measured using a five-point or a seven-point scale (e.g., very dissatisfied, somewhat dissatisfied, neither satisfied nor dissatisfied, somewhat satisfied, and very satisfied).

Purchase Intent: Self-reported likelihood of purchasing a company's products or services (Chapter 22).

Brand Metrics

Brand Strength: A brand's ability to differentiate the offering from the competition and create customer value through meaningful associations. Unlike brand equity, which reflects the value of the brand to the company, brand strength (also referred to as brand power) reflects the value of the brand among current and potential customers (Chapter 16).

Brand Equity: The net present value of the financial benefits derived from the brand. Brand equity is a function of brand power, as well as a number of additional factors reflecting the company's utilization of the strength of its brand (Chapter 16).

Price and Incentives Metrics

Cross-Price Elasticity: The percentage change in quantity sold of a given offering caused by a percentage change in the price of another offering (Chapter 17).

Incentives Ratio: Percentage of sales that involves an incentive relative to the company's total sales (Chapter 18).

Pass-through Incentives Ratio: Percentage of the incentives provided to customers by a given channel (e.g., a retailer) relative to the incentives provided to that channel (Chapter 18).

Price Elasticity: The percentage change in quantity sold relative to the percentage change in price for a given product or service (Chapter 17).

Communication Metrics

Advertising Awareness: The number of potential customers who are aware of the offering (Chapter 19).

Advertising Frequency: The number of times the target audience is exposed to an advertisement in a given period (Chapter 19).

Advertising Reach: The size of the audience that has been exposed to a particular advertisement at least once in a given period (Chapter 19).

Awareness Rate: The number of target customers who are aware of the offering, relative to the total number of target customers (Chapter 19).

Comprehension: The degree to which the target audience understands the message embedded in the advertisement.

Cost per Point (CPP): A measure representing the cost of a communications campaign. CPP is the media cost of reaching one percent (one rating point) of a particular demographic (Chapter 19).

Cost per Thousand (CPM): A measure used to represent the cost of a communications campaign. CPM is the cost of reaching 1,000 individuals or households with an advertising message in a given medium (Chapter 19).

Exposure: The number of times a given advertisement has been seen by the target audience (Chapter 19).

Gross Rating Point (GRP): A measure of the total volume of advertising delivery to the target audience. GRP is equal to the percent of the population reached times the frequency of exposure (Chapter 19).

Net Promoter Score: A metric designed to measure customers' satisfaction based on their willingness to generate word of mouth about the company and/or its products (Chapter 19).

Recall: The degree to which the target audience remembers an advertisement (Chapter 19).

Share of Voice: A company's communications expenditures relative to those of the entire product category (Chapter 19).

Target Rating Point (TRP): A measure of the total volume of advertising delivery to the target audience. TRP is similar to GRP, but its calculation involves using only the target audience (rather than the total audience) as the base (Chapter 19).

Top-of-Mind Awareness: The first brand identified by respondents when asked to list brands in a given product category (Chapter 19).

Distribution Metrics

All-Commodity Volume (ACV): A measure of an offering's availability, typically calculated as the total annual volume of the company's offering in a given geographic area relative to the total sales volume of the retailers in that geographic area across all product categories (hence, the term "all-commodity volume"). Also refers to the gross sales in a specific geographic area (i.e., total sales of all stores; Chapter 20).

Inventory Turnover: The number of times the inventory is replenished, typically calculated as the ratio of the annual revenues generated by a given offering to the average inventory (Chapter 20).

Same-Store Sales: A metric used in the retail industry comparing sales of stores that have been open for a year or more and have historical data to compare the current year's sales to the same time frame last year (Chapter 20).

Share of Shelf Space: Shelf space allocated to a given offering relative to the total shelf space in a given geographic area (Chapter 20).

Trade Margin: The difference between unit selling price and unit cost at each level of a marketing channel (Chapter 26).

Additional Readings

Farris, Paul W., Neil T. Bendle, Phillip E. Pfeifer, and David J. Reibstein (2006), *Marketing Metrics: 50+ Metrics Every Executive Should Master*. Philadelphia, PA: Wharton School Publishing.

Hubbard, Douglas W. (2007), *How to Measure Anything: Finding the Value of Intangibles in Business*. New York, NY: John Wiley & Sons.

Lenskold, James D. (2003), *Marketing ROI: The Path to Campaign, Customer, and Corporate Profitability*. New York, NY: McGraw-Hill.

Index

Terms listed in this index are grouped into four categories: (1) marketing concepts, (2) financial concepts, (3) marketing frameworks, and (4) companies, products, and brands.

Marketing Concepts

Financial Concepts

Marketing Frameworks

Companies, Products, and Brands

LaVergne, TN USA
06 January 2010
169051LV00006B/5/P

9 780982 512630